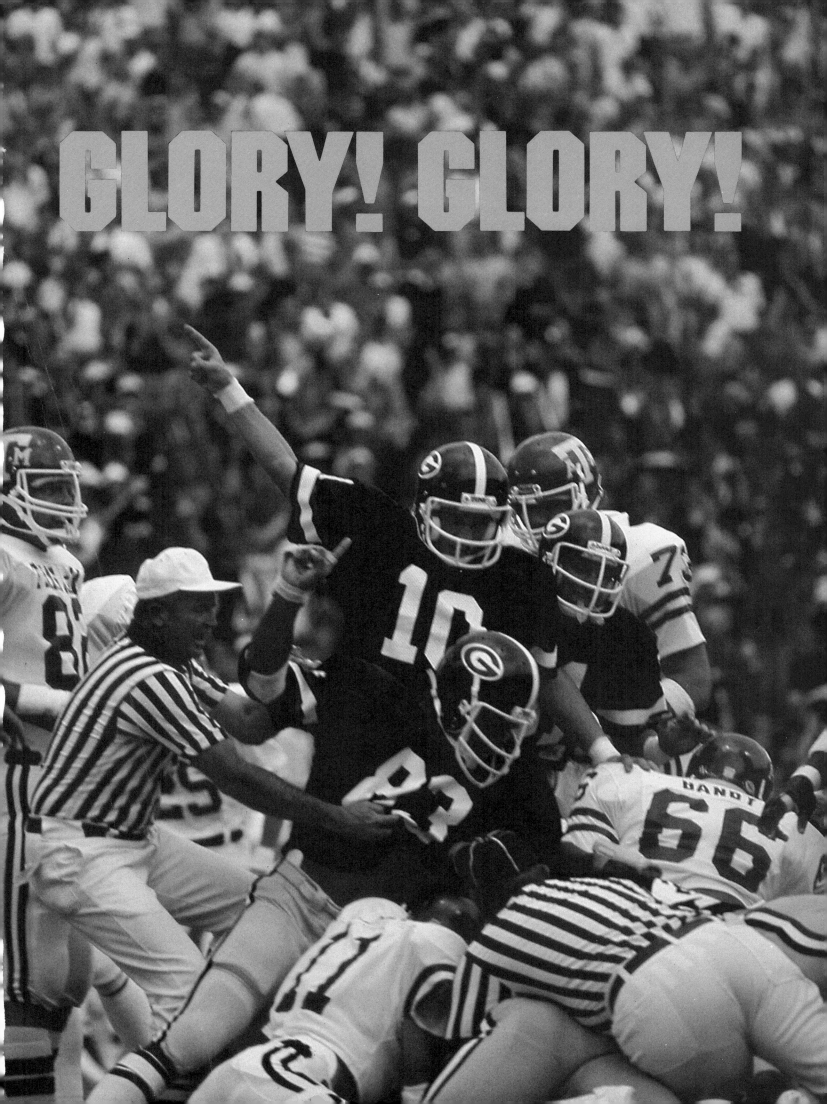

GLORY! GLORY!

GLORY!

Georgia's 1980 Ch

GLORY!

ampionship Season: The Inside Story

BY LORAN SMITH WITH LEWIS GRIZZARD

Special Photography by Wingate Downs

PEACHTREE PUBLISHERS LIMITED

Published by
PEACHTREE PUBLISHERS LIMITED
494 Armour Circle, N.E., Atlanta, Georgia 30324

Design by David Russell

First edition

Manufactured in the United States of America

LC 81-81924
ISBN: 0-931948-18-5

To my wife, Myrna, my biggest supporter,
who also gave me Camille and Kent,
the only wealth that I have.

CONTENTS

INTRODUCTION

To Georgia football fans, sons and daughters of the Red and Black, loyal friends of the University, the book you hold in your hands is The Second Greatest Story Ever Told. Second only because we who belong to these red clay hills and pine forested plains are a God fearing people.

When Buck Belue curled on the football for the last time on that agonizing afternoon of January 1, 1981, in the Superdome in New Orleans, you knew someone would write a book.

We are fortunate it was Loran Smith who decided to commit the great event to history, and that he invited Lewis Grizzard to collaborate with him. Loran has an insight and perspective on this drama that is nonpareil. And Grizzard. What can you say about Lewis except that the son-of-a-gun writes like Herschel Walker runs.

This is not just another sports book. It is a professionally told story of human struggle and achievement. The casual reader will find it interesting and entertaining. But for the true football fan, for all who deeply love the University and their state, it is a treasure.

Georgia's march to the National Championship exceeded a mere series of athletic contests and the Sugar Bowl certainly was more than a game. It was hot pursuit of perfection against terrifying odds. Herschel at Knoxville, Buck Belue and Lindsay Scott in Jacksonville. Slip the hangman's noose and spit in his eye!

Southerners gave such an effort in 1864. But Sherman stomped us. Georgia came close with Sinkwich and Trippi and perhaps a couple of other times. Close doesn't count.

We live in times of disappointment. Vietnam, the Mayaguez, the debacle in the Iranian desert. We had come to accept failure.

This Georgia football team would not accept failure.

It's not such a big deal to win a national championship when you're decidedly bigger and stronger and deeper than every opponent. These Bulldogs didn't do it that way. They won it on a lot of talent and coaching, but also on heart and soul and guts and a spirit that's been building in Athens for decades.

It wasn't even all Herschel Walker. The cast of heroes is large, and many are identified for the first time in this book.

Not all wore a uniform.

There's a kid growing up in Mobile, a guy painting a house in Jesup, an assistant coach who abandoned his family on Christmas Eve, a stubborn old basketball coach, a young man named Wayne McDuffie who had a vision. A lot of it ought to be fiction.

Read on and know this Championship didn't start in Knoxville, Tennessee, on a September night in 1980. It started years ago on a grade school field in Valdosta, in a backyard in Cobb County, in a hiding place in Barcelona, Spain, for examples. It's a helluva story.

This Championship is more precious because Vince Dooley brought it to Athens without compromising the University in any fashion. No embarrassments, no recruiting scandals. Read Chapter Two, Book Two, and learn what Scott Woerner says about that.

This is the University of Georgia: Poor kids from the tobacco fields of South Georgia, sent to Athens by struggling mamas and daddies in hopes they can come home and do better; rich kids from Atlanta driving sporty cars; kids whose great-grandfathers and great-grandmothers graduated; pretty girls, Ag Hill, the fraternities and the sororities. They all come to Athens, and the city and the University enfold them and make them one. Forever. The football team is one of the main things to hold on to.

Thus they journeyed to New Orleans. In red, in love, in hope, and in some trepidation. To be together for a moment that had never come before and might never come again.

New Year's Day. In the lobby of the Fairmont Hotel Dooley and Erk and the team ride single file down the long escalator to the buses. Faces absolutely frozen. It must have been like that on the landing crafts at Omaha Beach and at Iwo Jima, at the foot of Cemetery Ridge.

It was the greatest game a Georgia team has ever played. The sportswriters never really grasped that. Notre Dame could have kept the ball until Easter, and Georgia still would not lose!

Jimmy Carter is a spectator. A Georgian who went all the way and then lost.

These Georgians will not lose!

Herschel Walker! Thank God that magnificent young man is not cutting pulpwood in Johnson County. Thank God for Earl Warren.

Interception by Fisher. Interception by Woerner. Finally, Belue to Arnold and a first down. The impossible dream!

Barbara Dooley has her arms around Joel Eaves. She is crying. Joel has his arms around Barbara and he is crying. He is crying but he cannot speak.

It is a scene by Cecil B. De Mille.

Dooley is on the shoulders of his players, engulfed by the red tide. Georgians have been reluctant to accept him, and he has been called by his Alma Mater. He has been tempted, but he has stayed with Georgia and now he has won it all.

Vince Dooley is a Bulldog forever. Georgia is Number One. Hail to Georgia down in Dixie! Glory, Glory, to old Georgia!

We won't just read this book, we'll drink it. We will read it, and re-read it, and one of these days we damn well may bronze it. Let these memories last forever.

Jim Minter

Vice President and Executive Editor
The *Atlanta Journal* and *Constitution*

BOOK I

The Foundation

Prologue

Rex Robinson, the Georgia placekicker, is standing near the Georgia 40-yard-line with his index finger pointed toward the roof of the Louisiana Superdome which indicates to the official in the Notre Dame end zone he is prepared to kick off the 1981 Sugar Bowl Classic. It is January 1, 1:30 P.M., Central Standard Time, the Superdome is filled with 77,895 paying customers, and millions watch on national television.

Georgia, the nation's only undefeated, untied major college football team—ranked No. 1—is about to attempt to defend its position and win its first national championship.

Green and gold are scattered here and there around the massive stadium, the green and gold of Notre Dame. But mostly it is red and black and red and black and red and black, the red and black of Georgia.

"GEORGIA!" screams one section.

"BULLDAWGS!" answers another.

Many have not slept in days. They have come from Macon and Columbus and Savannah and Colquitt and Baxley. "How 'bout them Dawgs!" It echoes to Slidell, across the lake. Look back on the season. So close in Knoxville, barely against Clemson, the thriller against South Carolina, the miracle in Jacksonville, then Auburn, and then Georgia Tech.

The Southeastern Conference title is Georgia's. The Bulldogs ended the regular season 11-0. An incredible season. A wonderful season. But it has not been enough. Vince Dooley, the Georgia coach, had said it best the night before the same New Year's Eve, as the throng of Georgia fans literally conquered the French Quarter:

"Somehow, someway," Dooley had said. "We must do it one more time."

It had been a month since the regular season had ended against Georgia Tech, a long month of waiting and wondering and figuring. If the approaching matchup against Notre Dame had not brought about enough anxiety, there was the matter of Dooley, too, who had strongly considered leaving Georgia to return to his alma mater, Auburn, as head coach.

As I stood on the sidelines in those last, exasperating moments before Robinson's kick, I wondered why it had to be so hard for Georgia to convince a doubting world it deserved to be, at this point, on top and fighting to stay on top.

Undefeated Georgia, I was thinking, is actually an underdog to once-beaten and once-tied Notre Dame. The night before, I had heard a Notre Dame fan chide a Georgia fan:

"Just who did you play?" the Notre Dame fan asked.

"We played Georgia Tech, for one," the Georgia fan shot back.

Notre Dame had been tied by Georgia Tech, 3-3, of course, which first sent the Bulldogs to the top of the rankings. But the oddsmakers figure Georgia doesn't have the talent, except for the incredible Herschel Walker. And its schedule was soft, they say. They figure Georgia got to the Sugar Bowl on luck, and luck runs out in the big games.

And Notre Dame is awesome in its size and its power, and Notre Dame is so used to wrecking aspirations to be No. 1. Ask Bear Bryant and Alabama. There is also the Notre Dame myth of a divine overseeing of its football fortunes. Can that be?

Probably not. I agree with Chuck Mills, who suffered through so many losing seasons as coach at Wake Forest. "We pray before our games, too," said Mills, "but I've noticed God always seems to be on the side of the team with the biggest and fastest players."

Notre Dame had come onto the field before the game obviously aroused. If the Irish had not come to win the last game for their embattled and retiring coach, Dan Devine, they had come to win the game for themselves. They had been "embarrassed"—Devine's words—in their regular season finale with a loss to Southern California.

The number of things that can run through your mind in such a short time. I am searching, groping, hoping, looking at every angle as the game—finally, mercifully—is about to begin.

Maybe destiny owes Georgia one, I am thinking. The school has been in the football business for 89 years, and no national championships. Georgia has come close, but the prize always went to other teams.

Those were the days when Southern teams had to prove they were clearly better to win such a title. Regional voting prejudice would block the dreams of Southern teams. The Civil

Erk Russell and his troops before the battle of New Orleans. Would this be Georgia's greatest moment ever?

War should be forgotten, the sooner the better, but I allowed myself to conclude it is not always the South that perpetuates regional prejudices.

Jimmy Carter, the president, is among this crowd today. He is a lame duck president at this point with only three more weeks to serve. I did not vote for him because I felt he lacked something, he did not inspire my confidence and I could not vote for him simply because he is a Georgian.

But, it is particularly galling that there are those who credit his shortcomings to his being a Southerner, or who claim he had no business holding to the office because of his birthplace.

There is some of that in the air here. You can feel it. A Notre Dame player being interviewed by a sportswriter made a comment about his future being exciting because his degree was of great significance and would mean something.

"Which is more," he snickered, "than a lot of folks around here can say."

Georgia's throng of supporters got more than even for such looking down the nose. There were less-than-tasteful references to the Pope, and the cheer-of-the-night on Bourbon Street New Year's Eve had been:

YOU GOT THE HUNCHBACK!
WE GOT THE TAILBACK!

"I can't stand Auburn," a Georgia man said. "I despise Florida, and Georgia Tech ain't even worth wasting a breath on. But *I hate* Notre Dame."

That is because it is easy to hate Notre Dame. Notre Dame represents the ultimate in college football, it is the home office of college football. They never made a movie about Kansas football or Florida State, or the University of Texas at El Paso.

Everybody knows about Notre Dame. You can be an All-American at Notre Dame because of the great tradition and a terrific publicity department. Win a couple of big games, and Notre Dame is automatically ranked No. 1.

But beat Notre Dame, and you have beaten the best, or at least the best tradition. You have beaten the Yankees, the Canadiens, the Celtics, and the Steelers.

Georgia and Notre Dame had never played football against each other before this. I had wondered why. My research, as usual, had led me to Dr. John Stegeman, son of the former Georgia coach, athletic director, and dean of men, Herman Stegeman, and to Dan Magill, the long-time sports information director at

Georgia, the historian, the chronicler of every Bulldog deed, great and good.

Georgia and Notre Dame had met often in baseball when it was the primary collegiate sport, but Notre Dame early fell into a rivalry with Georgia Tech, according to Magill.

"In the early 1920s," said Magill, "the football rules committee, headed by Amos Alonzo Stagg of Chicago, wanted to outlaw the backfield shifts being used by Knute Rockne at Notre Dame and Bill Alexander at Georgia Tech. Rockne and Alexander became friends while fighting to keep the shift."

A number of Georgia coaches had Notre Dame backgrounds, including George Haffner, who directed the Georgia offense in 1980. Harry Mehre, Georgia's head coach from 1928 and 1937, was a Notre Dame center. Jim Crowley, one of Notre Dame's Four Horsemen, was backfield coach at Georgia from 1925-28. There were others: Frank Thomas, Rex Enright, Ted Twomey, and Harry Wright, who coached Georgia's line under Wally Butts in the 1950s.

All that history and all those connections, but it is 1981 before the Bulldogs and Irish ever play a football game. It will take three hours to play. Will it be the biggest ever, the crowning moment of those 89 years? "Glory, glory to ol' Georgia!" they have sung all these years, but will it be this day, this game that is most glorious of them all?

Look back. Look back to when Georgia achieved its first national recognition. It was late in the afternoon of October 8, 1927, in the Yale Bowl in New Haven, Connecticut, and it

Harry Mehre, Notre Dame center, Georgia coach in the thirties.

all came about in a pile of hay on one end of the field.

Georgia's head coach in 1927 was George (Kid) Woodruff, a successful businessman, who had agreed to coach the team for a dollar a year. It was Woodruff who had won a game against Sewanee during his playing days as the Bulldog quarterback, with a new twist to the Statue of Liberty play.

As the fog fell on the mountains of Tennessee, Woodruff dropped back to pass. He pulled off his headgear and threw it downfield, slipping the ball to his halfback. Sewanee, in the fog, chased the helmet instead of the ball, and the halfback raced unmolested for the touchdown. Georgia wins.

A week before the Yale game in 1927, Woodruff announced his retirement. He had long dreamed of beating Yale and bringing

LEFT: Out of the past. Glenn (Pop) Warner was Georgia's first paid football coach. TOP: Kid Woodruff later coached the team for a dollar a year. BOTTOM: Herman J. Stegeman led the Bulldogs from 1920 until 1922.

6

national attention to Georgia, but this was his last chance. The '27 team was his best team, later known as the "Dream and Wonder Team." It featured two All-American ends, Tom Nash and Ivy (Chick) Shiver.

When Yale played other Eastern teams in those days, the Yale Bowl was normally filled to 70,000 capacity. Those without Yale connections had difficulty getting a ticket. So, each season, an inter-sectional game was scheduled early in the season, with tickets going for a dollar each, giving outsiders their one chance to see Yale play.

Still, only 15,000 showed for the Yale-Georgia game in 1927. But a local radio station broadcast the game, and the crowd doubled by the third quarter when Georgia took a 14-10 lead.

Yale came back and four times worked its way inside the Georgia 10-yard line, only to be denied. In the last minute of play, however, Yale completed a fourth down pass for what was apparently a touchdown. But during the week before the game, the field had been covered with hay to protect it from rain. Before the kickoff the hay had been raked into piles at both ends of the field, partially obscuring the goal lines.

When the Yale receiver came down with the apparent winning touchdown pass, he came down in one of the hay piles with Georgia's Roy Estes on top of him. Two officials signaled touchdown, but Estes held the receiver where he landed until another official came over to check. They were a yard short of the goal line and the touchdown was disallowed. Georgia ran out the clock.

The victory almost brought Georgia a

Battle of Broken Jaw. Frank Sinkwich rambles in the 1942 Orange Bowl despite injury to his jaw. Sinkwich is the only Bulldog ever to win the Heisman Trophy.

national championship that season. A Rose Bowl bid was offered the Bulldogs, contingent upon beating Georgia Tech. In the mud on Grant Field, however, Tech won, 12-0.

There were other great moments: the 15-0 win over Yale led by the immortal Vernon "Catfish" Smith in the Sanford Stadium inaugural game in 1929, the great teams of the forties with Charley Trippi and Georgia's only Heisman Trophy winner, Frank Sinkwich.

A Rose Bowl victory in 1942 over UCLA would have likely given the Bulldogs a national title, but there was no poll at the end of the regular season, and Ohio State, which had not played in a bowl game, kept its pre-bowl No. 1 ranking.

On this day, however, I had to think back to 1959. I was there, in Sanford Stadium, in 1959 when Fran Tarkenton passed to Bill Herron and the world came to an end.

Georgia came into the game 7-1. It had to defeat Auburn to win the SEC championship. Pat Dye, now the Auburn head coach, had recovered a fumble at the Auburn 35 with three minutes left. Auburn led, 13-7.

Tarkenton moved Georgia to the Auburn 13. Fourth down. Tarkenton faded back, looked right, then at the last moment, turned and floated the ball to Herron, all alone in the left corner of the end zone. Durward Pennington's extra point gave Georgia the championship, 14-13.

When Tarkenton completed that pass, I was in heaven. We were classmates, we were

friends, and I was convinced life would never be so beautiful. I worked in the dining hall at old Payne Hall where the athletes lived. It was a part of my track scholarship arrangement. I had to serve meals to my friends, Saturday's heroes.

I also wrote sports for the school paper, *The Red and Black.* I wanted to brag about my friend, Francis Tarkenton. I wanted to interview his coach, Wally Butts, but I was frozen with fear.

He had charm and wit, Butts, but he was also caustic and often venomous with his remarks. He could graphically dress down anyone who failed in his judgment. The players who lasted under him, loved him. Some couldn't take it and left with bitter memories.

After the Auburn game I went to the old field house to ask Butts for an interview. He was taking off his khaki pants when I apologetically told him I wanted to write a story about my friend Francis Tarkenton who had just won the SEC title for Georgia.

"I don't see why the hell you want to write about him," Butts barked. "He's never thrown a block in his life."

I withdrew in a state of shock. It was later I learned Butts resented Tarkenton's lack of a strong arm so much that it frustrated him deeply.

As many marvelous moments as Georgia had in the past, the darkest ever came soon after the 1959 championship season. Butts would resign in 1960 and later become embroiled in

controversy over a story in the *Saturday Evening Post* which strongly suggested he and Bear Bryant tried to fix the Georgia-Alabama game in 1961 when Butts was athletic director.

The day the story appeared, Butts was in the basement of his home in Athens on Highland Avenue where he had entertained governors and sports celebrities.

I had to go there. As much as I feared him, I respected him, too. He was shattered. The phone rang and it rang and it rang. Well-wishers, mostly. After one particular call, Wally Butts broke down and cried.

I cried, too, as I left his house.

Later Butts would be granted a $460,000 settlement from the *Post* by a federal jury. But the ordeal had taken its toll. No doubt it shortened his life.

The Georgia athletic program had never been lower after Johnny Griffith's final season in 1963. I wondered, then, what, or who, could save it.

I would have my answer when a silver-haired gentleman named Joel Eaves would come to Georgia's rescue as its new athletic director, who would shock the state by hiring a young man, Vince Dooley, only 31, to become head football coach.

Seventeen years later I am taking one last quick glance at that same Vince Dooley as he stands, arms folded across his chest, on the Superdome sidelines. He must be dying inside, but he looks like he's the calmest man in the house.

Dooley is Catholic, of course, a former altar boy from Mobile. He's even got some Irish in him. At a Sugar Bowl party Notre Dame athletic director Moose Krause had whispered to Dooley that he had been considered as a possible successor to Dan Devine at Notre Dame.

"You're one of us, you know," he had said to Dooley.

Not today. Not at this moment. Today, he is Torquemada. He must punish the Catholics. Georgia needs this. *Georgia deserves* this. Notre Dame has worn the brass ring before, but never, never, never, Georgia.

Robinson has kicked the ball. It is floating above the artificial turf toward a Notre Dame receiver. Eighty-nine years of football history and it has come to this.

"Somehow, someway," Dooley has said. The ghosts of Rockne and Gipp and Leahy are probably circling above, but "somehow, someway . . . we must do it one more time."

PREVIOUS PAGE: Georgia Greats. A smiling Charley Trippi dashes for a 68-yard punt return for a touchdown against Tulsa in the 1946 Oil Bowl. ABOVE LEFT: Catfish Smith, who scored all Georgia's points in the 15-0 upset of Yale in the 1929 dedication game at Sanford Stadium. ABOVE: Wally Butts and Fran Tarkenton with 1959 SEC championship trophy.

9

JACKSON STREET DAYS

Vincent Joseph Dooley, fourth born of William Vincent and Nellie Dooley of 258 South Jackson Street, Mobile, was a depression baby who joined the population on September 4, 1932. Three sisters had preceded him. A brother, Bill, would come along 17 months later.

Times were hard all over when Vince Dooley was a child. They were especially tough at the Dooley house, which a bulldozer would eventually sweep away. On its site now sits the Mobile City Auditorium.

Dooley's father, who grew up an orphan in New Orleans and never knew his parents, was the chief electrician for the National Gypsum Company. Electricians made peanuts. His father also moonlighted as an electrician for the *Mobile Press Register* in order to keep his family fed. Vince and Bill Dooley saw very little of their father in their boyhood days. When they did see him, they noticed he always looked as if he needed sleep.

Nellie Dooley did what she could. She was a typical mother. Her only mission in life was to help her family survive. She was a good woman whose objective was to provide for the children. She made their clothes and stretched every penny. She took in boarders for extra money. There was always a seaman needing a room and meals. A boarder at the Dooley house was always treated like one of the family.

Imagine this: One boarder continued to keep in touch with Vince over the years, and when Georgia wound up in the Sugar Bowl in 1981, his daughter called the Georgia coach for tickets. As hard as they were to obtain—even for Dooley—so fond were his recollections of the days when the woman's father slept in the back room, she got the tickets.

Nellie Dooley was not blessed with good health. And money that should have gone for pills for her heart problem often was used to buy things for her family. She was repeatedly warned by her doctor to take her medicine but she spent her money on the girls, Vince, and Bill.

The hard times she was exposed to and giving her family priority, no doubt, would send her to an early grave. She died while Vince was a freshman at Auburn, playing a football game against the Alabama freshmen at Tuscaloosa. She died knowing her son was on the way to getting a college education, something that pleased her very much.

The number in the Dooley household in Mobile would continue to increase. An older sister, Margaret, had married and moved out of the house. Her husband, a pilot, was ferrying a plane from Memphis to Mobile. The plane crashed and Margaret's husband died. She moved back in with her parents and brought along her four children, two boys and two girls.

The boys, Bud and Tootles, were later placed in a boys home while the widowed sister kept the two girls at the Dooley house on Jackson Street. When Vince and Bill had finished college and were assistant coaches, each took one of the boys and became responsible for his education. Tootles moved in with Bill, and Bud became a member of Vince's family.

In Vince Dooley's early days there were no allowances, no spending money at home. Often, the family was behind on the rent. There were threats that the water would be turned off because their father was behind on the bill. William Dooley worked day and night, but the wolf continued to scratch at the door. *Times were hard all over.*

Vince and Bill learned the hard life of the streets. They were exposed to the tough environment of a port city. "We grew up in a hurry," Vince says now. "We saw a lot of life at an early age."

"Thank goodness it wasn't the drug era," adds Bill, now the athletic director and head football coach at Virginia Tech. "We tried everything. We could have been bums. It could have been bad."

10

Baby Vince. Born September 4, 1932, when times were tough all over.

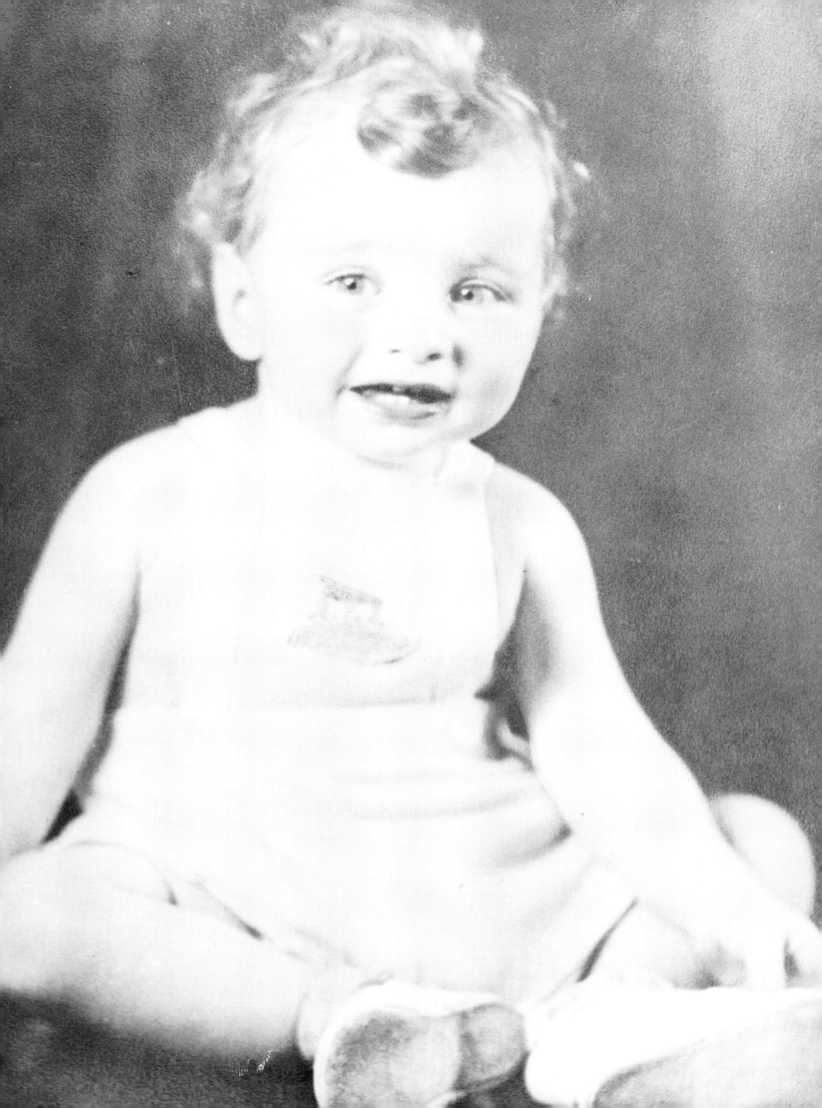

Short pants. Sports would change young Vince's direction.

Those were the days of jumping a freight train to Leakesville, Mississippi, for an hour's stay, and then back home on another freight; of fishing along the Mobile River, of summers visiting cousin Stevie over on Polecat Island, two acres of high ground and 140 of marsh. Cousin Stevie, he knew how to live. Home was a shack with no electricity or running water. Stevie trapped rainwater with a bucket on his roof. He fished, he hunted, he raised his vegetables until a hurricane ran him off Polecat and into Mobile.

Those were also the days Vince Dooley was one of the toughest kids on the block. He was exposed to a tough environment, and he had a terrible temper. Also, by the time he was in the eighth grade, he and most of his friends had been exposed to cigarettes and alcohol.

He had a good base, Dooley says now, but it wasn't easy. His mother stressed that he do right. And so did the nuns at grade school, the Sisters of Charity, and then in high school, the Brothers of the Sacred Heart. Ray Dicharry, his high school coach, was perhaps the one who helped him the most.

He was constantly in fights. He fought with his older sisters at home because of his trigger-quick temper, and he picked on little brother Bill. He would fight anybody, especially Bill. Some of it was roughneck wrestling matches, but there were honest-to-goodness fisticuffs. Bill was named William Gerald, the "Gerald" for a nun, Sister Gerald Marie, a friend of the family. "Look, it's Gerald Marie," Vince would taunt his brother, and the fighting would begin.

"I suppose most of our fighting," Bill Dooley remembers today, "was just being typical brothers. Vince would want me around him until some of his older friends came by, and then he'd try to get rid of me. I'd say, 'To hell with you,' and there would be a fight."

What changed Vince Dooley was the influence of the church and sports. Dicharry taught him that if he didn't control his temper he could never "be something in sports."

Dooley had an undying love for sports, or street games in those days, games like makeshift hockey. You play it on roller skates—all the poor kids get roller skates for Christmas—and you beat a tin can into what must pass for a puck, and then you rip a limb off a palm tree and you've got a stick.

"We had no idea hockey was played on ice," Vince recalls.

There was also something called "stoppers." Poor kids have great imaginations. "Stoppers" involved going to neighborhood grocery stores to collect bottle caps. You throw the bottle cap into the air and hit it with a broomstick. The rules follow those for baseball—sort of. A stopper hit a certain distance was a single, a little farther, a double, etc. If your opponent caught the stopper you were out. Dooley still has a chipped tooth, a souvenir from slamming into the curb making an out.

"It was for the Jackson Street stoppers championship, and my team won," he laughs. "It was worth it."

According to his brother, Vince Dooley

"went straight" as he began high school at Catholic McGill Institute. He found out he couldn't continue his wandering ways and make his grades, and without the grades, the school would not allow participation in athletics.

Basketball was Dooley's game. He was a pioneer jump-shot artist. He didn't call it a jump shot, but it was the forerunner of that technique. It was Sister Patricia who taught him the "hesitation shot," and to make the hesitation shot, he would jump over a chair and then shoot. He became the best basketball player for his age in Mobile.

He had played a CYO (Catholic Youth Organization) game in which his team had won 50-2. The other team managed to score only when Horse McCarthy came across the center line dribbling down for a layup. He began to lose control of the ball, made a vain attempt to shoot, and the ball bounced off an opponent's head, into the basket.

At McGill Dooley made the football team his sophomore year, but was rarely used. Had it not been for his best friend, Bobby Duke, he might have given up the game after that one season. Vince Dooley and Bobby Duke. They were legends.

They met at McGill and their friendship grew quickly. It was through Duke that Dooley gained two assets he had not had before—spending money and transportation. Duke's father was a route man for the Sam Joy Laundry. On weekends, Bobby Duke worked for his father.

Dooley managed to get himself appointed as an assistant route man for Mr. Duke, and soon he and Bobby were working from 6 A.M. until school time and on Saturdays picking up laundry from the freighters docked in Mobile Bay. They also had a neighborhood route. The pay was lousy—$2.50 each for working all day Saturday—but then they could double-date Saturday night in the 1941 Chevy panel-bodied Sam Joy truck.

So who was complaining about having to date in a laundry truck? Vince Dooley was an upperclassman at Auburn before his father owned a car. And while he was at Auburn it was this same Vince Dooley who would take girls for walks around campus and then ask if they would like to sit in his car. The fact he didn't own one didn't stop him. He would find a friend's car, invite the girl in and then hope his friend didn't show.

Vince Dooley and Bobby Duke were

TOP: Before football came Dooley's first sports love, basketball. The "hesitation shot" artist is No. 3 (far right, first row), pictured with his McGill teammates. BOTTOM: Dooley (No. 13) and the McGill Institute backfield.

dedicated laundry men, but one ingenious performance almost cost Bobby's father his job. On a rainy Saturday they decided to wear their bathing suits while delivering the laundry.

Get the picture: The door bell rings, you open, and here stand two kids in their bathing suits with your laundry.

"We even had a slogan," Bobby Duke recalls. " 'Rain or shine, Sam Joy's on time'."

Clever. Only the customers didn't think so. They phoned one of the Chinese brothers who owned the laundry and complained about the "nude delivery boys."

Bobby Duke and Vince Dooley eventually became inseparable. Their friendship would carry on to Auburn where they played in the same backfield. I mentioned Duke's influence on Dooley's career, but before I explain that, it is necessary to look at a couple of more relationships Vince Dooley had during his days in Mobile.

There was Grady Schaffer, for instance. They were the best of friends, too, before Bobby Duke came along and before Vince went straight. It was Grady Schaffer who convinced Vince Dooley to enter into a pact with him never to take schoolwork seriously.

Grady was street-wise, too, and tough. It was Grady Schaffer who nearly ended the young life of a kid named Johnny Jones who committed what Grady considered an unforgivable crime—he stole Grady's potato salad sandwich.

"Grady was something," Dooley recalls. "He would do the weirdest things. Like in the middle of an electrical storm, he would walk out in the rain and thunder and lightning and pray."

Grady was crushed when his friend Vince decided to hit the books in high school. But the pair remained in touch, even when Dooley went off to Auburn and Grady joined the Marines. Grady would later become a Los Angeles policeman. Grady died when his wife shot him in a domestic quarrel. Many from the old Jackson Street gang, including Vince Dooley who was a pallbearer, made it to the funeral.

Then there was little brother, Bill. They fought. I mentioned that. But they had their times together, too, and they still do today. They were competitive as youngsters, and they remain that way. The competition ignites quickly on a tennis court or on a fishing trip. There is always a bet on who will catch the first fish.

But their compassion and understanding for each other is just as visible. After working for Vince during his early years at Georgia, Bill went on to head coaching jobs himself, at North Carolina and now at Virginia Tech. During the football season they talk on the telephone each Friday. It is a high point in the week for both of them.

As kids the fighting had stopped by the time they reached high school. One reason is little brother Bill had grown up. He was not the easy mark he had been and Vince became less antagonistic. Big brother was no dope.

When they were in high school the two Dooley brothers would grab a couple of blankets and a change of clothes and hitchhike from Mobile to the Gulf Shores where they would sleep on the beach and do odd jobs for meal money. They were the original beachcombers.

And there were all those girls, girls whose parents had money, visiting for house parties. The Dooley boys would pick out an unsuspecting young lady, and wind up getting themselves invited to dinner.

"We were awful," Bill Dooley says. "If the girl was pretty, we'd take her dancing after dinner. If she wasn't, we'd disappear after we ate."

During their college days Bill and Vince took trips together in the summer, to Florida, to Cuba, somewhere different to explore—and to plunder.

Bill Dooley took to football immediately. He was also enrolled at McGill. But Vince, he was the school "hesitation shot" sharpie, the basketball man with all the moves. So back to Bobby Duke.

It was a hot, August morning in 1948. Bobby Duke wheeled up to the Dooley residence on Jackson Street and yelled to Vince who was sunning himself on the roof of the two-story house. The Dooley brothers roomed together and their window opened onto the roof. They called that spot the "Crow's Nest."

Usually, when Bobby Duke arrived at the Dooley house in the Sam Joy Laundry truck, he never turned off the ignition. Vince would come bounding out of the house, and away they would go. This time it was different. Vince wouldn't come down. Bobby Duke had arrived to take him to the opening football practice, and Vince didn't want to go.

He had made the traveling squad his sophomore year, but he had spent most of the time sitting on the bench. Who needs football when you're already a basketball star? Plus, Vince Dooley had been out late that night, and it was so pleasant sitting there in the sun.

Bobby Duke, a halfback for McGill, wouldn't let up. Finally Dooley consented. McGill had everything it needed for a good season except a quarterback. That is where the coach, Ray Dicharry, put Vince Dooley, and he was a starter in a matter of days. Dicharry ran the single wing, and Dooley, with his basketball experience, knew how to handle the football.

He was smart. He was a competitor. He was

Big Three at McGill. Dooley (left), best friend Bobby Duke (center), and Bubzy Partridge led team to 1949 Mobile city championship.

strong and he was tough. "The surprising thing, too," Duke remembers, "is he did so well as a passer. He really didn't have a strong arm, but he was accurate, and he worked on his passing."

The combination of Duke and Dooley led McGill to the city football championship in 1949. There were no state playoffs in those days. They were both recruited heavily.

By this time Vince Dooley was a changed person. He had learned to control his temper, he was captain of both football and basketball teams and was making good grades. No more life on the wild side. He was doing well in school, he was still earning money working for Sam Joy, and he realized an education was important. With an education he could avoid working in the Mobile shipyards, which is what

he had earlier considered would be his lot in life.

He had become a responsible young man. There was common knowledge he still had a wild streak, but he could be counted on to do what he said he would do, especially in church. Whenever Archbishop Toolen came to town, Dooley was always called upon to serve as altar boy for early Mass. The priests knew they could count on him to be prompt and handle his assignment correctly and efficiently.

He learned that, it would seem, from a father whose life was so filled with responsibility. "A commitment is a commitment." I have heard Vince Dooley say that so many times. It was his father who taught him. He remembers his mother constantly reminding him "manners will take you where money won't."

Vince Dooley chose to continue his education and his athletic career at Auburn. He liked the school, and the coaches agreed he could play basketball as well as football.

Auburn. How strange. As kids, he and brother Bill would spend Saturday afternoons close to the radio, listening to Harry Wismer broadcasting the Notre Dame games.

. . . *Dancowicz, the center, is down over the ball and Bertelli takes the snap.* . . .

When games were close, the Dooley brothers would say a rosary for the Irish. They had never heard of Auburn or Alabama or Mississippi State where Bill Dooley would play.

Vince Dooley's deal at Auburn was he would stick to football his freshman year and then be eligible to play basketball. As soon as football season ended his sophomore year, he

Quarterback Vince Dooley of Auburn in 1954 College All-Star Game in Chicago.

immediately came out for basketball. His coach was Joel Eaves.

The 1951-52 Auburn basketball team had been working for weeks by the time Dooley walked onto the floor. A starting lineup had already been determined, but Dooley would eventually become a starter.

"He was a smart player," Eaves says. "He could move the ball, and how he could shoot. He liked the game. He loved it. You could see that in him. If he had stuck with basketball, he would have been an all-conference player. If he played today, he would make somebody an excellent point guard."

But Dooley would have only one season as a collegiate basketball player. During his junior year as the Auburn football quarterback, a lineman missed an assignment against Ole Miss in Memphis. Dooley pivoted to get away from the onrushing tackle and took the blow to his left knee. The injury required surgery. After the operation Dooley again tried to play basketball, but he reinjured the knee and was forced to give up the sport that was his first love.

He was able to finish his football career at Auburn and was chosen for the College All-Star game in 1954. He spent two years in the Marines, then came back to Auburn as an assistant to Shug Jordan, who had called him "a coach on the field" as a player. In 1961 he was made head freshman coach. He responded with two undefeated teams in three years.

You go back and you wonder about his life. He was a poor child, on the streets at a young age. What if he had listened to Grady Schaffer? What if Bobby Duke had not convinced him to forget his suntan and go to football practice with him that August morning in 1948?

That was the day he got serious about football, and from that day forward his life has centered around the game.

August, 1948, in Athens: Wallace Butts was still the toast of the town. Two seasons before, his Georgia team had gone undefeated and untied. It had whipped North Carolina in the Sugar Bowl to finish No. 3 in the nation. Many felt the Bulldogs deserved No. 1.

After going 7-4 in '47 the prospects for another great season were undeniable. In 1948 the team went 9-1 and won the SEC title. Johnny Rauch was the quarterback. He would make All-American. Joe Geri and John Donaldson were still around, and there were some outstanding linemen: Homer Hobbs, Gene Lorendo, Hamp Tanner, Porter Payne, Weyman Sellers, Bobby Walston and Jack Bush.

The backfield also had the Reid brothers, Bernie and Floyd, and John Tillitski.

Butts was worshipped in those days. World War II was becoming a distant memory, and there was an abundance of football players. Georgia fans were ready to give Butts a lifetime contract. They would have probably elected him governor.

But what, if anything, endures? Lean years and much trouble were ahead for Butts and for Georgia. And the man who would eventually lead the Bulldogs out of that wilderness was sunning himself on a Mobile rooftop.

RIGHT: The late Shug Jordan for whom Dooley played and coached. He called Dooley "a coach on the field." BELOW: 1948 Georgia Bulldogs. SEC Champions with 6-0-0 record.

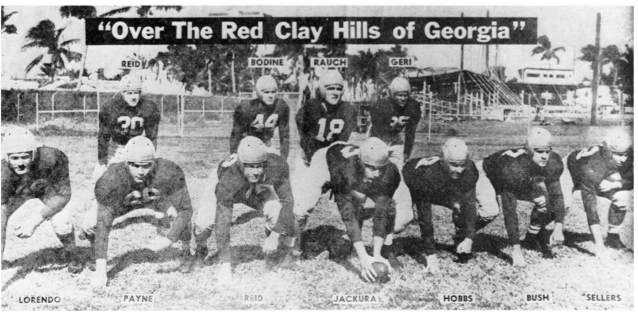

"Over The Red Clay Hills of Georgia"

REID   BODINE   RAUCH   GERI

LORENDO   PAYNE   REID   JACKURA   HOBBS   BUSH   SELLERS

"That Bright Young Coach"

O mer Clyde Aderhold, president of the University of Georgia, had stopped in Newnan, Georgia, to make an important telephone call, one of the most important in his school's athletic history.

He dropped a dime into the slot on top of the phone and called Auburn University, Auburn, Alabama, and asked to speak to the head basketball coach, Joel Eaves, who was in his office.

The time was 11 A.M. in Newnan, 10 A.M. in Auburn. The date was November 22, 1963.

Aderhold and Eaves had met the night before in the Heart of Auburn Motel. It was there Aderhold had offered the silver-haired Eaves the position of Georgia athletic director.

Aderhold had given Eaves until the next morning to make a decision.

Eaves took the job. The announcement would have been even bigger news that day, but it was overshadowed. Two hours after Aderhold and Eaves talked, John Kennedy was assassinated in Dallas.

What Georgia people knew about Joel Eaves was that he had been a successful basketball coach at Auburn. But the inevitable question came, "What can he do for our football program?"

Georgia was deep in the football pits when Eaves arrived in Athens. Facilities were awful. There was little money in the bank. Georgia Tech had whipped the Bulldogs three straight. The Wally Butts-Bear Bryant-*Saturday Evening Post* episode had lasted what seemed like forever.

Johnny Griffith had replaced Butts in 1961 after Butts had resigned. He inherited a disaster. He never had a chance. The alumni went for his throat in 1963 after three straight losing seasons.

The alumni were barking at Aderhold as well. Find somebody to straighten out this mess, they said, and find him fast.

Eaves, with his gentle, yet firm manner, had impressed Aderhold, who was nearing retirement.

"He doesn't scream and rant and rave like those other basketball coaches," he would say.

Joel Eaves was the son of a brickmason. He had grown up in Atlanta near Grant Park. He cut grass, delivered papers and caddied for 70 cents a round at James L. Key golf course. He

18

played three sports during his college days at Auburn. He coached basketball at Atlanta's Murphy High and later returned to Auburn to coach his alma mater's basketball team to 14 straight winning seasons.

But, again, big deal. What could he do for Georgia's pitiable football program?

His first decision brought more negative reaction than any subsequent decision he would make. Georgia needed a football coach. The alumni wanted a name, someone who had won before.

Eaves gave them Vincent Joseph Dooley, a 31-year-old nobody who was the freshman coach at Auburn.

It is December, 1963, and the athletic board is in a state of shock. They have gathered in the Georgia Center for Continuing Education. Eaves has just announced his choice for head coach.

Until that moment only Dooley, Aderhold, Gov. Carl Sanders, sports information director Dan Magill and Eaves had known. A group of pallbearers had never looked so depressed.

Young Vince Dooley congratulated by Tech's Bobby Dodd after Dooley's first win over the Yellow Jackets, 7-0 in 1964. End Barry Wilson (86) is now a Tech assistant.

Picture Day in Athens. "Vince Who?" with a slow prospect.

20

"I can tell you two things about him," Eaves, with his peculiar candor, told the group. "He's got a big nose and he won't panic." Eaves was right on both counts, but that day all the athletic board knew for sure was that Dooley did, in fact, have a prominent nose.

President Aderhold certainly hadn't heard of Dooley, who had quarterbacked Auburn's 1951-52-53 teams and who had later coached under Shug Jordan and with Eaves at Auburn.

A handful of press had gathered to meet and interview the new coach in the old president's dining room at the Georgia Center. Aderhold was asked to make a statement about Dooley, a handsome fellow who then wore a snap-on tie and who had combed his hair straight back, making him look more like a bouncer at the VFW club than a major college head football coach.

Aderhold couldn't remember Dooley's name, not for the life of him. When he talked, Aderhold had a habit of dipping his knees and jingling the considerable change he always seemed to have in his pockets. He cleared his throat and set out to compliment the new coach, obviously hoping the name would come.

"Uhhhh, we are proud to, er, have this, er, bright young coach to come with us. He, uh . . . this bright young coach comes highly recommended by the folks at Auburn University."

He continued to look at Dooley and search for his name, but it never came. Finally, after praising the "bright, young coach" a number of times, he jingled his change violently one more time and turned to Eaves and made perhaps the most profound statement of his administration.

"In the future," he said, "when you have questions on athletics, call the athletic director, don't call me."

Eaves took that statement as irrevocable, and it would come to trouble him at times during his remarkable career at Georgia. I was associated with him, directly or indirectly, for 14 years. He is from the old school, from the school that says when you run something, you do the running and you run it right and nobody—nobody—should interfere with you. Communicating with, and answering to, a committee was not only impractical to Eaves, it was ridiculous.

From the very start he was a tough-minded, unyielding administrator. He picked young Dooley when probably nobody else would

have. When he retired, in 1979, there could be no question he had built a solid program at Georgia, one ready for national accomplishments.

He was frugal. He was more than that. At times he was downright tight. He was making sure no unnecessary lights were left on in the Georgia athletic offices long before it became the fashion to conserve energy. He didn't believe in borrowing or deficit spending. He didn't understand accountants' symbols and codes, nor did he speak the lingo of bankers. He simply squeezed every dollar an extra time before turning it loose. He treated the Athletic Association's money as if it were his own.

Eaves stood for honesty in a time when college athletics seemed fraught with cheating. If you want to provide a deterrent to illegalities in college athletics, you do what Joel Eaves did. He swore he would fire any member of his staff who violated the first rule.

He had many sides as Georgia's athletic director: A shy and withdrawn side, a tough side, a sentimental side, a stubborn side, a sensitive side. Unfortunately for him and for the many who had business relationships with him, they saw only one side, and often it was that part of him that could be immovable.

There was the matter of the state legislature's tickets. In the past the state's lawmakers would pick the best home game on the Georgia schedule and request a number of tickets. Eaves told the legislature, essentially, to go to hell, no matter how much money it had appropriated for the university that year. Give up a hundred single game tickets for Georgia Tech or Alabama, Eaves reasoned, and you have lost the possibility of a hundred season ticket sales.

"The tickets to Georgia football games are for Georgia fans who support us by buying season tickets," Eaves said. "The legislature can order season tickets like everybody else."

There was pressure. Politicians went screaming to the chancellor of the university system to pressure Georgia President Fred Davison, who had succeeded Aderhold, to force Eaves to change his mind.

Eaves never budged in his thinking, but he ultimately did have to compromise. Still, he remained critical of politicians, and many of them felt he considered their entire lot undesirable characters.

Two nights before Georgia lost to Arkansas in the 1969 Sugar Bowl I sought out the late George L. Smith of Swainsboro in New

Orleans. He was speaker of the house and for years one of the most powerful men in Georgia.

In his position he had been invited to the game as a guest of the university by the president's office. As a member of the official party he would receive a per diem check, drawn on the athletic association, for meals.

I was then business manager of athletics. I found him in Brennan's to deliver the check. He politely refused it.

"You are my friend," he said. "You're from Wrightsville and I'm from Swainsboro. We're neighbors, and I like my neighbors. I also like my university. I am a Georgia Bulldog, and I like being a Bulldog. But you go tell your Mr. Eaves I don't want anything from him or his athletic department."

Regardless of his scraps with politicians and his displays of stubbornness, Joel Eaves performed a miracle at Georgia. Consider:

—By 1969, five football seasons under his "nobody"-coach Vince Dooley, Georgia Tech was still looking for its first victory over a Dooley team; there had been two conference championships, and four bowl trips.

—By 1969 facilities had become a showcase. Sanford Stadium had been decked, and there was surplus money in the bank.

—Georgia fans had begun worrying about the basketball program. When Georgia people began worrying about basketball in those days, it was an assurance the state of football affairs was close to perfection.

—During his career at Georgia, which spanned 5,699 days, there was only one losing football team, and the Bulldogs won 18

Southeastern Conference titles. AND, Eaves would quickly point out, the ink was forever black.

He made it through bypass heart surgery in 1977, and he was in the stands when Rex Robinson kicked off for Georgia at the 1981 Sugar Bowl, shooting for a national championship.

What must have been going through his mind! The day Aderhold called from Newnan. The press conference to announce the Dooley hiring. Dooley's first game, a crushing 31-3 loss to Alabama and Joe Namath in Tuscaloosa. The first victory, the next week, 7-0 against Vanderbilt on a hot Saturday night in Nashville.

And that first season, that 1964 season, what a season it was. It ended with Georgia's sixth victory, a 7-0 defeat of Georgia Tech, captained by Bill Curry on a rainy day in Sanford Stadium. Georgia immediately accepted a bid to play Texas Tech in the Sun Bowl.

Dr. Don Ewalt of the bowl was at the game, all the way from El Paso. As he offered the bid, he passed out sombreros for the coaches. Later he said he was impressed with Georgia's hospitality. President Aderhold had hugged him.

It was not a national title, not even a conference championship, but it brought Georgia back from the dead, and it proved Joel Eaves and that "bright young coach" from Auburn knew what they were doing.

Eaves' genius cannot be denied. Neither can the fact he had to perform his job, the last several years, with a broken heart.

Georgia opened its 1968 season against Tennessee in Knoxville. We stayed in a motel

Pair of aces. Lynn Hughes (left) and Preston Ridlehuber were two of Dooley's first stars at Georgia. Ridlehuber quarterbacked the Bulldogs to a big upset over Michigan in 1965 and Hughes went on to make All-American at safety.

Upset in Jacksonville. Georgia placekicker Bobby Etter (11) scores the winning touchdown against Florida in 1964 after recovering a fumbled snap on a field goal attempt. The Gators fell, 14-7.

near the airport. Following breakfast the day of the game, Eaves watched sleek jetliners take off and land with precision.

"It's amazing how those big things fly," somebody said to him.

"Yeah," he replied. "Makes you wonder why it takes so long for them to learn how to stop something like cancer."

The cancer was Joel Jr.'s, his son's. Even then, I think he knew Buddy would not recover. Buddy Eaves died in 1974. He was 24 years old. His father still cannot, and will not, talk about the death.

Eaves was the best athletic director Georgia has ever had. He brought integrity back to the program. Whatever he failed in public relations, he made up for with sheer human kindness.

He fought Tennessee athletic director Bob

Woodruff forever. If Woodruff said at 10 o'clock in the morning that the sun was up, Eaves would disagree. If Woodruff said "black," Eaves would say "white." It was a personality clash, nothing bitter, just two stubborn warhorses always pulling in opposite directions.

When Woodruff's wife, Margaret, fell down a flight of steps and was critically injured, Eaves called Woodruff every day for over a week. When she died, Eaves made special arrangements to get to her funeral.

"I think athletic people are closer," Eaves said of his response to Woodruff's plight. "I think we understand one another."

23

Dooley and the Bear. A sweet victory ride for the Georgia coach after the 18-17 upset of Alabama in the opening game of 1965.

"Say It Ain't So"

At the front door of the charming old Casa Blanca Hotel, which is anchored into the georgeous blue waters of the Caribbean in Montego Beach, Jamaica, Vince Dooley and I were greeted by our favorite cab driver.

"Taxi, mon?" said Brockett.

Brockett was our friend, our guide, our confidante, but we could never figure why. Certainly not because we were big tippers. I can—under certain influences—become a careless tipper, but never when I'm around Vince Dooley. Dooley can best be described as a calculated tipper, regardless of influences. In fact, he calculates everything.

We declined Brockett's offer for cab service this particular evening, choosing instead to walk the dusty main street, past the several vacation hotels, to a night spot called Club de Camp.

It was winter of 1969, and already Vince Dooley had won two Southeastern Conference football championships for Georgia. He had not yet lost to Georgia Tech, he had been to four bowls, and he had recruited all-Americans like Bill Stanfill and Jake Scott. Vince Dooley was at the top of the mountain. He was making the chapel bell ring in Athens on Saturday nights, and he was enjoying the financial, social and emotional status that comes with such heady success.

There were still a few dissenters around, those who didn't like Dooley's air-of-stiffness personality, those who didn't like his run-oriented offense, those who felt the forward pass should be employed at Georgia like an automatic rifle.

I've never seen Dooley beam more than he did at a dinner in the late sixties with Georgia Senator Richard B. Russell in Washington. The late senator from Winder, just up the road from Athens, chastised those who would have more passing by saying, "I like a fair amount of circus with my football, too, but you have to run to win."

Those early years were great years for Vincent Joseph Dooley, not yet forty. As we walked this evening, a Jamaican street band sang out:

This is my island,
In the sun. . . .

I thought to myself, Vince Dooley has found his island in the sun, too. At Club de Camp we sang with the band, gave a clumsy performance of the limbo and sipped Red Stripe beer. There is still nothing Dooley enjoys more than relaxing in a new environment where there are no alumni, no fans to talk about football. In those settings he can put aside everything except what is happening at the moment.

But I wanted to talk this night, I wanted to probe this man, about his thoughts concerning the Georgia football program and the future of it. There was small talk, on my part, here and there about certain problems, especially that of real or imagined insensitivity of athletic director Joel Eaves to certain Georgia alumni and that of athletic department public relations in general. Those things greatly troubled me in those days.

I couldn't get anything out of Dooley. He smoked his pipe and ignored me. Later, however, after we had returned to the patio of the Casa Blanca and were enjoying the cool evening breezes and the peaceful sounds of the Caribbean splashing against the hotel, I blurted out, "You know, Vince, I could never work for another school. Georgia is the only school I'll ever work for."

I didn't make that statement expecting a response, but I will never forget the one Dooley offered.

He said a man's feelings for his alma mater should be real, but that as a coach, he recognized there was no reason why he couldn't enjoy a professional association with another school.

"Ideally," he said between puffs of his pipe, "in this business you need to change jobs at least one time."

Already he had passed up one splendid opportunity to go elsewhere. In time he would pass up another. That he has remained at one school for seventeen years in a profession known for its high turnover rate is probably a tribute to the patience of both coach and alumni wolves.

Dooley's first season, 1964, ended in triumph, a 7-0 victory over Texas Tech in the Sun Bowl for a 7-3-1 record. Dr. Aderhold was happy. The athletic board was happy. They had the alumni off their backs, and the athletic director was running the show, and they could already tell he knew how to manage a dollar and that he would keep them free of red ink.

And the new football coach was working out so well, too. Vince Dooley was being hailed as a miracle worker all over the state and southeast. Miracle workers don't usually cash in, and Dooley was following suit. For the magic he performed in Athens in 1964, he was paid $14,500 in salary and $100 per Sunday for his television show.

Joel Eaves and Vince Dooley had worked closely at Auburn. They spent hours on the road together scouting opposing teams. It was a warm, genial relationship, but one that Eaves, the elder, dominated.

That didn't change when the pair took over at the University of Georgia. Eaves, during Dooley's first season, even made his young coach check with him concerning how many players could fly with the team when it went out of town on a road trip. Eaves and Dooley fought at times, but they did it eyeball-to-eyeball, behind closed doors. They had enormous respect for each other, but Dooley had his gripe—he wanted more control and more independence in running his football team. At the same time, he was resolved not to hurt Eaves in any way. It was Eaves who had given him his chance to be a head football coach. Without Eaves he might even today be an obscure history professor somewhere in the state of Alabama.

But two years after arriving unknown and unappreciated in Athens, Dooley finally gained that independence he was seeking.

The 1965 season began incredibly. Georgia upset Alabama on national television with the Kirby Moore-to-Pat Hodgson-to-Bob Taylor flea flicker, 18-17. Dooley was a genius. A couple of weeks later his team went to Ann Arbor and upset defending Rose Bowl champion Michigan. Dooley and Georgia got national recognition.

The season could have gone on to even loftier heights had not a rash of injuries and bad luck struck the Bulldogs. In the Auburn game, for instance, fullback Ronnie Jenkins fumbled away what could have been the winning touchdown on the Auburn one-yard-line with time running out.

Dooley's head was low as I drove him back to the Coliseum from Sanford Stadium that afternoon.

"Why did I do it?" he asked aloud. "Why did I give the ball to Jenkins? Why did I do it?"

The Auburn loss was especially tough because it was his second straight against his alma mater, and Dooley wanted to beat Auburn badly. When he and Eaves left Auburn two years earlier there had been no tears, no going-away party and no well-wishes. Some bitterness between Eaves, the head basketball coach at Auburn, and Shug Jordan, the head football coach, had filtered out to Dooley, as well. I've been with Vince Dooley after every game he's lost at Georgia. I still feel the one that hurt as much as any was that 1965 loss to Auburn.

The season did end on a happy note for Georgia, however. Dooley surprised Georgia Tech in Atlanta with an unbalanced line and

again he defeated the Yellow Jackets, 17-7. The surprise attack caused Tech head coach Bobby Dodd to give his assistant coaches a fierce tongue-lashing.

Meanwhile, out in Norman, Oklahoma, the winds and the alumni were howling. Gomer Jones, who had taken over the University of Oklahoma football fortunes after the legendary Bud Wilkinson had retired, had fallen into great disfavor. He would eventually be canned, and the Sooners would be looking for a successor.

It was Wilkinson himself who suggested Oklahoma approach the thirty-three-year-old Dooley from Georgia. Wilkinson had retired at Oklahoma to make an unsuccessful run for the U.S. Senate. Later he had taken a job as a color analyst for NBC college football broadcasts. He and Jim Simpson were in Athens for Georgia's upset of Alabama in the '65 opener. After the flea-flicker put Georgia in

It's all over in Ann Arbor. Georgia startled the nation in 1965 with an upset of the defending Rose Bowl champions, Michigan, on the Wolverines' home field. At bottom left, Dooley and his assistants ride toward the dressing room on the shoulders of their players.

Former Oklahoma coach Bud Wilkinson with Dooley before the nationally televised opener with Alabama in 1965. Georgia would upset the Tide and Wilkinson, who covered the game for NBC, would recommend the Bulldog coach be hired to take over the faltering Sooner fortunes.

reach, 16-17, Wilkinson, who was on the Bulldog sideline to do a post-game interview, said to Vince, "We've got to go for two!" as Dooley called time out to consult with his assistants. A few weeks later, Wilkinson told Dr. George Cross, Oklahoma's president, the man who could put his football program back together again was in Athens, Georgia, and was probably his for the taking.

Oklahoma had the money, oil money. In December of '65 the school asked permission to interview Dooley. Dr. Aderhold must have considered suicide. Dooley went to Norman to interview, and the entire state was in an uproar.

In the end there were several factors that kept Dooley in Athens:

—Lawyer M. E. (Buster) Kilpatrick of Atlanta drew Dooley a tax-sheltered annuities program, more logical and more rewarding in the long-run than the cash bundle (rumored $40,000 per year) Oklahoma had offered.

—There was the promise of more independence in running the football program at Georgia.

—Wife Barbara, though willing to go to Oklahoma had that been her husband's final decision, preferred the trees and hills of Athens to the flatlands of Norman.

Eaves met Dooley in the Riviera Hotel in Atlanta to make the counter offer to Oklahoma. The details were worked out and Dooley told Eaves he would stay. Then, Dooley would reveal later, the normally mild-mannered athletic director "danced around the room like a little kid, jumping on the beds and hollering."

Eaves rejoiced. I rejoiced. The entire state breathed a collective sigh of relief. Dooley was staying in Athens. The first Southeastern Conference championship would follow the next season, in 1966. Another title would come in '68. The seventies would bring a few down years, and another title in 1976, and Dooley would even suffer through his first losing season (5-6) in 1977.

I recall, during a couple of those less-than-glorious seasons, the scattered "Dump Dooley" bumper stickers that surfaced. Perhaps Pepper Rodgers, the deposed Georgia Tech coach, explained the business of football coaching better than anybody else:

"It's a lot easier being a doctor," Pepper explained. "You operate on a patient, do your very best, but if he dies, all you have to do is walk out and tell the family, 'I did all I could'.

Not only do they forgive you, they still have to pay you, too. Lose a game as a football coach because some nineteen-year old dropped the ball and the alumni want your hide."

Still, after the Oklahoma offer, Dooley never talked seriously with another school until 1980. Many had sent feelers, but Dooley always rejected them. Not only did he not respond to those feelers, he also refused to allow anything to be said about them publicly. He has often remarked, "It's work to keep your name out of the papers regarding other jobs."

So the glorious 1980 season came, and eleven straight victories later it is Sunday morning following the victory over Georgia Tech on Saturday. It is Georgia's third straight win over Tech and Dooley's thirteenth in seventeen tries. Georgia is ranked No. 1 nationally, it has another SEC title, and it can win its first national championship by defeating Notre Dame in the Sugar Bowl. Ah, it is Georgia's finest hour. What could happen to spoil it?

It was that story on the front page of the *Atlanta Journal-Constitution* sports section that very morning, November 30, 1980. Auburn University might, indeed, call Vince Dooley home to take over its entangled football mess, and Vince Dooley might, indeed, accept the challenge.

I met Dooley in his office that morning to tape his weekly radio show. As we finished, Dan Magill walked in and offered his congratulations on the season.

Magill paused at the end of his congratulatory remarks and then added, "Say it ain't so."

"Close the door," said Dooley.

I felt a sinking feeling in my stomach. When I had read the story earlier, I figured it was more newspaper rumor than anything else. Now I was certain there was something to it.

"This is between just us," Dooley began, "but Auburn *is* going to make a serious effort to try to hire me. I've had unofficial feelers, but I won't negotiate that way. I have told them they have to observe protocol, and if they contact Dr. Davison and go through the proper channels, I will have to talk to them."

The sinking feeling in my stomach continued. So did Dooley.

"The Auburn people are upset with their program and all the divisiveness over there," he went on. "I know they're going to make a substantial offer. I've got to listen. It's home.

29

It's my alma mater. The two of you understand that, don't you?"

Magill and I nodded. Dooley then made us a promise.

"If they come to me," he said, "I will evaluate the situation from all standpoints, and I will make a quick decision. I won't drag it out."

The room was silent. Finally, Magill spoke up.

"You've done a marvelous job here," he said. "The Georgia people won't want to lose you. I hope there is some way you can stay."

I mumbled something like that, too. I forget what. I was preoccupied with my own rationalization of what was happening here. I had, in the past, considered Auburn luring Dooley back, and I had expressed that consideration often to assistant coach Bill Hartman, a close friend. But Hartman had steadfastly disagreed.

"He just won't ever go," Hartman had said.

But what was it Dooley had told me that night at the Casa Blanca Hotel in Jamaica? A coach should move at least once. Where better to go than back home? And Auburn needed him now, *really* needed him now. And they could pay, and they could meet any demand he might make.

I tried to look on the other hand. He is at the pinnacle of his career at Georgia, ranked No. 1, undefeated, untied, with a chance to win a national championship. He would give that up? He would leave, perish the thought, Herschel Walker?

I went back and forth and back and forth. There was the matter of Fob James, of course. Fob James and Dooley played in the same backfield at Auburn. They are close friends, they sometimes vacation together. And who is Fob James? Governor of Alabama, that's who, an Auburn man who is probably sick and tired of seeing his school get clobbered by Bear Bryant and Alabama year after year. He'll work to bring Dooley back, of course.

But what of Bryant? Who, in his right mind, would take a job where you have to beat Bryant to keep the alumni happy? The other angle, however: Bryant is nearing retirement. When he goes, won't Alabama have the usual problem trying to find a successor to a legend? Wouldn't a new, successful head coach at Auburn then be rolling in the finest of clover?

As we walked out of his office that morning in November, Dooley asked if his wife, Barbara, was keeping our children while my wife, Myrna, and I took a week's trip to Phoenix. I told him, no. Myrna had decided not to ask because she felt it would be too much for Barbara who was still recuperating from surgery following the mid-season automobile accident in which she and Vince had been involved.

I followed Magill out the door and back downstairs to his office. When we reached his office I said, "Dan, he's gone."

"You bet your boots he's gone," said Magill.

The next three days were madness. There was story after story in the newspapers, most of which were certain Dooley would accept the Auburn offer, which turned out to be a startling $1.8 million AND the full athletic directorship which Dooley still did not have at Georgia.

The fan reaction was, well, interesting. From Vince-the-Victorious a day or two ealier, he was now Vince-the-Villain. He was raining on the parade. There were two schools of dissenting thought:

—If he's that disloyal, said some, then let him go. How could a man seventeen years at Georgia, now on top of the football world, even consider going back to Auburn, alma mater or no alma mater?

—A person should consider all offers, said others, but can't it wait? Won't negotiating the possibility of leaving hurt Georgia's chances in the Sugar Bowl? "We've waited all our lives for this moment," an alumnus from South Georgia had said, "and now the man who led us to it seems to be spoiling it."

Dr. Hanly Funderburk, president of Auburn, made the call Dooley had insisted upon. He called Georgia president Dr. Fred Davison, who had succeeded O.C. Aderhold in 1967, and asked permission to talk to Dooley about the Auburn job at the Southeastern Conference meetings which would begin Monday in Birmingham.

Protocol dictated Davison give his agreement to the meeting. Back to Bryant: he was head coach at Texas A&M when Alabama, his alma mater, successfully brought him home. He was asked later why he had returned.

"Mama called," he replied.

Now, "Mama" was calling Dooley. There was tremendous pressure and sentiment from Auburn to hire Dooley. Auburn would further make public its intentions and its dedication to change by quickly announcing the firing of its current head coach, the beleaguered Doug Barfield.

The day after he was fired, incidentally—while Dooley was negotiating for the million-eight—Barfield had to pull jury duty at federal court in Montgomery. Each prospective juror had to give his name, address and occupation. Barfield stood before a hushed courtroom and said:

"Doug Barfield.

"Auburn, Alabama.

"Unemployed."

Dooley and Davison met in Davison's hotel room Sunday afternoon in Birmingham. Dooley explained his reasons for wanting to listen to the Auburn offer.

"If I were trying to hire a coach," Davison had said, "I would want somebody like you too."

Dooley returned to his room and called his lawyer, Nick Chilivis, in Atlanta and asked him to fly to Birmingham as soon as possible to be with him during the meetings with the Auburn selection committee the next day.

Chilivis arrived Monday and the two went in for a morning meeting with the Auburn representatives.

"I am interested, of course," Dooley opened, "but I have to be satisfied that leaving Georgia would be in my best interest."

The meeting dragged on through the morning. There was no break for lunch. Sandwiches were ordered to the room. At the end of the session that afternoon there was still to be no major announcements. Dooley called Athens and made a statement for release by sports information director Claude Felton which said, essentially, there had been a meeting, but there was no decision. The mood in Athens was glum and the concensus among even athletic board members was that their head coach was gone.

Monday night Dooley was scheduled to speak in Orlando. He kept his commitment. He was flown there by Allan Parks, who was the starting Auburn quarterback when Dooley was a sophomore.

After the Orlando meeting he went out to dinner with former LSU coach Charley McClendon, who now runs Orlando's Tangerine Bowl.

"He wasn't there all evening," said McClendon later. "He sort of came and went, like he had so much on his mind."

That night Dooley slept at the home of a former Athens Touchdown club president, Harold Brewer, who had just moved to Orlando. It was a sleepless night. He was burdened with fatigue when he arrived at the Atlanta airport the next day to be met by Bill Hartman and former Georgia player and athletic board member Don Leebern. Dooley wanted to learn from Hartman and Leebern the climate in Athens. He wanted to make an objective decision, but he didn't feel he could if the atmosphere was negative or bitter toward him. During the drive back to Athens, Hartman, for years a close and trusted adviser to Dooley, assured him Georgia still considered him its head coach and wanted no change in that situation.

Dooley arrived home at 755 Milledge Circle in Athens at 4:15. He had no time to bring his wife up to date. He was to meet with Davison at 4:30 at Davison's campus office in Lustrat House. Chilivis had previously met with Davison for two hours alone. Dooley had felt it would be helpful for someone other than himself to try to further articulate his reasons for reviewing the Auburn offer. He also wanted to point out—contrary to various newspaper reports—that no decision had been made. He had not even had time to talk over the situation with his family. It was not a negotiating session between Davison and Chilivis. Positions were simply stated. All parties wanted to make certain that communications would be open, candid, and direct.

The athletic board had met in emergency session Monday night to discuss what would happen if Dooley should leave. They had to formulate some sort of plan, with the national championship game only a month away and the recruiting season in full swing. There is little doubt the board would have named Dooley's chief assistant Erskine Russell the head coach for the Sugar Bowl. After that, no plans were made.

When Dooley and Davison finally met that Tuesday afternoon, they did not start with negotiations. First they reminisced and perhaps it was at that point that the pendulum began to swing back into Georgia's favor for Dooley to remain in Athens.

Dooley and Davison first met during Dooley's first year in Athens, 1964. Davison was then dean of the School of Veterinary Medicine and a serious football fan. He and Dooley were both members of the Athens Rotary Club. They sat together often in meetings. And often they drove to nearby Jefferson and other neighboring cities to attend makeup Rotary meetings. They became friends. They became close.

31

Davison later moved to Atlanta to become vice chancellor of the university system. When he was named president of the university in 1967, Dooley couldn't have been more pleased. He felt Davison liked athletics but would support athletics with the proper perspective. He would not be a rubber stamp for whatever the athletic department wanted, but he would see to it his athletic department was of the quality many other presidents seek, but seldom get. The Dooley-Davison trips to Jefferson began again.

Both sides were honest and open and candid that day in Lustrat House. If Dooley were to stay at Georgia, the matter of the athletic directorship would have to be cleared up, once and for all. At Auburn he had been offered BOTH jobs—head football coach AND athletic director. At Georgia, he still lacked full control. Some backgound is necessary to fully understand Dooley's position:

He is still a relatively young man, forty-nine, but Vince Dooley, I am certain, has no plans to continue coaching until retirement age like Bryant at Alabama, for instance. So, where does a man like Dooley go after leaving the sidelines? The athletic director's chair, of course.

"I've got to have a place to step up to if they kick me out," he has so aptly put it in times past. Win the world championship and they love you. Put losing seasons back-to-back and . . . well, recall Pepper Rodgers' statement.

Consequently, when Joel Eaves indicated he would retire at sixty-five in 1979, many assumed Dooley would take on the dual position of football coach-athletic director. He wanted both jobs. He felt he had earned that position. He had not played footsie with other schools. He had displayed a deep commitment to Georgia and he felt, frankly, he was an exception to the rule of not giving one man both jobs.

But Fred Davison had been concerned about the problems that could arise from combining the two positions. He liked Dooley and respected him, of course, and he obviously appreciated him. But he obviously felt Dooley's future was secure enough that he would not need to aspire to have both jobs. If Dooley did want to become athletic director, and give up coaching, Davison was prepared to create an avenue for such a move.

But consider Dooley's side again: He really had no assurance of such a move, especially if those back-to-back losing seasons came. And

what if Davison moved on to another job? Where would that leave him?

It is probably too late to do anything about the basic structure of college athletics, but the college presidents could have done something smart many years ago if they had had the foresight to do so. It might have been done in Knute Rockne's era or even earlier as the college football boom gained such a grip on the public. If they had made coaches teachers, as they should be, and had integrated them into the pure academic process and given them tenure, the problem wouldn't be what it is today.

Who can blame the coaches for wanting fat contracts and then breaking them for a better deal? You coach successfully for ten years and you're forty-five years old, in the prime of life, and you have back-to-back losing seasons and, bam, you're gone. Sometimes it gets out of the institution's hands. Politics are there and always will be.

You have to win to keep your job. It's that simple.

In June of '79, Eaves retired. But Dooley did not get the full athletic directorship. A compromise was struck. Reid Parker, a good man miscast, became athletic director for administration and Dooley became athletic director for sports.

It was, however, Dooley and Davison who had drawn up the compromise, and Dooley was never bitter about the arrangement as some believed. Obviously it did not offer the security of an outright athletic directorship which long-term was a liability for Dooley, but in the day-to-day office routine, it posed him no problem. He and Parker not only got along, the operation was smooth.

However, there can be no question that full control of the athletic department was a drawing point to Auburn, and if Georgia were to keep Dooley, it would likely have to make a similar offer. That, of course, would eventually be agreed upon between Dooley and Davison, but what Dr. Fred Davison had done for Dooley five years before may also have entered deeply into the coach's mind when he made his final decision to remain at Georgia. Dooley admitted later thinking about the incident as he talked to Davison that Tuesday.

The 1974 season had ended on a sour note, a loss to Pepper Rodgers and Georgia Tech in the Athens mud. Then Georgia agreed to play Miami of Ohio in the Tangerine Bowl, which Dooley would later agree was a mistake. The

Bulldogs, with a poor regular season and no business in a bowl, lost. An Atlanta sportswriter said the Georgia program had "no class."

Summer came and Dooley was entering the last year of a four-year contract. The "Dump Dooley" stickers were out. Even the athletic board was grumbling, especially about the bowl trip. Dooley's future was a daily topic of speculation in the state's newspapers.

As the 1975 season approached, Dooley had a serious problem—how to prepare his team when there was so much conversation as to whether or not he would be around after the first game, or after the end of the season. The question was prominent on everybody's mind as Dooley began to make final preparations for the start of summer practice in early August.

As the team reported for the annual Picture Day, Davison was meeting with the athletic board. In an unprecedented move he orchestrated a move with the board to give Dooley a three-year extension on his contract. The staff and the players did not have to concern themselves with Dooley's status after that, and the result was a 9-2 regular season and a Cotton Bowl trip. If a president ever had a direct hand in a winning season, it was Fred Davison in 1975.

Dooley never forgot that gesture by Davison. He also never forgot the times Davison came into the Bulldogs' dressing room after a game, hoarse from cheering unabashedly for his school's team.

The Dooley-Davison Tuesday meeting lasted into the early evening. Neither man has ever made public exactly what was decided in the meeting, but it is relatively easy to figure Dooley was promised the full athletic directorship as soon as it could be worked out.

Dooley was finally able to go home to talk the situation over with his family.

There was the matter of his children, all four of whom had grown up in Athens . . . as Bulldogs. An eldest son had another year of football at powerful Clarke Central High. His daughters had friends and boyfriends. Athens had been home for the Dooleys for seventeen years.

Dooley, when he arrived home that evening, still had not made up his mind. It had been a whirlwind three days, from Athens to Birmingham to Orlando, back to Atlanta and then to Athens for the meeting with Fred Davison. There had been no quiet time.

Dooley had promised he would not drag out the decision. The time had come to make one.

Dooley and Davison at press conference in 1980. Did a gesture by the Georgia president keep his football coach away from Auburn?

He was at home, alone with his wife. They talked. Vince Dooley *calculates everything.* He outlined each of the sessions—with Auburn and with Davison—to his wife. He talked about the pros and cons of each situation. He was interrupted only once. Jesse Outlar, sports editor of the *Atlanta Constitution,* came by. The state, as was the case fifteen years earlier, awaited his answer.

He was already leaning, he admitted later, toward staying. In Auburn, they still thought just the contrary. Plans were already being made for a press conference to announce the new appointment.

Late into the night they talked, Vince and Barbara Dooley. At one point, as he talked, Dooley wandered into a sitting room just off his den. In that room the walls are covered with the pictures of his All-Southeastern Conference players, of which there have been many.

Suddenly Dooley fell silent. He gazed at the pictures.

"Barbara," he said to his wife, still in the den, "we've got too much invested here. All these players, all these teams. I love Georgia too much to leave."

He walked back into the den. He smiled at his wife and she smiled back at him. They embraced. It was over.

A
Study In
Commitment

The warm waters of the Caribbean are royal blue. Vince Dooley's broad back is white, as is the bald spot on the top of his head. His face is covered with a snorkel mask. He is searching the ocean floor, which he can do for hours.

There is something about Dooley's love for the water that says a lot about the man. He has stamina and durability in the water. He likes the challenge of the sea. He is confident in an environment where others may become tense and apprehensive. There is adventure in Vince Dooley's soul.

I have seen him and known him in a variety of environments for many years, but aside from thrilling moments in football, I have never seen him more exuberant than a few years ago when he discovered a queen conch shell during that snorkeling episode a few miles out from Grand Cayman Island.

A queen conch is a rare find, and it was not purely an accident that he discovered the treasure. He worked at it during a long afternoon of exploration. I watched him from our boat, which was operated by a Caymanian named Churchill.

Dooley drifted along with the tide. Churchill watched him too.

"He's drifting too far," the Caymanian said. But Dooley worked on and on. He was in his own world where no one else existed.

LEFT: The student and his teacher. Dooley and his coach at Auburn, Ralph (Shug) Jordan, after a Georgia victory over the Tigers clinches a Southeastern Conference title, one of four. ABOVE: Dooley was tightlipped and pensive as his team warmed up for the 1981 Sugar Bowl in New Orleans.

When he came back aboard the boat, Churchill warned of the dangerous currents late in the afternoon. Dooley didn't hear him. He was too pleased with his discovery to worry about his personal safety.

"Look at this, Billy," he grinned, almost like a little boy, to his brother, "a queen conch." He held it aloft and displayed as much emotion as he did when he was carried from the field following the Sugar Bowl in 1981.

He grew up on the water, fishing the Mobile River. He still fishes as hard as any man I have ever seen. On vacations I have known him to fish for a week, starting at six in the morning and stopping only at dusk.

He is an excellent spearfisherman. Perhaps too good. Once in Jamaica he took after a flounder and chased it for hours. Again, the challenge. Match wits against the fish and the ocean and see who wins.

Dooley wins. He speared the flounder, but he had dived too deep. When he came back to the boat, his nose was bleeding badly.

"You idiot! You stupid idiot!" wife Barbara chastised him, out of her own concern for his well-being.

But that is his way, this intricate, complex man. Whatever he does, he does with great gusto, with intensity, and I mentioned how he feels about a commitment. *A commitment is a commitment.*

He is consumed by that which he pursues. On a flight home from a two-week tour in Italy, Dooley decided he would spend the entire flight reading a biography of Benito Mussolini. The day before we caught the plane to New York he had searched every bookstore in Rome until he found an English translation of the Il Duce biography.

He had a window seat in the plane and I had the aisle. Between us was Barbara. Vince read his book. I organized notes I had made on the trip. And I slept. Barbara became more and more displeased with our silence and our preoccupation. Before the trip was over, her Lebanese temper was to the boiling point. She chastised her husband relentlessly.

"I'm not going to share any more of our time with Mussolini!" she declared.

Dooley looked up only once during the tirade, with that wry smile of his, expressing amusement more than anything else. The tirade continued most of the trip. But Dooley continued with Mussolini. He had tuned everybody, and everything else, out. He can do that. It could be a marriage liability, of course,

but that tuning-out ability is probably very helpful for a football coach.

His intensity, his concentration, I think, is why he has been successful in his profession. I have also often wondered what kind of a teacher he would have been. Had a few things gone differently, maybe that is what he would have become.

He has a master's degree in history. Politics intrigues him. Soon after he arrived as Georgia's coach I discovered he spent a great deal of time in the university library. I decided that was unique for a college football coach, and I wrote a feature story for the Athens newspaper. The wire services picked it up and the article was played prominently in several Southern newspapers.

Frank Howard, who was still coaching at Clemson at the time, saw the story and remarked to an Atlanta Touchdown Club audience: "Tell Dooley when he loses a few football games, that library will be a nice cool place to hide from the alumni."

Vince Dooley has remained an enigma of sorts to Georgia fans. He has given them championship after championship, but they still wonder about what they call his coldness, his aloofness. A few times he has opened up for public consumption. On Christmas morning, the day before the Georgia team was to leave for New Orleans. I picked up the *Atlanta Constitution* and read an in-depth feature on Dooley, the best, I think, that has ever been done on the man and his relation to his profession and his family.

Dan Barreiro authored the piece, and it was Barbara Dooley who uncovered the man she has lived with, borne four children for, and loved for twenty years.

BARBARA DOOLEY ON HOW SHE MET HER HUSBAND: "Our first conversation was really something. He said, 'Hi, I'm Vince Dooley.'

"I said, 'Well, so what?'

"That really blew him away. He was the big Casanova on the Auburn campus and everybody was supposed to know him. But I really didn't know the name. I think that intrigued him, because I was one of the few girls who wasn't after him."

It was four years later they finally married.

BARBARA DOOLEY ON HER MARRIAGE: "I don't want to knock his family, but he was not brought up in a warm atmosphere. His parents [who are both dead] loved him, and he loved them. But from what I can gather, there was very little outward emotion. There was no

Vince Dooley discusses strategy with George Haffner (top left), braves the chill in Lexington, Ky. (top right), and enjoys 1973 Peach Bowl victory over Maryland, 17-16.

hugging and touching. I have really tried to analyze this because it's bugged me for years.

"I think he thought, as he was growing up, that any outward sign of emotion was sissy, so he suppressed it all trying to be a man. I was raised totally differently, touching, hugging, and kissing. This has been the hardest thing for us to come together on. He married me, so I'm just supposed to know he loves me, but I was raised where you say 'I love you' all the time.

"It was something we had to deal with, and you have no idea how much the man has grown at home. He makes a point of touching the children now. He puts his arms around us at night. He sees how important it is. The coldness people see in him, it's not really coldness; it's not knowing how. He was taught not to cry or touch, but he's not the same man I married. He's warmer now. I watch him. He's making an effort. I appreciate that."

BARBARA DOOLEY ON HOW HARD HER HUSBAND WORKS: "During two-a-day practices, he gets up at 5:30, he goes to work,

and he comes in at midnight. He works seventeen hours a day. He loves it. I wish he loved me that much. I would love to get seventeen hours a day."

BARBARA DOOLEY ON WHY PEOPLE THINK HER HUSBAND IS ALOOF: "Vince is not a performer. He's not a showman. And people are going to have to accept Vince for the kind of man he is. He wears well, once you get to know him, whereas some people overwhelm you at first, then burn out. The more you get to know Vincent, the more you want to know him."

BARBARA DOOLEY ON HER HUSBAND'S EGO: "He's secure. He doesn't need it."

Secure. His search for security in his first days at Georgia may have been what brought on his unfriendly, aloof, distant image.

He was not a social climber in those early days, but he was not unaware of what was being said about him: "What's wrong with the man? Doesn't he have a personality?"

He and Joel Eaves simply felt the athletic staff should remain private until they could determine exactly who the loyal Georgia people were. Plus, the athletic department was in deep disarray. There was little time for anything else besides work.

Also they knew Georgia people were split and only winning would bring them together. Socializing with various groups would serve no useful purpose, especially in Athens where feelings remained sensitive about Wally Butts, who still lived in the community and who was still bitter about what he and his family considered to have been unfair treatment by the university.

Aware of these feelings, one of the first things Dooley did when he got to town was to make a friendly call on Butts, who often wrote him complimentary letters after a Bulldog win and a don't-let-them-get-you-down letter after a tough loss.

Dooley found security in those early days the only way he had ever known: Stick to yourself, think things through, and work night and day. He preferred to socialize with his coaches and with those close to his staff. He did not want to be distracted nor display a casual attitude toward his considerable challenge.

He was right in this attitude, but it was to disappoint many in the community who felt he did not appreciate their interest in Georgia football. Athens was bigger than Auburn, but it functioned socially much the same way. The most important man in the community is the

Vince Dooley, the hunter. Matching wits against his prey. That was in the past. He's now a fisherman.

A last farewell from Bobby Dodd. Dooley's third straight victory over the legendary Tech coach came in 1966 when the Bulldogs whipped the previously undefeated Yellow Jackets, 23-14. Dodd would retire after Tech's subsequent trip to the Orange Bowl. Georgia would defeat SMU in the Cotton Bowl.

football coach. Athens wanted to treat him like a new preacher in a small town. Take him food from the garden, invite him out and give him a happy-to-have-you welcome.

I think if he had it all to do over again he would have been more responsive. But he was only thirty-one. And some of the people weren't all that warm to him. They had wanted a "name," remember, and they had gotten Vince Who? Dooley felt the atmosphere of doubt and disapproval, so he stuck to proving he could do the job and ignored his social standing in Athens.

And one thing he knew then, and it still goes today: Be the most entertaining, charming fellow this side of Bob Hope, but it won't

amount to anything if you don't win. Lose, and they would be saying, "Vince Dooley is certainly entertaining, but we need somebody who is serious about football."

He has improved greatly as a speaker, however. At first he was factual, direct, and to the point. He said what was going on with his football team and then he sat down. He never left them laughing, and he never hustled the big shots or slapped any backs during the pre-speech cocktail hour.

"A man can't change his personality," he would say to me when the critics bore down on him in the seventies.

But he did. Not in a way that would be dishonest. He just showed his human side

39

"Win the 1976 Southeastern Conference title," Dooley said to his team, "and I'll shave my head like the rest of you." The Bulldogs responded with a conference championship, and Dooley responded with this hair-raising experience.

more and he smiled more. Riding through the campus, I would see him wave at a student. I'd say, "Who was that?" He wouldn't have the slightest idea, but he knew he was being recognized and he was practicing good public relations. He was tired of people falsely accusing him of not speaking. The loyal I'd-do-anything-for-my-school alumnus always expects his head coach to speak first and to carry the conversation. Tell funny jokes and slip them some inside poop.

My longtime banker and friend, John (Kid) Terrell of Athens, puts Dooley's role into perspective as well as anybody: "I'm proud of Vince and appreciate him because he's Georgia's coach. His personal life should be his own business. I don't have to drink with him to appreciate him. If he'll ring the Chapel Bell on Saturday nights, I can find somebody to drink with."

Vince has changed. Smart men do. Still, he's no fun to be around when he's edgy,

40

especially if he's lost a game or two. He doesn't publicly show his displeasure at losing, but it is there.

I feel I have known better than anybody else how it hurts for him to lose. We do a post-game radio show for the Georgia network from the locker room after each Georgia game and there were plenty of times when the first questions I asked, no matter what, would make him angry. It didn't bother me. I didn't feel it was anything personal. But friends began to comment they thought something was wrong between us, and that Dooley was taking out his frustrations on me. When people in the broadcast business began to say the same thing, I became concerned and less understanding. I decided to complain.

I had never listened to any tapes of the broadcast, but I decided to do just that three years ago to try to determine how our conversation sounded. We did, in fact, come off as though there was friction.

When I approached Dooley with my concerns, he said he did have a problem with some of my questions. He felt that I led with questions that defended Georgia. He didn't want that. He didn't want it to sound as if Georgia could do no wrong.

We agreed to work on the situation. I said, "Okay, after your first loss this year, I'll say, 'Vince, what in the hell is wrong with the coaching?'"

He laughed. That was the last thing that was said. The show was the best ever in 1980. Georgia won every game.

But Vince Dooley's relationships with broadcasters, fans, alumni, what of it? How does he get along with his players? More than anything else, he has always been honest with his players. As they get older, I imagine they appreciate him more. Like children, players would rather have it their way, even if what they want is not in the best interest of the team.

Chip Wisdom played linebacker for Dooley and then coached for him for eight years. He left after the 1980 season to become defensive coordinator for Memphis State. He has a bright future and will probably be a head coach himself someday.

Chip Wisdom knows Vince Dooley, the coach. His thoughts:

ON DOOLEY, THE MOTIVATOR: "The best thing he did to motivate when I was playing was he would always draw a clear picture of what was at stake in a given ball game or season. He would dramatize and clearly define what our role was in any given situation. In doing so, he made it perfectly evident to everybody on the football team what we could accomplish by winning."

ON DOOLEY, THE LOCKER ROOM SPEAKER: "There's no Lombardi, hellfire and brimstone in him. He never raises his voice, or challenges your courage or manhood. He never tries to con you or give you a sad story so you will play on your emotions. What he does is treat you like a man, like a mature individual. He says, here's what's in front of you, here's the plan the coaches have, but you're the one that has to do it."

ON DOOLEY, WHEN HE LOSES: "I don't think the blame is all his when we lose, but he accepts it. He does so openly, and he doesn't wait for somebody else to get around to it. Players appreciate that."

ON DOOLEY, WHO HAS NEVER MET AN OPPOSING TEAM THAT ISN'T A POWERHOUSE: "I think the way he builds up

The brothers Dooley. Bill (left), a former assistant at Georgia, is head coach and athletic director at Virginia Tech.

41

every opponent is psychologically sound. You always need to have respect for your opponent. I don't think Vince Dooley has ever expressed fear of an opponent, but he always expresses respect for what they are capable of."

ON DOOLEY, THE CRITIC: "I have never known him to run down an individual player on an opposing team or his own team."

There have been grumblings from players that Dooley doesn't attempt to be close to his team. There are two sides to that coin. The other is, does the head coach have the time to get close to seventy-five athletes?

Erskine Russell, Dooley's long-time assistant head coach and friend, says bluntly that the biggest change he has seen in his boss in the seventeen seasons they have been at Georgia is his attitude toward his players.

"He's much closer to them now than ever," suggests Erk. "He's made a big effort in that direction."

Any man who reaches the top of his profession, and Vince Dooley has certainly done that, is unique in some respect, but I believe that he may be the most unusual of all those in his profession.

He never followed the script. It is a tribute to him of the highest order that he overcame what he overcame to be where he is today.

A man many knew to be shy—maybe even a loner—makes it in a profession where you have to expose your personality at every turn, a private man who has had to perform publicly, a man who appreciates the depth to people but is often forced to exist on shallow relationships. He could legitimately be cast as a pipe-smoking professor of history. Yet, for much of his life, formal education had absolutely no appeal to him.

Like so many of his generation he came from a limited environment. He was able to pull himself up by his bootstraps. He avoided becoming a juvenile delinquent and it might have been a closer call than people realize. He's made something of himself, and he's done it on his own terms. He's learned to adjust to others, but he has not lost sight of

The Bulldog Braintrust. Dooley and defensive chief Erskine Russell (background). He and Dooley have a unique relationship. Dooley has allowed him to develop his own public personality and identity which few head coaches would permit. In return he has given Dooley 17 loyal and successful years of service.

his goals nor compromised his beliefs and his way of doing things.

When Vince Dooley became a head coach he thought things through as he always has. He figured out who he was and where he was professionally. He assessed his environment and his occupation and set about making things work. The central theme was the job and how he would run it. He would change over the years, but in the beginning he was going to do it his way and not worry about the falling chips. He knew if he didn't produce he could disappear into some obscure job in some distant town and Georgia people would remember him as a statistic and nothing more.

Knowing the nature of his business has always enabled him to keep things in perspective. He has adjusted because he is a decent human being and because he is smart enough to make adjustments that make sense in trying to achieve the objectives in his work.

The critics and the tough times haven't, and won't, break him. He believes in himself and he also knows that if you coach long enough,

hard times will eventually come. Nobody has ever escaped this reality, because college football is a keenly competitive business. The other side has pride and resources and determination, too. They don't play dead for you on Saturday afternoons.

Vince Dooley is what he is. He has never displayed a false image, though he is a careful protector and preserver of certain images.

What he is, is a polished Mobile street fighter and competitor. And, he's a winner. That cannot be disputed. He's got a Jackson Street "stoppers" championship, a chipped tooth and a national collegiate football title to prove it.

Before the battle. Dooley in a pre-game conversation with legendary Ole Miss coach, Johnny Vaught. By the end of the 1966 season, Vince Dooley's second coaching year with the Bulldogs, he had defeated three of the most successful coaches in the SEC: Vaught, Bear Bryant of Alabama, and Bobby Dodd of Georgia Tech.

I boarded the Delta flight in Atlanta, headed for the American Football Coaches Association annual meeting at the Diplomat Hotel in Hollywood, Fla. It was January, 1972. On the airplane with me was the lonely, sad figure of Bud Carson, who had just been fired as the Georgia Tech head coach.

He had lost to Ole Miss in the Peach Bowl, and the wolves had gone for his throat. Funny, I was thinking as I watched him, he was within sixty-five yards and a minute and twenty-nine seconds of probably keeping the job he had inherited from the Tech legend, Bobby Dodd.

In the final regular season game of 1971, Tech and Georgia met on Grant Field Thanksgiving night in front of a national television audience. Carson had two straight wins over the Bulldogs. He was almost to get a third. Georgia trailed 24-21, with the ball on its own thirty-five, with 1:29 left on the clock.

Here came quarterback Andy Johnson down the field with Georgia. Just as the clock was about to run out, the Bulldogs scored and whipped the Yellow Jackets, 28-24. Had Tech held on, Carson might have escaped the axe. Carson deserved his reputation as one of the hardest-working coaches in the business. Georgia people always felt the Tech alumni had done them a great favor in replacing Carson. But he was "illegitimate," not to the manor born, not a "Tech man," and that is probably what lost his job for him, in the long run.

On that January flight to Florida, Carson was flying first class (they generally expect you to have those kinds of privileges after they fire you), and I was riding tourist. But I talked a stewardess, who happened to be a Georgia graduate, into allowing me into the first class cabin for a visit with Carson.

He seemed eager, and pleased, to have company. He was not reluctant to discuss his dismissal by Tech. His pride was stung, you could sense that. He didn't understand that "Tech man" thing. Figures released in the Atlanta papers had indicated he was, among other things, the lowest paid major college head coach in the country.

Carson complimented the Georgia program, the Georgia facilities. Then he made a statement that startled me. "You know, what I needed at Georgia Tech is what Vince Dooley has in Erk Russell—somebody who could forearm them into their place when they get out of line."

It was obvious Bud Carson didn't know the Erskine Russell I know—the leader, the motivator. NOT, the enforcer. I tried to explain. Looks, I said, can be so deceiving.

Erskine Russell. Vince Dooley's top aide for all the seasons at Georgia. The secretary of defense. The assistant head coach. Erk. Just plain "Erk."

Paint his picture with words:

Totally bald since anybody can remember. And that ever-present (during the season) skinned forehead which has been ruptured time and again during pre-game drills as he butts his helmeted troops and psyches them for battle.

The faded, torn and tattered black sweat jacket he's worn on the sideline for years, exposing him to September's heat and humidity and November's cold and rain. He's there—bareheaded and barearmed—giving the signals to his defensive captain.

Biceps bulging. Thick thighs churning when he runs. Forearms threatening. Cast his part to Charles Bronson.

Yeah, looks can be deceiving. There's not a mean bone in Erskine Russell's body. And I can find hundreds who will fight anybody who disagrees.

Erskine Russell is a gentle man, tough, but the kind of tough that has brought respect and devotion from those who have played under him. I will never forget the first practice session he and Dooley held at Georgia. It was August, 1964. Russell had arrived in Athens from an assistant coaching job at Vanderbilt.

Georgia, remember, was in the pits. No talent, or that was the prevailing belief. Not with Russell. He burst through the practice gates that first time in '64, assembled his first Georgia defense, looked them in their eyes and said, "You're good enough to play for me and you're good enough to win."

Win they did. Seven games and an incredible

Erk. Bleeding Bulldog red.

The master of defense. His teams bend, but rarely break.

second-place finish in the Southeastern Conference. The Florida game was something that year. Florida was supposed to cream Georgia.

Late in the game, the score tied, 7-7, Bobby Etter, 140-pound kicker, lined up for a Georgia field goal attempt. There was a bad snap. Etter picked up the ball and ran it in for the touchdown. Georgia won, 14-7.

The locker room in Jacksonville's Gator Bowl was bedlam. President O.C. Aderhold was hugging Dooley, players were screaming. Erk's emotion got the best of him. He jumped on a table and led a resounding cheer:

DAMN GOOD TEAM!
DAMN GOOD TEAM!

Remember his words months earlier when he first met his "damn good team": "You're good enough to play for me and you're good enough to win."

If Dooley is reserved with his players, Erskine

Russell more than fills the gap between the coaches and the players. He's a man's man, if that archaic phrase still stands in these times. Erk won't let you down. You *know* that. That is why so many of those who have played for him have played so hard for him on Saturday afternoons.

Three years after that incredible upset of Florida in 1964 the two teams were hooked up again in a close game. Florida wound up winning, 17-16, because Georgia tackle David Rholetter did such a good job blocking. The Bulldogs lined up for an extra point and Rholetter blocked an onrushing Florida linebacker with such force that the Florida player flipped head over heels and his foot blocked the Georgia kick. That one point was the margin of the Gator victory.

The Georgia team was disgusted with itself. A fight broke out after the game. That infuriated Dooley. He is a man of control. He expects his team to be. But Russell, he is a man of emotion. I can still see him now, hugging a couple of big linemen who had played their hearts out for him, only to lose by that one, lousy point.

Tears were rolling down his face.

Erk Russell is fifty-four years old. Imagine that. Fifty-four and he still loves the game with a little-boy affection that has never worn off. And it shows, and it spills over to the alumni, to the fans. If I have heard it once, I have heard it a thousand times from Georgia people: "Erk Russell—I love the man."

He came from Birmingham, 2210 28th Street in Birmingham, to be exact. He lived within sight and smell of the blast furnaces of the steel mills, which were only a couple of first downs from what he still calls "The Hollow," a playground. The making of Erk Russell was at that playground.

"There was a wading pool where I learned to swim," he remembers, "three clay tennis courts with steel nets, and a rock-hard baseball diamond which became a football field in the fall. In the summer I would go to the park at seven in the morning and stay all day. When my mother wanted me to come home, all she had to do was walk out our back door and yell."

He still recalls his best Christmas ever, the one when he found an Acme tennis racquet, a J.C. Higgins baseball glove and a football helmet under the tree. He played it all, and he played it well. He was a master of the arts of

Erk, then and now. Growing up near the sight and smell of the Birmingham blast furnaces. BELOW: With Herschel Walker in 1980. The Russell philosophy never changes: "Team" first; "me" second.

horseshoes and marbles, but it was football, basketball, tennis and baseball that sent him through college. He lettered in all four sports at Auburn.

Erk Russell is a private man in many ways. He will not discuss his family background. "I had a good home, I lived in a good neighborhood and grew up with good friends. What more could you want?"

But all wasn't happy at home. His father had a bout with alcohol. He had a three-year-old sister to die of spinal meningitis when he was six.

And there is another tragedy in his life he will not discuss. No way. No matter how hard he is pressed. There was Erk's middle son, Don. It happened suddenly. The child accidentally hung himself. He was three.

"We never talk about it now, and we didn't after it happened," says Jean Russell, his wife. "But I know it was tough on Erk. He was so fond of Don. Don was a big, happy baby, and so lovable. He always seemed to be on his daddy's lap.

"After he died, Erk carried his picture in his billfold for a long, long time. The only thing he ever said to me about it was that whenever he would look at that picture, he would think, 'What's the use of living when things like this can happen?'"

But that may be the only pessimism, the only negativism, he has ever known.

It is a tribute to Erk Russell that despite a deep personal loss, he has still managed to spread goodwill to all those who have come in contact with him.

"He is so even, so wonderful," Jean Russell says. "I believe he was born that way. You can't develop that sort of disposition."

He is a man of constant good humor. Once, I discovered, he had scored the final four points in an Auburn basketball game to defeat Southern Illinois, 50-48, in a big upset on the road. I asked him about this particular athletic success.

"I felt I owed the Auburn team that much since the guy I was guarding had scored forty-six of the other team's forty-eight points."

And there's his story of his wife forcing him to a costume party the night after a bitter Georgia loss. He protested strongly.

"I don't even have a costume," he complained.

"No problem, honey," his wife replied. "I'm going to sprinkle a little perfume on your head and you can go as a roll-on deodorant."

Erk's oldest son, Rusty, played defensive end for his father, concluding his career on the 1975 team that upset Florida, clobbered Georgia Tech and went to the Cotton Bowl. Rusty is now a Georgia assistant.

Before that Cotton Bowl game I interviewed Rusty for a Dallas television station. I asked him what it was like to play for his father. His answer was classic:

"He has made certain there has been nothing in our relationship that would bother the other players on the team. The only problem I have is what to call him. I feel sort of silly calling him 'Coach Russell'."

There was a pause. Then he grinned and said, "But I sure as hell ain't gonna call him 'Daddy'."

It remains a mystery, of course, why this defensive genius with outstanding leadership and motivational abilities never became a college head coach. That's all he ever wanted to do, coach.

There were interviews and all sorts of rumors over the years. Iowa State called once, and there was something about his going to The Citadel. But nobody with a big job, a key job, ever knocked on his door and said, "You're our man."

One of the reasons is that Erk has never promoted himself. To be a head coach, you've got to blow your own whistle occasionally.

You apply for the job, then you get recommendations. You keep an ear to the ground. You make it your business to let those doing the hiring know that you are available. Erk never followed that script. He is simply not aggressive in pushing himself.

Jobs would open. We would discuss them. He would say to me, "You know the athletic director there. Why don't you call and recommend me?"

One, for purely selfish reasons, I didn't want to see him leave Georgia. Two, he needed to show the interest himself.

"Maybe I should have been more aggressive," he says now, "but I don't want to worry people about hiring me for a job. I figure if they figure you are good enough that they will call you and offer you the job."

Vintage Erskine Russell.

I think the closest he came to being a head coach was in 1980. Had Dooley chosen to take the Auburn job, I think the Georgia athletic board would have named him head coach without question.

He's fifty-four now, recall, so maybe that was

his last shot at the big office, but he won't complain. Erk is Erk. Plus, he has already surpassed his lifetime ambition. He wrote in his high school annual that his goal was to "succeed Mr. DeYampert." J.W. DeYampert was his high school coach.

He did eventually become a high school head coach at Grady in Atlanta. He admits he would have remained satisfied had he never been offered the opportunity of a collegiate assistantship.

In recent years I've even heard him say he wouldn't mind spending his last seasons on the sidelines with high schoolers around him.

Kids. He loves them. He has a way with them. He *relates*, in today's vernacular.

"I can't imagine being involved with kids we spend so much time around and not having a great relationship with them," he says. "We have so much in common. We have those common goals. You know how they feel when they win. You know how they feel when they lose. You know how they hurt when they hurt."

Vintage Erk Russell again. "I love the man," they say.

For the record, so do I.

In the heat of battle. A man of emotion.

51

A DAWG NAMED BELUE

On autumn Saturday afternoons, Ben Belue, class-ring salesman of Valdosta, Georgia, always listened to Bulldog games. He was a Georgia fan, always had been. He'd turn the radio loud, stretch out on his living room floor and wait for Larry Munson to unfold the Bulldog story of the day.

His son would listen, too, Benjamin Franklin Belue. But you don't call a kid *Benjamin Franklin* down in South Georgia. *Ben* would have worked, of course. Even *Frank*. But how about *Buck*? That's perfect. There are sports names, and then there are sports names. *Buck Belue*. I've heard few better.

Ben Belue idolized his son, and the son returned the feeling. He tried to do everything his father did in his early years, and that included joining his old man for those afternoons of listening to Georgia football.

But as the years passed, and young Buck Belue got old enough to develop a mind of his own, there was something about Georgia he didn't like. Here was a kid developing "the arm"—the ability to throw a baseball from centerfield to home plate when the other kids his age couldn't get it past second base; the ability to throw a football long and straight.

What he didn't like about Georgia was inspired by critics of Vince Dooley who felt the Bulldog offensive attack was too conservative, that it needed more passing. A kid with "the

TOP: Valdosta slugger Buck Belue also wanted to pla[y] baseball at Georgia. RIGHT: The determined quarterbac[k] faces Notre Dame in the 1981 Sugar Bow[l]

arm'' wants to be able to put the ball in the air.

Years later a man named Wayne McDuffie would escape the harsh winds of Stillwater, Oklahoma, to change Buck Belue's mind about that. But know simply that the young man who quarterbacked the Georgia football team in 1980 had no intentions of ever wearing red and black during those days of listening to Georgia games with his father.

Ben and Buck were inseparable in Buck's tender years. It was one of those father-wants-son-to-be-a-great-athlete sort of things. As soon as his son was old enough to hold a bat, Ben Belue was pitching him baseballs in the yard. In the fall they threw the football. Ben Belue *lived* for his son to develop athletically.

Valdosta meant Wright Bazemore and Valdosta High, of course. Bazemore was the legendary coach at the legendary high school

ABOVE: Little Boy Belue. A fancy for football at age 7 and a happy 12th birthday. FACING PAGE: Valdosta High star with his coach, Nick Hyder.

where they not only won state high school championships, they won *national* high school championships and they turned out star players by the score.

Ben Belue talked to Wright Bazemore. What are good practice routines for a kid Buck's age? What should I try to teach him? How far along should he be? Bazemore gave the answers and Ben Belue followed the orders. Some kids you can ruin that way. Some you turn into stars. Ben Belue got lucky.

His son was a Little League baseball star, naturally. He played centerfield. He pitched. He never played on a team that didn't win.

Bazemore saw him. One of the reasons Bazemore was successful at Valdosta was his scheme of scouting all the developing boys in town to find out who was the best pure athlete. He would be targeted as Bazemore's future quarterback. The word would go forth to the junior high coaches.

Bazemore so tapped Buck Belue, who was a starter for his junior high team, at safety, when he was in the seventh grade. Few seventh graders ever made the starting lineup in junior high. When Bazemore sent the word down to play Belue at quarterback, he was dropped from number one safety to number three quarterback. Buck Belue quit the team. His father was crushed, but his father had the good judgment to allow the youngster to work out the problem by himself.

His son went back to the team—and number three quarterback—in two weeks.

"I got tired of spending my afternoons playing in a tree house," he said.

He started at quarterback as an eighth grader in junior high football. People began to take notice. In the spring he was even invited to take part in practice with the Valdosta High varsity—a thirteen-year-old going against seventeen-year-olds. That is boys against men.

"At the start of spring practice they would send one of the assistant coaches over to the junior high in a little red Datsun pickup," Buck remembers. "About eight or ten of us would pile in during our sixth-period P.E. class and we'd head over to varsity practice."

They love their football in Valdosta. They did then. They do now. Bazemore built a dynasty. He did it by developing his players early. Still, you wonder about the kids, skinny junior high athletes knocking heads against the top high school players under the hot South Georgia sun. That is the stuff decisions to play other sports are made of.

Buck rolls for Valdosta. Georgia gained his attention by switching from the veer to the "I" formation.

"By the end of spring," Buck Belue recalls, "the eight or ten of us in the truck were down to two or three. But I never thought about quitting again, no matter what. I'd gone through that."

Buck made his debut into the hallowed Valdosta High football arena during that spring of 1974 when Valdosta held a football "jamboree" with Waycross, Moultrie, and Lowndes County teams. In a spring jamboree each team plays a quarter against each of the other three opponents.

The first time young Buck Belue went into varsity action he threw an eighty-yard touchdown pass. The entire town buzzed with anticipation of what their child quarterback might eventually become.

They didn't have to wait long. Bazemore had become athletic director by the time Belue started Valdosta High. Head coach Nick Hyder listed Belue as, again, third-team quarterback when fall practice began. But by the second day one of his other quarterbacks quit the team, and another was injured. Valdosta opened the season with Freshman Buck Belue at quarterback. He would remain in that position until the final game of his senior year, which happened to be against Clarke Central in Athens.

"During all that time," Hyder recalls, "he never missed a practice. It was rough on him at times, too. Some of the older players didn't particularly care for a kid being their quarterback, and they decided to make it rough on him. One day I looked in the huddle and Buck's jersey was torn off, his nose was bleeding, and there were scratches all over his face.

"I said, 'Buck, I'm going to take you out, son. They're killing you'.

"He pleaded with me not to. Then, it dawned on him. 'You can't take me out, coach,' he said. 'You don't have anybody else to put in here.'"

It was an unheard of season in Valdosta in 1974. The team went 3-7. But they went 10-2 Belue's sophomore season, then 9-2, and then 12-2 in 1977. His senior season, Valdosta and Clarke Central played for the state AAAA championship in Athens. Valdosta missed a field goal late in the game, and Clarke Central won, 16-14.

The recruiters were all over Buck Belue. He had talent, yes. But he had more. He had what they call "big-play ability." Nick Hyder, his high school coach, had said it about him: "He does what it takes to win. If it takes ninety miles an hour, he'll go ninety-one. If it takes fifty, he'll go fifty-one."

Enter Wayne McDuffie. Enter Wayne McDuffie, visionary, who, in 1977, had a great deal to do with Georgia's ability to soar to national heights three years later in 1980.

McDuffie is from Hawkinsville, Georgia, but he had played at Florida State. ("The only school that would take a chance on me.") Later he coached at New Mexico and then at Oklahoma State, in Stillwater. He had been involved with football in other sections of the nation, and he was familiar with recruiting philosophies all over.

Georgia had a lousy season in 1977, Dooley's first and only loser so far. But it was Wayne

McDuffie, by then the Georgia offensive line coach, who saw the new day breaking. Georgia, he reasoned, was shooting at too small a goal, the Southeastern Conference title. Shoot higher, he said, and maybe you don't fall as short if you miss.

"Dammit," he told the other coaches, "you can compete for the national championship at Georgia. I've been on more college campuses than anybody, and I've never seen a better program, better facilities, or a better all-around place to go to school, to play football, and to live.

"Also," he went on, "the state is full of football players. You get the best athletes in the state of Georgia, and you can compete with anybody."

McDuffie even pointed out what the fan support in Georgia meant to recruiting and competing nationally:

"The people in this state love football, and if you play for the University of Georgia, you'll never be forgotten whether you make it great in the pros or not."

He gave an example—former Georgia quarterback Mike Cavan, now a fellow member of the Bulldog staff.

"If the State Patrol stops me, it's forty bucks. I played at Florida State. Mike Cavan gets stopped, and they let him go. Mike's like a Baptist preacher. He doesn't pay full price for anything. The people take care of their old quarterback."

McDuffie had the role of recruiting Buck Belue to Georgia. It wouldn't be easy. Belue was still concerned about what he perceived to be a lack of interest in passing at Georgia. But McDuffie wanted him badly. He was convinced there was something special about him.

"He's got ice water in his veins," he would tell Dooley. "He looks at you with that cold stare, and he never tips you off to what he's thinking."

Bazemore had seen something in him, too, at an early age.

"I never saw a better player as a youngster," he says now. "But, I don't think Buck still knows how good he is. He is one of those players that don't go all out on every play. He's always under control, and he keeps something in reserve. That is why he can step forward and give you the big play under pressure. If he went all out, I think you might see one of the greatest quarterback talents there is."

McDuffie could *smell* what Belue could do at Georgia. Big-play man at quarterback. Get some receivers—like Lindsay Scott at nearby Jesup—to go with him, and the climb to a national championship would be on.

But first he had to convince Belue to put his name on a Georgia scholarship. Tennessee and South Carolina were very much in the running.

Now back to the end of the Valdosta-Clarke Central game in Athens in December, 1977. McDuffie was at the game, of course. He spoke to Buck. He spoke to the Belue family, and then he said goodnight.

While Buck was still in the shower at the Clarke Central gym and while his family waited for him before the long drive back home to Valdosta, Wayne McDuffie had a brainstorm. He jumped into his '77 brown Pontiac and headed down U.S. 441 to Interstate 75. He checked into the Holiday Inn in Valdosta at 3:30 in the morning.

The Belue family walks into the front door of their house the next day, after driving all the way from Athens, 250 miles away, and their phone is ringing.

"It's Wayne McDuffie," said the Georgia assistant. "I'm here in Valdosta."

Buck had answered the telephone.

"You're where?" he asked.

"I'm in Valdosta at the Holiday Inn. I wanted you to know how bad I want you to come to Georgia. Bad enough to drive down here last night."

On Monday afternoon he met with Belue at the home of Butch Brooks, the Valdosta baseball coach. Buck said he had finally ruled out South Carolina. It would be either Tennessee or Georgia. McDuffie went to work. He had a couple of hole cards.

First he talked about his concept of a national championship. He also talked about staying home in the state of Georgia.

"Think of your parents," he said. "It's a lot closer to Athens than it is to Knoxville."

But there was still that nagging idea about the Bulldogs' passing attack, or lack of one. McDuffie was ready for that, too.

He had done some research. Every fan has the image of professional teams throwing on every down, but McDuffie studied the ten previous Super Bowls and found out each winner was a run-oriented team. Some even ran the ball as much as seventy-five percent.

These teams also had something else in common. Although they ran more than they passed, they all had a big-play quarterback. Georgia wanted its quarterback in that mold.

McDuffie went at Belue with both barrels.

He promised Georgia would be opening up more. Dooley had already indicated he would leave his veer offense and go to the "I" in 1978.

And he promised Dooley would go along with Belue's desire to play baseball for four years at Georgia, even though he would have to miss spring practices.

He told Buck Belue if Georgia could dominate the state in recruiting in 1977, it could be the groundwork for a national championship.

"If you come to Georgia," he said, "others will follow."

Young Buck Belue listened. He listened for two hours. McDuffie went back over it all again and again. Belue's response gave no indication what he was thinking. Occasionally he cleared his throat, or he would gaze off into the distance, or he would rake his hand through his mop of curly hair. He had his feet propped up on Kay Brooks' coffee table, the picture of supreme confidence.

McDuffie was seething on the inside. He wanted this picture of confidence moved to Athens, but he also wanted some indication of where the youngster stood.

"I wanted to bang on the walls," he laughs now, "but I had to look like I was calm."

At 5:30 Buck, still offering no indication of his plans, said goodbye to McDuffie and went home to celebrate his eighteenth birthday. McDuffie headed back to the Holiday Inn. He was exhausted, frustrated. He called Butch Brooks and suggested a little nighttime rabbit hunting. They were making plans for the hunt when the operator cut into the conversation.

"We have an emergency call for Coach Wayne McDuffie," she said.

It was Buck Belue on the line.

"Coach McDuffie," he began, calmly as ever, "I've talked all this over with my family. . . . "

McDuffie's heart was pounding. The next sentence was his recruiting life or death. It was a year of work and sheer agony squeezed into a half-second.

"And I've decided," Buck Belue continued, "to come to Georgia."

McDuffie broke into a big grin. He said enthusiastically, but holding his control, "Welcome to Georgia, Buck. You'll sure look good in red."

A few more pleasantries were exchanged, and Belue invited McDuffie over to the house for a celebration. It was final. It was official.

McDuffie put the phone back on the hook. Then, and only then, did he let go.

He screamed at the top of his voice. He beat the wall of the Holiday Inn.

At the celebration at the Belue home McDuffie set about to locate Dooley who was on a recruiting mission in Alabama. A call to Barbara Dooley did no good. Even she didn't know how to find her husband. McDuffie called assistant coach John Kasay. He didn't tell Kasay the news, he only said it was an emergency and he had to find Dooley. Kasay tracked down the head coach.

When McDuffie finally got Dooley on the phone, he said, "Coach, what would you say if I told you Buck Belue was going to Tennessee?"

"You're fired," Dooley replied.

"To this day," McDuffie says, "I think he meant that. But when I told him the truth, I could see him grinning through the phone."

So, step one. Buck Belue was in the fold. Until Herschel Walker came along, no Georgia recruit ever received as much attention.

The next step was to get the news to Jesup, get the news to the state's premiere receiver, Lindsay Scott, that Buck Belue was going to Georgia. Belue wanted to throw to Scott, but would Scott agree that it was Belue he wanted throwing to him?

Probably not. When Belue signed that December day in 1977, Scott had not yet made it official, but he had already told the University of Tennessee to get a scholarship ready because he was ready to sign.

Belue in the Georgia fold with Dooley. He was step one to the bid for a national contender.

Put Down
That Trumpet,
Son

John Donaldson played in the backfield with Charley Trippi on Georgia's undefeated Sugar Bowl team in 1946. Later, he was an assistant coach under Ray Graves at Florida. But when Vince Dooley arrived in Athens in 1964 and gave Donaldson the chance to return to his alma mater as a Bulldog assistant, he quickly took it.

He would leave once, for an attractive business offer, but then he would return again to the Georgia staff. In 1973, however, they called him home to Jesup, Georgia, and Donaldson couldn't resist. He became the Wayne County High School head football coach.

Why would a man leave the collegiate level to go back to South Georgia to deal with 15-year-olds? Maybe there was more than just football calling Donaldson back. What didn't suit him about Athens was John Donaldson can't go a day without at least a little fishing or hunting. Jesup gave him the opportunity to coach and also enjoy the outdoor life. There would be no recruiting hassles. The life would be perfect for him.

So we go to Jesup on a lazy summer day in 1974, and John Donaldson is working at his boyhood home on Plum Street. The house is in need of repair.

Strolls into the scene a skinny black kid named Dennis Scott. He asked for work.

"I'd never laid eyes on him before," Donaldson recalled, "but I gave him the job. Before long, I knew this was a special kind of kid. He was always on time. I could tell by the way he worked, he was a mature, responsible young man. I really liked him."

You don't actually "recruit" high school athletes, but it doesn't hurt to ask. Donaldson inquired if Dennis Scott ever played any football.

Never tried it, said young Scott. He played in the band.

Wait a minute, said Donaldson. Musicians are easy to find, football players aren't. He went to work on Dennis Scott and when summer practice opened, he had the junior-to-be on his team.

He was small, 5-10, 150, but he had speed and he had moves. He became a reserve back. In a big game against rival Waycross, the starter suffered a broken leg and Donaldson called on Dennis Scott.

The first play, he took a hit in the mouth and chipped a tooth. Waycross worked him over.

"But he didn't quit," Donaldson said. "He answered back, blow-for-blow. I knew I had a football player after that night."

60

Now the plot thickens. It is the following spring, and spring football practice is about to begin. Dennis Scott has discovered he likes football and he likes John Donaldson. He wants to do all he can for the team. He mentions his kid brother.

"He's in the band, too," he told Donaldson, "but, Coach, he's taller and bigger and better than me."

"What's his name?" Donaldson asked.

"Lindsay," replied Dennis Scott. "He'll be a sophomore next season. He plays trumpet."

Donaldson was interested. If the kid had speed like his brother and was the same solid citizen Dennis was, he wanted Lindsay Scott on his team. He even did some checking into the Scott family history. Donaldson thinks speed is hereditary. He asked his assistant coach, Arthur

Williams, about the Scott brothers' father, Raymond, who had played for a local all-black school during pre-integration days.

"Raymond Scott," said Arthur Williams, "could fly."

That was enough for Donaldson. Put down that trumpet, son, you're going to learn to play football. Lindsay Scott quit the band and came out for football his sophomore year at Wayne County High.

He played rarely his initial season on the team, but by the time he was a junior it was evident he would become one of the state's premier high school athletes.

"He was some football player," said Donaldson. "He had the quickness and the great hands. He had the speed. He could jump. I figured if I put him out wide, they would have to double cover him every time."

Lindsay Scott caught 26 touchdown passes for Wayne County his junior year, and that without a quarterback with a powerful arm. The idea, most of the time, was to throw it short and over to the middle to Lindsay and let him do what he could from there.

"Our streak play," Donaldson explained, "was I would tell the quarterback to throw the ball straight down the field as hard as he could. I knew Lindsay would get it if it was thrown deep enough because he had so much speed. Unfortunately, we could rarely get the ball deep to him. If he had played with a quarterback like Buck Belue, there is no telling what kind of records he would have set in high school."

Scott also played safety on defense.

"He would have made a great safety in college," said Donaldson. "He enjoyed hitting, and he hit hard."

The recruiters flocked in. Lindsay Scott was a wanted man. He could break open a game. Get Lindsay Scott and you have instant offense.

Recall that Georgia has signed quarterback Belue from nearby Valdosta. What they need for this down-the-road dream of a drive for a national championship is a receiver to go with Belue. What they need, what they *must have*, is Lindsay Eugene Scott.

Mike Cavan, the former Georgia quarterback under Dooley, and now a Bulldog assistant, was obsessed with signing Scott. That is putting it mildly.

Lindsay Scott was a case for Cavan. He had already committed to Tennessee once, then changed his mind, then changed his mind again. He would, in fact, be a part of Johnny

61

Lindsay Scott grows up. (Clockwise, starting above) At age 6, age 8, and at 15, breaking into football at Wayne County High. There was time for basketball, too.

LEFT: In action for Wayne County. The "streak" play in which the quarterback throws the ball as far as he can downfield, and the coach hopes Lindsay can run under it. TOP: Look familiar? It's Lindsay Scott scoring on a 70-yard touchdown pass in the last 40 seconds to win for Wayne County High. A few years later, on a hot day in Jacksonville. . . . ABOVE: John Donaldson. Back home in Jesup, he found a jewel of a receiver for Georgia.

Majors' rebuilding program in Knoxville, a member of the recruiting class of 1978.

But Cavan wouldn't give up. You never know in college recruiting. A kid tells you in October: "I'm going to Georgia." You don't rest easy. You are dealing with impressionable teenagers and they do change their minds.

On the Saturday in December when high school athletes are first allowed to sign scholarship agreements, Lindsay Scott did not make it official with Tennessee. That was at Tennessee's request. That was a big bungle by the Big Orange.

The Volunteer recruiters who were in charge of Scott were told to hold off the signing until the following Wednesday when Majors, the new Tennessee coach, could come to Jesup and do the honors.

The delay turned out to be a crucial move, a big plus for Cavan and Georgia. When that Wednesday rolled around, Scott had decided he wasn't sure. He was still interested in Georgia. The battle of nerves, of recruiting cat-and-mouse, was on.

Cavan was determined. Christmas Eve came, and still Scott hadn't made up his mind. Cavan left Athens, headed home to Thomaston to be with his family. But when he arrived he couldn't stand to be away from Jesup and Scott, Christmas or no Christmas.

Cavan phoned a friend in Jacksonville, Tommy Dudley, a pilot and associate recruiter. Dudley left his family, too, and flew to Thomaston to pick up Cavan. He dropped him off in Jesup.

Cavan headed straight to a local men's store, owned by Georgia partisan Jimmy Sullivan. Who was walking out the door but Lindsay Scott.

"Lindsay," said Cavan, "I can't be anywhere else on Christmas but with you. I told my family I had to leave them because it's that important for you to come to Georgia."

"Coach Cavan," replied Scott, "you're crazy."

But Cavan had a feeling. It had been with him during the entire recruiting run at Lindsay Scott. He felt the youngster wanted desperately to sign with Georgia, but didn't know how to get out of his earlier involvements with Tennessee.

Mike Cavan spent Christmas Eve, 1977, alone in a motel room in Jesup, Georgia, banking on that feeling.

A couple of days later he was joined by fellow coach Wayne McDuffie, hero of the Buck Belue signing. They sat up late, plotting their next move. They finally went to bed, but there was little sleep. At six o'clock, they decided they must go to the Scott house. Don't let the sun catch you sleeping in a recruiting battle.

On the way they found an open restaurant and ordered two cups of coffee to go. They arrived at the Scott house at 6:30. As they pulled into the yard, Tennessee coaches Bob Harrison and Bobby Jackson were walking in the front door.

"Oh, hell," said McDuffie.

"We're going in, anyway," said Cavan.

They got out of the car and walked to the front door. They were met by Lindsay Scott's mother, Johnnie Mae. She was adamant.

"These folks were here first, Mike," she said to Cavan. "You've got to wait outside. You just can't come in."

The strain of it all was getting to Johnnie Mae Scott.

Cavan's mind was racing. How could he get into the house? He had to get into that house. He looked down at his cup of coffee.

"You gotta let me in, Johnnie Mae," he said. "I ain't got no sugar for my coffee."

Johnnie Mae Scott sighed, then relented.

"Okay. You can come in," she said, "but you have to stay in the kitchen."

Cavan and McDuffie were in the Scott's kitchen, the two Tennessee recruiters were in the living room with Lindsay's father, Raymond, and Lindsay was still in his bed, staring at the ceiling.

Cavan and McDuffie waited and waited. Two hours passed. The Tennessee coaches wouldn't budge. Johnnie Mae Scott fretted. Back and forth this thing had gone. First, Tennessee, then Georgia, then Tennessee again, then who knows? When she couldn't take it anymore, she went into another room and put a gospel record on her stereo and turned the volume full blast.

Three hours passed. It is 9:30. Cavan and McDuffie have had it.

"You find Lindsay and tell him let's get this damn thing over with," McDuffie said to Cavan. "I'm going in there," he continued, pointing to the living room.

Cavan strode back to Lindsay's bedroom. On the wall were posters and jerseys from dozens of schools. He had seen every campus he had wanted to see. This is recruiting, recruiting of a "blue-chipper."

Lindsay Scott, on this late December

morning, had finally made up his mind. He wanted to sign with Georgia. But he didn't know what to say to the Tennessee coaches.

They had been so nice to him, so appreciative of him; they had talked of the great plans they had for him. If only they would just go away. If only he didn't have to walk in that living room and face them. It would be so easy.

But recruiters don't go away. They have to be literally *run off*. Otherwise, they fight to the very last minute, hoping there will be a change in a recruit's thinking. Recruiting is what drives most coaches out of the business. Little wonder. McDuffie says it best: "You've got to compete just as hard in the living room as you do on the field."

McDuffie is in the living room with the Tennessee coaches. Cavan is sitting on the edge of Lindsay Scott's bed. He starts talking. This is it. THE moment. Cavan is almost certain Scott is his, but you are never, never sure.

"Look, Lindsay," Cavan says, "you've got to go out there and tell those people what you are going to do. You gotta tell 'em you've made up your mind and you're going to Georgia and that's final."

Lindsay agreed.

Cavan suddenly had this flash in his mind: He had just heard the youngster commit to him, but he could still see him walking into that living room and uttering the dreaded, hateful word, "Tennessee." *Recruiting is what drives most coaches out of the business.*

Lindsay arose from his bed, dressed, and walked into his living room with Mike Cavan. The tension was heavy. An Academy Award was about to be announced.

Lindsay, his long and lithe body a perfect picture of a wide receiver, breathed deeply and said, "I've thought it over, and I've decided the best thing for me to do is go to the University of Georgia."

Cavan leaped over to Raymond Scott's chair and started singing and shouting and hugging the man. Then he went to Lindsay and hugged him.

"Wonderful! Great!" he shouted. "This is the best news I've ever had in my life! Did you hear him, Mr. Scott? Your boy's going to Georgia! He'll be great!"

It was over. Everybody in the room knew it, including the Tennessee coaches.

"We'll see you fellows later," said McDuffie, grinning, as he ushered them to the door.

First, Buck Belue, the exciting quarterback from Valdosta, had been yanked away from the clutches of Tennessee. Now, the other half of a desired passing combination, Lindsay Scott, had sent the Big Orange packing.

When could Georgia, then, make its move, its thrust at a national championship as Wayne McDuffie had forecast? The next season? The next? How about three years down the road, when Belue and Scott and other outstanding recruits would have had time to mature and develop?

And what else would Georgia need? Linemen? Of course. The good Dooley teams have always been known for their powerful offensive and defensive lines. A great kicking game would be important, too. A young fellow named Rex Robinson was already on the scene by now. He would fit into the plan.

But a running back, what about a running back? All the great teams have a great running back. Pittsburgh in 1976, when it routed Georgia for the national title in the Sugar Bowl, had Tony Dorsett.

A running back, that was the missing link in Georgia's football future in 1978.

Turn the page.

The Seige of Wrightsville, Georgia

Willis Walker and Christine Taylor grew up on dirt-poor farms in Wrightsville, Georgia, county seat of Johnson, an hour's ride out of Macon. Not far from Wrightsville, flows the Oconee River, which rises north of Athens and meanders past Sanford Stadium on its way south.

Willis and Christine were childhood sweethearts. They met at a small country school, Tucker's Elementary. Later, they attended Doc Kemp School, where blacks got what was supposed to be a high school education in those "separate-but-equal" days before integration.

They married on February 29, 1955, at a minister's home.

February 29, 1955:

Vince Dooley was a second lieutenant with the Marines, stationed at Parris Island, S.C.

Francis Tarkenton was playing basketball for Arnold DeLaPerriere at Athens High School. The coming fall, he would lead Weyman Sellers' Athens High football team to the state championship. Then, he would begin what was to be a brilliant career at the University of Georgia, followed by his rise to stardom in the National Football League.

February 29, 1955: I was a slow, but deliberate end for Red Bullock's Wrightsville High Tigers. I wanted to be better than I was. I wanted that desperately. But there was no hope.

After his marriage, Willis Walker farmed for his meager living. Four children came along. Willis took to farming with Rex L. Jackson. The house where the Walkers and their children lived at the time is now used to store hay.

Then a fifth child was on the way. Christine Walker had to travel all the way to Dublin, 11 miles, to see a doctor. Wrightsville had no hospital, not even a small clinic.

Her doctor was Fred Chambless. It was a decision he made that may have saved Christine Walker from serious problems with her fifth pregnancy. His patient from Wrightsville had phlebitis, which can be dangerous to pregnant mothers and their newborn. The doctor made the decision to move Christine Walker to Augusta where she could have specialized care.

On March 3, 1962, at 8:21 P.M., Christine Walker delivered her fifth child with no complications, a healthy, eight-and-a-half-pound boy.

She had a first name for her baby, "Herschel," for the child's paternal grandfather. She had planned to give him the middle name of "Cearneles"—a name she liked—but she changed her mind. A nurse walked into her room at the Talmadge Memorial Hospital one day while she was holding the baby and suggested she include a "junior" on the end of Herschel's name.

"He just looks like a 'junior'," said the nurse.

But there was a problem. Christine Walker had named her oldest son "Willis, Jr." No problem. She simply made Herschel's middle name "Junior," which may cause some problems for Herschel in years to come. Imagine, when Herschel gets his own family, Herschel Junior Walker, Jr., not to be confused with Herschel Junior Walker, Sr.

There was another problem with the baby's name. A typist at Talmadge Memorial misspelled his first name on his birth certificate and it came out "Hershey."

It remained that way until 1978 when Herschel Junior Walker applied for his Social Security card. His mother took down the family Bible and went to see Charlotte Beal, judge of the Johnson County Probate Court and custodian of vital records, who straightened out the problem.

Dr. Fred Chambless, who now lives in Rome, did not remember Christine Walker as his patient when I informed him of that fact in January of 1981. Yet his decision to send her to Augusta may have saved her from complications, and may have saved infant Herschel Walker from harm as well. In this unfolding story of the success of the University of Georgia's 1980 football team, Dr. Fred Chambless played a role not to be forgotten.

It was a struggle in those days for the growing Walker family. A sixth and seventh

Herschel Junior Walker. A doctor's good judgment, a healthy baby, and the rest is history.

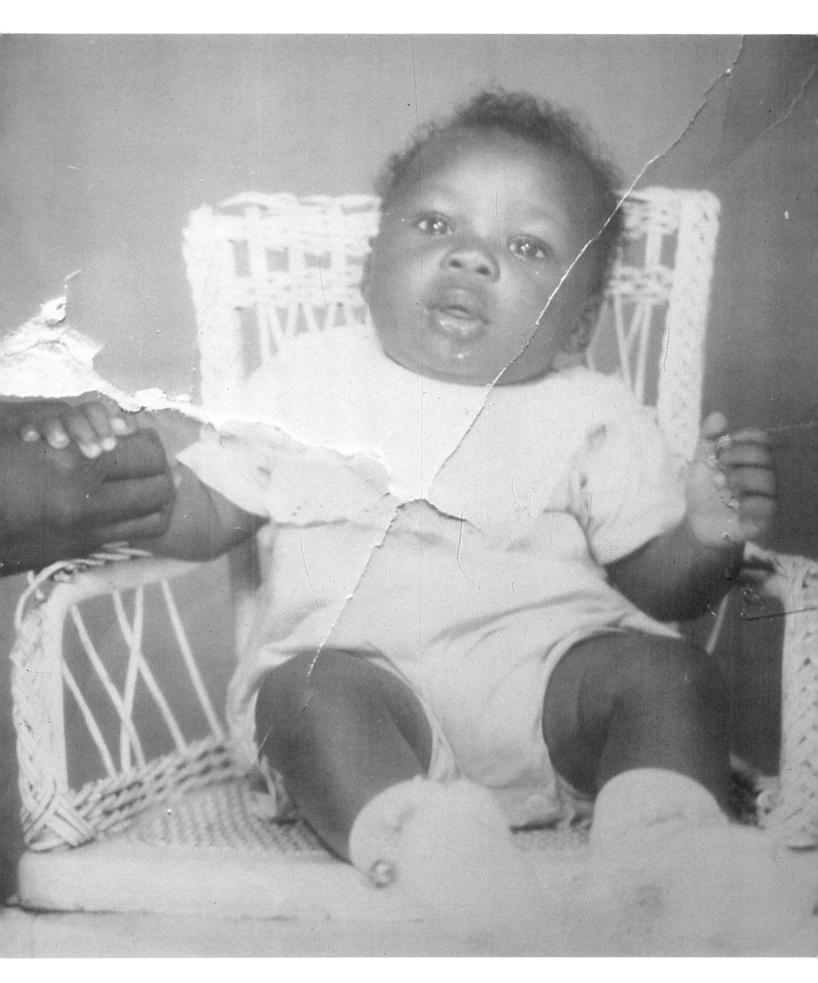

child would come along. Willis Walker would eventually have to give up farming and go to work at a nearby kaolin plant. His wife, a small, neat, quiet woman, would have to work, too. She is still at it today, toiling eight hours in a Wrightsville factory that produces trousers.

She has her memories of her little boy, Herschel. When she remembers him as a child, she *beams:*

"He was always shorter than the other little boys. I worried about him. He was a runt was what he was. I think he was always worried about being so short when he was growing up.

"But he could eat when he was a little boy. That child loved peas. We called 'em red hull peas. He would eat those peas as long as I would put 'em on his plate.

"Herschel was the best child you could have. He had a few fights, but all little boys fight. I only had to spank him once, when he teased his sister, Veronica. She cried until I came home from work, and then I spanked him. But I never had to do it again.

"He would always mind me. He would always listen to me. But he would never tell me what was wrong when something was bothering him. He would just go to his room and write down his thoughts. I used to try to find copies of what he was writing, but he hid them from me. Herschel never gave us any problems, but he never talked to us when he got upset. He was always able to work things out for himself."

As a child Herschel shared a room with his younger brother, Lorenzo. Willis Walker was finally able to move his family out of what would become the hay barn. He bought a house across the railroad tracks, up a dirt drive, on a hill, a few miles out of town on Idylwild Road.

At night Herschel spent much of his time in his room, thinking to himself or writing poetry.

The old Walker house. Now it's used to store hay.

68

He rarely went to sleep before one in the morning. Yet he was usually the first to arise the next day.

"He got so little sleep," his mother remembers. "I worried about him, but Herschel was always different."

Willis Walker never had time for sports in his life. He is a pleasant man, open and kind, who has known little else but work in his 44 years. But he encouraged his children to take part in athletics, especially after integration brought the opportunity and the facilities to do so at Johnson County High School.

Herschel Walker first became interested in competing athletically in his own backyard, however. He was slow to develop physically and he was having trouble keeping up with his older brothers and sisters.

"There was always an argument at night about who could run the fastest," Willis Walker recalls. "One of the children would say, 'I can

Willis and Christine Walker.

outrun you,' and then there would be all this talk, and all this bragging, and the next day they would all be outside racing."

Herschel had trouble keeping up. He was 14 before he could outrun his older sister, Veronica, who would become an outstanding athlete herself. But what his parents saw in Herschel was his determination, even when he was being left in his sister's dust.

"Herschel always wanted to win," his father continues. "If he couldn't win the first time, he would keep on trying, and every time he lost, he would try to figure out some other way he could win."

It was Tom Jordan, an assistant football coach under Gary Phillips at Johnson County High, who discovered the awkward, but ambitious, sixth-grade athlete, Herschel Walker.

"He was not very big then," says Jordan, now coaching in South Carolina, "and he was worried about growing. He wanted to develop fast. He would ask me all sorts of questions, and it was obvious he was dedicated. He had a reading deficiency as a sixth-grader, but he said he was going to overcome that, and he did. He worked at it just like he worked at everything else."

Jordan remembers Herschel Walker as maybe the third best athlete in his class his seventh and eighth grade years. He still hadn't developed physically.

His mother worried. He was so small. He would want to play football, of course, and Christine Walker had other sons to play football, but they were bigger than Herschel.

One Sunday afternoon when Herschel was about to enter the Junior High program, Tom Jordan decided to visit Christine Walker. He knew she was worried about her son's football interest.

"He told me Herschel could get hurt at anything," Christine Walker said. "He told me if I stopped him from playing football, that he might get involved with something a lot worse. I studied about it, and I decided to leave Herschel alone."

In the eighth grade Herschel almost quit football on his own accord. He wanted to move up to the varsity, to be with his older brother, Renneth, even if it was for practice only. The varsity coaches wouldn't allow it. He was still too small. According to his mother, Herschel thought the coaches were trying to hold him back. The kid had ambition. It took a great deal of convincing to keep Herschel down on the farm one more season.

Working on the weights in Wrightsville. A body beautiful on a diet of Gatorade and hamburgers?

The physical development he had longed for finally began in the ninth grade. Herschel made the varsity team. As a sophomore he started as the fullback in the "I" formation, which meant he was used primarily as a blocker. He also played defensive end.

The headlines, the attention, the notice began when he was a junior tailback. His body had blossomed, the incredibly strong calves and thighs, the massive upper body, the huge neck. He was over 200 pounds (his diet now, according to his mother, was strictly hamburgers and Gatorade), and he had run the 100-yard dash in 9.9.

He began to pile up amazing amounts of yardage for Johnson County High. His feats were legend, and by the time his junior year ended, he had attracted national attention. The onslaught of recruiters, the tons of letters, the hundreds of telephone calls were about to begin.

* * * *

The Johnson County schoolhouse is made mostly of concrete blocks. It is gray and square, chilly in the winter and steamy hot as classes wind down in late spring. Many of the kids who seek education there still expect to remain in the county and find life's work in the fields or as pulpwooders.

Some will find jobs with the one or two local industries in town, and some will find work in Dublin or nearby Sandersville, or maybe Warner Robins, or Macon. Others, a few lucky ones, will go on to college, and their accomplishments will be dutifully reported by *The Wrightsville Headlight*, which we always jokingly called the "Taillight." The *Headlight* will cover anything the college kids do, provided their mamas bring in the information.

Simply put, as the year 1979 rolled around, there hadn't been much big news in Wrightsville since the Civil War. Certainly, no great athletes ever emerged from this village of 2,300.

Oh, now and then there was a Roy Thompson or an Al Chamlee, and one year there was a running back with great speed, William Scott. He signed with Clemson, but he didn't last more than one season. The athletic abilities were there, but not the scholastic.

As a matter of fact, before 1980, the last person from Wrightsville to have earned a college letter in athletics (and a degree) may have been me, for track with Spec Towns' Georgia team. Wrightsville, in other words, had never been a hotbed of athletic talent.

But came 1979, Herschel Walker's senior season at Johnson County High School. People in Los Angeles, New York, and Columbus, Ohio, were suddenly aware there was, in fact, a Wrightsville, Georgia, and in that town there was a kid named Herschel Walker who was big, who was strong, and who had a sprinter's speed.

Herschel had no idea what was about to happen, of course. Neither did his family. Neither probably did his coaches.

First, the National Collegiate Athletic Association (NCAA) contacted his coaches, Gary Phillips and Tom Jordan, even before the first game of Herschel's senior year, when the recruiting drive would begin from every corner of the nation.

The NCAA made it clear: It would be monitoring the recruitment of Herschel Walker. The coaches were warned: Some recruiters will try anything. Be ready. Herschel could even be declared ineligible if the NCAA found illegalities in his signing.

Phillips and Jordan devised a plan: All contacts with their young athlete must come through their office first. Herschel and his family agreed. If and when a school chose not to follow this plan, that school was eliminated from the running.

The recruiters came in droves. On Friday nights when Johnson County and Herschel played football, Lovett Stadium would have as many as 20 different schools represented, all trying to convince Herschel Walker to sign his name on their dotted line.

"We could have held a national coaching clinic in my office almost any day of the week that last six months before he signed," says Tom Jordan, who was assistant principal as well as an assistant football coach. Jordan's office was in the junior high building. Herschel would slip out of the high school and over to Jordan's office to avoid recruiters.

That worked for a time, but recruiters are a crafty lot. Soon they learned Herschel's every move and followed him constantly.

Although the family home was off limits to recruiters, that didn't keep them from using the telephone. Also, there were many calls after midnight.

One night Jordan received a call from a local service station owner.

"Coach," he said, "there's somebody here that says he's the head football coach at Ohio State, and he wants to talk to Herschel."

Jordan wasn't sure if he would meet an imposter or not, but he drove down to the corner and, lo and behold, there stood Earl Bruce, who is, in fact, the head coach at Ohio State. He had been in Florida and stopped by to see if he could convince Herschel to consider becoming a Buckeye.

The Walker family agreed to meet with Bruce briefly, although it was about time for Willis Walker to head to the kaolin plant to work the night shift.

The Ohio State coach left after midnight, and when and where he finally got to bed is anybody's guess. Had he been able to put Herschel Walker in a Buckeye uniform, he would have considered any inconvenience well worth it.

The first time I ever saw Herschel was at a football banquet in Wrightsville his sophomore year. I was sitting with my best friend, Hodges Rowland, an attorney, and a longtime family friend, Ralph Jackson, Jr., who had invited me down.

"Tell Coach Dooley that Georgia better watch out for Herschel Walker. He's going to be a great college prospect," Ralph said to me.

Wrightsville fell into the recruiting territory of, again, Mike Cavan. I told Cavan about my conversation with Ralph Jackson and I mentioned Herschel Walker.

"A prospect from Wrightsville?" he laughed. "Do y'all even PLAY football down there?"

It wasn't long before Cavan was coming to me and telling me the great things he had learned about Herschel Walker. It grabs a coach's attention when a young athlete has placed first in the shotput and then lined up in the starting blocks to run a 9.7 or a 9.6 100-yard dash.

As soon as Walker finished his junior year, Cavan almost took up residence in Wrightsville. If you couldn't find him at his office or at his home in Athens, you knew he would be 110 miles due south on Highway 15. It had become his responsibility to recruit the greatest athlete ever to come out of the state, and he didn't want to be accused of not being on the job. Local Georgia followers Bob Newsome and Ralph Jackson suggested Cavan spent so much time in Wrightsville, he should file a tax return from Johnson County.

Herschel's last football season at Johnson County High was nothing short of incredible. He rushed for 3,167 yards and 45 touchdowns.

Johnson County Superstar. The recruiters came from every corner of the country.

The 45 touchdowns for one season and his 86 career are national high school records.

He led his team to the Class A state high school championship, he was a consensus high school all-American and he was named *Parade Magazine*'s national high school back-of-the-year.

There was only one element in Herschel Walker's schoolboy career that bothered recruiters in the least: Class A schools are the smallest in Georgia. There was some negative speculation:

So Herschel Walker weighs 220 and he might one day run a 9.3. His competition has been nothing. He's been running against 140-pound defensive backs and 170-pound defensive linemen. What will happen when he steps in against the bigger and faster competition?

Mike Cavan brushed aside such thinking, however. He was convinced Herschel Walker would have been the best high school running back in America against any kind of competition. Cavan—and all the Georgia coaches—dedicated themselves to signing him. They had worked with such fervor the two preceding years to put together the talent it would take to make a run at the national title. But here was the missing link, here was the running back, the yardage machine.

They did not want to lose the most publicized back in America to an out-of-state school.

From the beginning, Cavan thought Georgia had an excellent chance of signing Herschel Walker.

"He knew how badly we wanted him," Cavan explains. "And he knew he had a great opportunity awaiting him at Georgia. But he took his time making up his mind for certain. We had to be patient."

Cavan got Lindsay Scott in 1978 with persistence. He would try the same with Herschel. From August to December of 1979, Cavan went to Wrightsville at least two days during each week, although he had other areas to recruit, and he had his own backfield coaching duties on the field in Athens.

In December, however, he was in Wrightsville five days out of each week—at least. Sometimes he would remain on weekends. He would keep this routine until Easter.

December passed and still Herschel hadn't signed. January came and went. Then February. Still, no word from Herschel. The pressure began to build. The calls were constant. Even recruiters who had been told Herschel had no intention of signing with their schools continued the push.

Finally there was an announcement that at least Herschel had narrowed his choices to three schools: Georgia, Clemson and Southern California. Coaches from those schools made an agreement. They would no longer talk to Herschel and his family, who had grown increasingly tired of the hassle.

The truce was broken by a Clemson recruiter who asked Herschel to meet with him in an obscure county cemetery. One of the local townspeople got wind of the meeting and called Bob Newsome and Ralph Jackson, who informed Cavan, who blew the whistle on the meeting.

"I did have an advantage," Cavan laughs now. "The town was pro-Georgia, and nothing would take place that I didn't know about it."

February turned into March. Easter Sunday was approaching. Herschel had made another decision. He would not be going to Clemson. It would be Georgia or Southern California, with its tradition of great running backs.

The family wanted Georgia. They wanted Herschel close by. They wanted him with his sister, Veronica, who was at Georgia on a track scholarship. Athens was only two hours away.

But there was beginning to be a problem with some of the Georgia supporters, both in Wrightsville and from around the state. They were tiring of Herschel's indecision. They were pushing at him.

There is a certain independence in Herschel Walker's makeup. He listens to his inner self. As his mother pointed out, he keeps his troubles to himself. He liked Georgia. He liked the Georgia people. But he felt he was being pushed.

"I didn't want to be told where to go or be pushed into any school," he would explain later.

He had tired of the invasion of his privacy. He had tired of the pressure. He even made the statement he might not sign with anybody—except the Marines.

"The Marines help people, and I've always thought about being a Marine. Maybe that's what I'll do," he said. He admits today he seriously considered that alternative to playing college football.

Easter Sunday morning came in Wrightsville. This was to be the day. Herschel had decided this would be the day he would end the speculation and the pressure.

The night before, he had not fallen asleep

until past two o'clock. But he was up at 6:30, a typical schedule for him. He jogged down the dirt drive of his home, across the railroad tracks, and onto Idylwild Road. He ran to where he was even with the Ray Carter home—about a mile away—then turned and jogged the mile back.

When he walked back into his house, his mother and his father and his sister, Veronica, were having breakfast. He walked in on their conversation. They were worrying out loud about Herschel's impending decision. They still wanted Georgia, but they still weren't certain Herschel did.

Herschel said nothing. He was frustrated. Would signing with Georgia be a copout? Didn't his inner self tell him maybe he should get away, far away, where everybody didn't know who he was, where he would be left alone, where they would have a chance, as he told himself, "to learn me as Herschel and not just as a football player?"

He walked outside and began to tinker with his motorcycle. He continued to think. He wanted to please his family, but he wanted to please himself, too.

Should he call Los Angeles? He had the number of the assistant coach who had recruited him. He continued to tinker with his motorcycle, a Kawasaki 400. He could call Los Angeles collect, and then it would be over. He could catch a plane the next day, and he wouldn't be a big splash out there; he could get away from the pressure, the attention.

He walked back inside the house, and the conversation at the kitchen table was still in progress. He listened. Suddenly, he had an impulse: Go to the telephone. Go and call Los Angeles. He would awaken the Southern Cal coach at that hour, of course, but he wouldn't mind.

It would be the most important wake-up call of his life, as a matter of fact.

The family continued to talk. Herschel was making up his mind. It would be Southern California.

He doesn't know today exactly what made him change his mind that morning. It was over. He had decided. But before he could dial the number in Los Angeles, it occurred to him his family did have a stake in all this. Go west to Southern Cal and he would rarely see his family. They would not be able to see him play that often.

Standing in the kitchen, he simply blurted it out:

"Okay," he said, "Call Coach Phillips and tell him I'll sign with Georgia."

That was part of the plan, too. When Herschel decided, Phillips would be the first to know. He would then notify the school.

Cavan, on this day, was not in Wrightsville. He was on a family Easter-egg hunt in Atlanta. Phillips contacted Bob Newsome and Ralph Jackson in Wrightsville, who knew how to find Cavan. He was never out of their company without letting them know where he could be reached. For six months, Cavan had been on standby to head to Wrightsville for any reason.

The call came through from Wrightsville to Cavan in Atlanta. Cavan screamed when he heard the news. His family, in the yard hunting for Easter eggs, thought he had been shot. Cavan called Dooley in Athens. He also alerted Steve Greer, who is head of recruiting. The three met in Athens an hour later and were quickly headed to Wrightsville.

The drive took two hours. It seemed like an eternity. If those they met and passed along the way had known their mission, they would likely have been followed into Wrightsville by the biggest caravan in the history of the state.

Gary Phillips had arranged an afternoon signing session. He, along with assistant Tom Jordan, Bob Newsome, and Ralph Jackson, met the three Georgia coaches when they drove into the Walker family's yard. Georgia had already used its three official visits with Herschel, so Dooley, Cavan, and Greer had to wait outside until Herschel had signed his name to the scholarship agreement.

The second that was done they went into the small house to offer their congratulations. That night Newsome threw a party at the lodge on his farm a few miles out of town. He and Ralph Jackson had worked the hardest to put Herschel in red and black.

The entire state celebrated. Herschel signing with the University of Georgia was front-page news. Dooley, meanwhile, did have one concern. He knew people would expect a lot out of Herschel Walker immediately. He knew the pressure for him to excel could be a problem. The day he signed, Dooley called his new recruit aside and told him:

"We don't expect miracles from you. We will never pressure you. We'll give you an opportunity, and all we want is for you to do your best. People may expect too much from you right away, but the coaching staff will be patient."

From the start, Herschel Walker was humble.

He predicted no great things for himself at Georgia. Maybe it was Tom Jordan who was most responsible for that attitude.

"Back in the ninth grade," Jordan recalls, "I can remember talking to Herschel about attitude, which was always so important to him. One of the things that we talked about was the loudmouth athlete. I couldn't stand that type, and neither could Herschel. I think it made an impression on him when we talked about those things."

From the beginning, Herschel Walker was quiet, soft-spoken, humble, a gentleman.

Before graduating from high school, he would reap even more honors. He was named Georgia's high school athlete-of-the-year by the Georgia Sports Hall of Fame. He ended his high school track career with a 9.5 in the 100-yard dash and a 21.5 in the 220.

The summer would come and go quickly, then it would be time to report to fall practice in Athens. The schoolboy days would be over. He would leave his mother's home. The pride of Johnson County would make the giant leap from the house on the hill, across the railroad tracks, and up the dirt drive to the big time of major college football.

* * * *

First, in 1963, came Joel Eaves. Shortly thereafter, arrived Vince Dooley. Then, came Erskine Russell to join the Dooley staff.

There were some good years, there were some great years, there were a few years that were disappointing.

In 1978 came Buck Belue and Lindsay Scott and other promising freshmen. Earlier, a significant crop of talent had been gathered—Scott Woerner, the brilliant defensive back and return specialist; Rex Robinson, the placekicker; offensive linemen Tim Morrison, and Hugh Nall, and Nat Hudson, and Jeff Harper, and Jim Blakewood, and flanker Amp Arnold. The defensive leadership was strong, too, with cornerbacks

Signing Day. After months of deliberation, Herschel signs on Georgia's dotted line. His sister, Veronica (left), was already at Georgia on a track scholarship.

Scott Woerner and Greg Bell, defensive end Robert Miles, safety Jeff Hipp, cornerback Mike Fisher, defensive end Pat McShea, linebacker Frank Ros, defensive guard Tim Parks, and rover Chris Welton.

Georgia would find two outstanding defensive linemen in 270-pound guard Eddie (Meat Cleaver) Weaver and tackle Jimmy Payne, 245 pounds, from Athens.

There would be others, too—Jimmy Womack and Ronnie Stewart, fullbacks; Nate Taylor, another linebacker; Norris Brown, the tight end; Carnie Norris, who would have to play behind Herschel Walker at tailback; and the punters, Jim Broadway and Mark Malkiewicz.

The Georgia team of 1978, led by Willie McClendon, was 9-2-1. Buck Belue was the hero of a 29-28 come-from-behind victory over Georgia Tech. Lindsay Scott returned a kickoff for a touchdown that helped defeat LSU in Baton Rouge.

The '79 team was a disappointment, at 6-5, but that disappointment soon passed with the signing of Herschel Walker on Easter Sunday, 1980.

There would be some changes when the 1980 season opened in Knoxville against Tennessee. One, Buck Belue, would be the No. 1 quarterback, no questions asked. The year before, he had shared playing time with senior Jeff Pyburn. The two-quarterback plan, which had worked for Dooley before, had not clicked as well as it had in the past.

Also George Haffner would arrive in Athens from Texas A&M to take over the duties as offensive coordinator for Bill Pace, who would be headed to, of all places, Tennessee to face his former colleagues and players across the field in the opener.

AND, of course, there would be Herschel Walker.

Seventeen years after University of Georgia president O. C. Aderhold had made that telephone call from Newnan to Joel Eaves in Auburn, the collection of individuals and circumstances had been assembled for Georgia's shot at its first national championship.

And what could a stolen pig and a linebacker from Barcelona, Spain, have to do with all of this? I was just coming to that. . . .

Herschel and Veronica in Athens. The family wanted Georgia; Herschel finally gave in.

BOOK II

The Season

And Along Came Herschel. . .

Each spring the University of Georgia football team throws a party and initiates freshmen into its brotherhood. The ritual goes back to the Wally Butts era when a local Athens restaurant owner, Bob Seagraves, hosted the party at his establishment a few miles out of town.

Seagraves' Restaurant has long since been swallowed up by residential expansion in Clarke County, but the spring party lives on. In 1980 the upperclassmen behind the party had an idea: Why not have a barbecue?

Terrific idea, but where does the pig come from?

We steal the pig.

Hot night in Knoxville. Georgia captains Frank Ros (48) and Hugh Nall (54) shake on it with the Volunteers.

One pig turned up missing from a University experiment pen.

The revelry continued late into the evening when the newly-initiated freshmen came up with an idea of their own: Why not dump the carcass of the pig over at a girls' dorm?

Boys, as they say, were being boys. But somebody blew the whistle and University police arrived on the scene to nab the pranksters and what was left of the pig. On duty with the University police that night, incidentally, was David Saye, a former Vince Dooley player at Georgia who probably had been involved in some sort of spring initiation himself.

As soon as word came that the police were looking for those responsible for stealing the pig, the upperclassmen who were involved turned themselves in. Among the group was the 1980 captain, linebacker Frank Ros.

News travels fast. The incident was covered by the Atlanta newspapers and even *Sports Illustrated*. Vince Dooley hit the ceiling. You can explain away such incidents—or pranks—as typical of fun-loving, active college athletes to people who are close to your program. But to your critics and detractors who relish the opportunity to go into action, here is an example of, for instance, the head coach's inability to control his players.

Dooley worried about the image of his 1980 team. His ulcer started acting up again. The list of names he had to discipline for the incident was a long one, and he spelled out the conditions of that discipline as sternly as a no-nonsense frontier judge.

All summer long, Frank Ros and a number of his senior-to-be teammates could be found painting fences around the athletic fields and doing all sorts of other manual labor for minimum wages, which they never pocketed.

The money went to pay for the stolen pig and for their scholarships. Dooley demanded, as part of the disciplinary measure, they earn their fall keep by working throughout the summer.

The severity of Dooley's discipline could have had an adverse effect on the 1980 Georgia team. The players involved could have sulked, could have turned against him. But they didn't. Frank Ros would talk about the ordeal later:

"We knew what we had to do and we did it," he said. "We agreed with Coach Dooley and we understood his actions. He had always been a fair man with us and we knew we had let him down.

"But even though we brought about a lot of bad publicity, spending that summer together made us a closer group. We spent the summer talking about the '80 season.

"Plus, everybody on the team had offered to help. I mean, everybody. To a man, they all came to my room and offered to chip in to pay for the pig. Their attitude was, 'What can I do

81

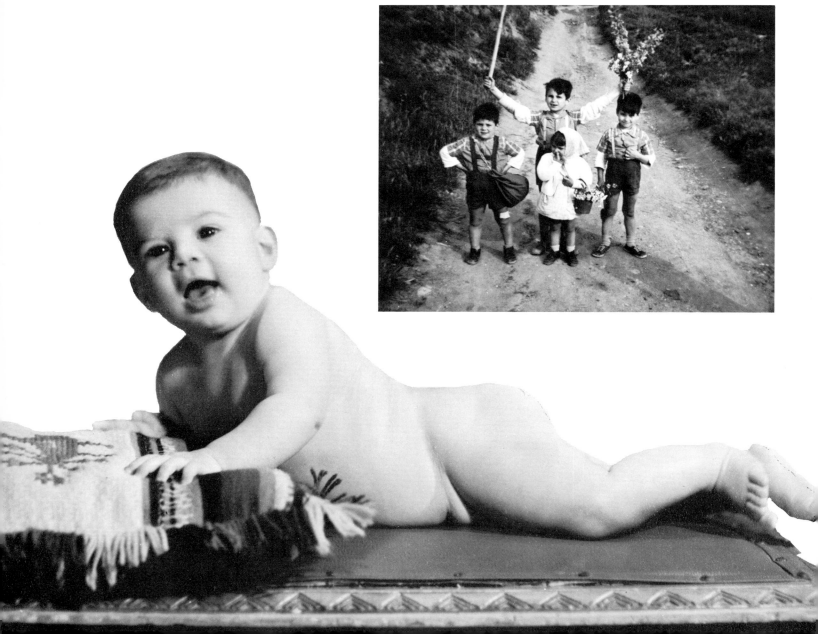

to help?' You could tell then we were going to be close. That incident brought us together."

Frank Ros, senior captain, would lead that team onto the field on Saturday night, September 6, in Knoxville, where Georgia would open the 1980 season against Tennessee in Neyland Stadium.

Francisco Ros. Born, March 1, 1959. Barcelona, Spain.

The day Frank Ros was born, Wallace Butts was conducting spring practice in Athens with a team that had lost six games the previous fall. It was maybe the best team in the country to lose six games.

The Georgia Athletic Association was preparing to retire No. 40, the jersey worn by Theron Sapp who scored the touchdown on Grant Field in 1957 that broke an eight-year losing streak to Georgia Tech.

Guard Pat Dye and quarterback Francis Tarkenton were rising juniors on that team, and that would make Butts forget the loss of linebacker Dave Lloyd who had quit the team with a year of eligibility remaining to sign with the Cleveland Browns.

Lloyd's decision to leave the campus did not bring about any tears in Payne Hall, the athletic residence, however. Lloyd was a powerful rock of a man who had incredible ability, but his unnecessary 15-yard penalties often caused his teammates great concern.

He intimidated his teammates. He often left morale in shambles. Without him in 1959, Georgia would win the Southeastern Conference championship and defeat Missouri in the Orange Bowl. The Auburn game had been the conference title clincher, climaxed by a classic Tarkenton-to-Bill Herron touchdown pass in the closing seconds for a 14-13 victory.

Standing on the north sideline that day had been Vince Dooley, the Auburn quarterback coach. He had just completed work on his Master's Degree in history, and he was still a bachelor.

Six seasons later he had switched sidelines. He was wearing Georgia red. On Thanksgiving Day 1965 he and his family drove to Atlanta to watch the Georgia freshman team, which included Jake Scott and Bill Stanfill, defeat the Tech freshmen in the annual Scottish Rite charity game at Grant Field.

That same day, six-year-old Francisco Ros and his family set sail aboard the *Independence* from Barcelona. They would sail past the statue of Christopher Columbus, on to New York.

Ros' father had been a laborer in a local factory. He had degrees in both business and engineering, but under the Franco regime in Spain you worked where you were told to work. The Ros family had cousins who had bucked the Franco system. They had faced the Franco firing squad. An uncle took flight to France and never again returned to his homeland.

Francisco Ros started school at three. The family needed extra money, so his mother worked. She could not afford a babysitter, however. She worked out a deal where Francisco could remain in a kindergarten. The schoolhouse was a two-story building. The girls attended classes upstairs and were kept totally isolated from the boys.

"You were seated," Frank remembers, "according to your performance and ability as a student. The smartest kid would sit on the first row and the next smartest behind him, and so on. Usually, the kid who sat on the back row wasn't the dumbest, he was just the youngest. Three grades were in one class together.

"I always had to sit on the back row. I was really too young to go to school, but I learned a lot in a hurry. It would help me later."

Francisco Ros would hear and learn his first English phrases aboard the *Independence*. That phrase would be, "Good Morning." His father had managed to get his family out of Barcelona and was headed to America for a better life. They would settle in Greenville, S.C., where he found work as an engineer in a textile factory.

Francisco—now "Frank"—entered Brushy Creek Elementary School. All he could say, still, was "Good Morning." But the early kindergarten training helped him. He could already multiply and do long division while his classmates were still learning their ABC's.

"I would have traded all my advancement for the ability to communicate," he says now. "All the kids looked at me like I was crazy. It was a lonely, confused feeling I won't ever forget. I cried. I cried because I couldn't communicate. The only thing I understood was the lunchbreak. When kids started out of the classroom door for lunch, I figured that out, so I headed home."

In Spain Frank Ros' classes had run from 9 A.M. until noon, then came the siesta, then classes resumed from three o'clock to six.

"As I headed out the door," Ros goes on, "a teacher grabbed me and pulled me back inside. She wanted to know where I was going, I guess. I didn't understand her. And I couldn't make her understand me, either. She finally

83

Captain Frank Ros during early childhood days in Spain.

pulled me into the lunchroom and got me something to eat. I was a chubby kid, and I liked to eat. Finally, there was something I could understand."

It took him three months to be able to begin communicating with his fellow students. He was into the middle grades before he began to fully comprehend the new language.

Football would come easier. He would grow to be strong and fast and earn four letters in football at Eastside High in Greenville and a scholarship to Georgia. His Americanization was complete.

He is still not a U.S. citizen but he plans to complete that process soon. He has been back to his homeland for visits. He has no intention of ever staying.

"Once when I went back to Barcelona where I was born," he explains, "I stood outside the steel gates in front of the little shack which we had shared with another family. I realized how lucky I was to have a father who would take me to America. I'll be forever grateful to him."

Frank Ros, 6-1, 218, black hair, brown eyes, fast and choppy speech, brought his team—in white jerseys and red pants—onto the turf at Neyland Stadium a few minutes before kickoff on Saturday night, September 6, 1980. The temperature was still in the 90s. The humidity was stifling. The crowd had swollen to 95,288, the largest crowd ever to witness a college football game in the South.

The game was rated nearly even. Georgia was coming off its 6-5 record in 1979, but it returned veteran talent on defense. For Tennessee, this was to be the year its hero-returned Johnny Majors would put the Vols back into Southeastern Conference contention. He had been lured from Pittsburgh where he had won the national title in 1976 with an easy victory over Georgia in the Sugar Bowl.

Tennessee had some questions at quarterback, and its best runner, Howard Simpson, had been thrown off the team in fall practice for disciplinary reasons. But the Volunteers had good defense, excellent offensive linemen, and a good kicking game.

The Tennessee advantage over Georgia came from the huge crowd, the artificial turf and a fellow named Bill Pace who had left Dooley's staff as offensive coordinator after the 1979 season to take a similar position under Majors.

Nine months earlier he had been running Georgia's offense. Now he was running Tennessee's. For six years in Athens Pace had

occupied an office with Georgia's defensive coach, Erskine Russell. They talked football most of the time. After all those years Pace knew how Russell thought and what defensive alignments he liked to call in certain situations. Pace had the advantage in going one-on-one with Russell because, further, he knew the Georgia defensive personnel and Russell didn't have that advantage with Tennessee's offensive players.

"When we worked together," Russell would say, "I used to mention to him, 'Bill, this sort of play gives us trouble or that kind of play gives us problems,' so he had a great idea of what might go against us."

Frank Ros met the Tennessee captain in the middle of the field. Tennessee won the toss. Rex Robinson kicked off the 1980 season, and, on the first play from scrimmage, the Volunteers fumbled. Georgia recovered at the Tennessee 24. Two plays later Norris Brown tried to run a reverse. He fumbled, and the Vols had the ball back at their own 21.

From that point nothing seemed to go right for Georgia. Tennessee started moving behind the passing of quarterback Jeff Olszewski, and the Bulldogs' offense was going nowhere. Barely into the second quarter, Buck Belue fumbled the snap from center deep in his own territory and Jimmy Womack, the Bulldog fullback, recovered in the Georgia end zone for a Tennessee safety and a 2-0 Tennessee lead.

The Bulldogs kicked off from their 20. Tennessee came driving. Olszewski took the Volunteers 54 yards in eight plays and scored himself from the Georgia four. At the half, Tennessee led 9-0.

Bill Pace went one-up on Erskine Russell and Georgia in the third quarter. Tennessee had possession, first down on its own 48. Olszewski passed for 16 yards to the Georgia 36. Russell signaled the Georgia defense to blitz. Pace guessed that was exactly what Russell would do.

Pace signaled his offense to pass over the middle. Olszewski dropped back. Here came the Bulldog blitz. The Tennessee quarterback tossed the ball to Mike Miller, who had cut in front of defensive back Scott Woerner. Miller took the ball and dashed into the end zone. Two plays and another Tennessee touchdown. The score was 15-0 with 4:02 to go in the third quarter.

Pace immediately sent word in that he had a two-point conversion play ready. He was still counting on his days with Russell to give him the edge. He remembered the Georgia defensive coach liked to blitz in a two-point conversion attempt. He called for a quick handoff. He thought it would be a cinch to score.

Russell did not call the blitz. He knew Pace would be looking for it. The Georgia line stopped the Tennessee running back and the score remained 15-0. That play would turn out to be the difference in the ball game.

But Georgia's chances seemed nearly hopeless at the time. The offense couldn't move. Tennessee had 15 points. There were only 19 minutes left to go. Tennessee students were chanting, "How 'bout them Dawgs!" behind the Georgia bench.

Russell:

"In the third quarter, I thought to myself that I had maybe hurt our team. We tried to do too much and prepare for anything and everything, and we had tried several times to cross up Pace, and it obviously wasn't working. The good thing was that, regardless of what was going on from the standpoint of our strategy, the team never really gave up. They kept believing something would happen."

Pace:

"I really felt good with those 15 points. We were doing basically what we wanted to do and what we expected to do. It boiled down to us not being able to put Georgia away."

First there was the fumbled punt. Jim Broadway of Georgia kicked to Tennessee's Bill Bates with three minutes to go in the third period. The Bulldogs' Joe Happe timed his tackle perfectly, and hit Bates the same time the ball did. Bates went one way, the ball went the other.

There was a mad scramble for the loose ball. Georgia had it, then lost it, then had it again. The ball continued to roll toward the Tennessee end zone. Recover in the end zone, and Georgia had a touchdown.

The ball finally rolled out of the end zone and the Bulldogs had to settle for a safety. The score stood, 15-2, at 3:19 of the third period.

What the play did was activate the Georgia sidelines, which had been quiet for too long. The team seemed to be waiting for something

Deeeeefense! Red helmets are all over the ball carrier and Georgia is fighting back from a 15-0 deficit to Tennessee.

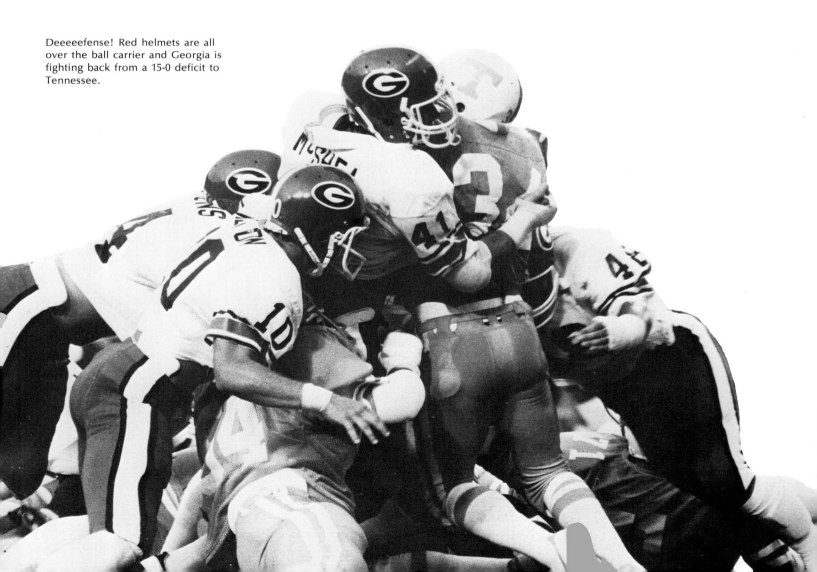

to happen. There were points on the board and now the Vols had to kick back to Georgia. But could the Bulldogs move the ball?

Belue connected with Lindsay Scott for 24 yards down to the Tennessee 16. There was less than a minute and a half left to go in the quarter. Something incredible, something historic was about to happen.

Herschel Walker did not start in his first collegiate game. Throughout pre-season practice Dooley insisted the young tailback sensation from Wrightsville be brought along slowly. There was even some indication Dooley had been disappointed with Walker in summer practice.

The week before the Tennessee game, we met at the hot dog stand near the end of the Clarke Central-Griffin high school game in Athens. I asked about Herschel.

"I'm afraid," said Dooley, "that Herschel is just a big, stiff back." At that point, Walker was still learning and had not displayed his marvelous talents to Dooley and his staff.

Dooley finally decided to use Walker in the

1

The Touchdown Debut of Mr. Herschel Walker. Georgia trailed Tennessee 15-2 late in the third period when the tailback from Wrightsville broke loose for his first Bulldog touchdown. (1) The Georgia line opens a hole and Walker blasts through.

2

second period in Knoxville when nothing else seemed to be working. He talked to offensive coordinator George Haffner, who calls the Georgia plays in the booth. "I'm putting Herschel in," said Dooley. "Don't be afraid to let him carry the ball."

He did nothing spectacular in his first running attempts, but at least now he had been in a college football game. Plus, on a second down and 14 at the Georgia 31, Belue kicked his fumbled snap toward the Tennessee sideline, and it could have been recovered by the Vols with disastrous results. But Walker, with his great speed, got to the ball and recovered for the Bulldogs.

Back to late in the third period: Walker is in the game. Haffner calls a pitch sweep. It is first down at the Tennessee 16. Belue pitches to Walker. There is a hole in the line. Walker bursts through. Near the goal line he meets Tennessee safety Bill Bates. It is no contest. Herschel Walker, with a full head of steam, his powerful thighs churning, runs completely over Bates, chewing him up and spitting him out

(2) He runs over one Volunteer defender, then splits a couple of more (3), and finally prances into the end zone from 16 yards out (4).

and leaving him stretched out on the Tartan turf. At the goal line he splits two more defenders and races in for his first Georgia touchdown.

The sideline went crazy. Georgia was back within a touchdown and it was the freshman who had electrified the house with his 16-yard dash into the end zone.

The speculation was over. *Herschel Walker was for real.* I walked over to Mike Cavan. He had recruited Walker. He had believed in him.

"How do you feel?" I asked.

"I don't want to hear anything else about Class A football," he said. The score after Rex Robinson's extra point was 15-9 with 1:03 left in the third period.

Three plays after Herschel had driven the Georgia fans wild, and had quieted the Tennessee students who were beginning to back away from the fence behind the Bulldog bench, Georgia got another break.

Olszewski fumbled and Georgia recovered at the Volunteer 25. With 11:16 to go in the game, Herschel Walker took another pitch and went nine yards for his second touchdown. The score was tied, 15-15. Robinson put Georgia ahead, 16-15.

But so much time remained. The two teams exchanged punts. Then, here came Olszewski again. He passed for 22 yards, then for 17. He moved Tennessee all the way to the Georgia five.

Pace sent down the call for a Power I formation and a play he had named "Sweep at 8." He called that same play "48" when he ran Georgia's offense. It was a pitch to the tailback who looks for a hole at tackle. It is a possession play that should, under the circumstances, gain three or four yards.

Olszewski pitches to Ford, who starts right, toward Georgia's defensive left. He sees a gap to the inside. The Tennessee right tackle is making an excellent block. Ford cuts to the hole.

The right guard for Tennessee has the assignment of blocking Georgia linebacker Nate Taylor, perhaps the most unlikely starting linebacker in all of college football. He's not big enough, not fast enough, not good enough, but he is a winner. He always seems to be around the ball. His timing on a play was never more perfect than in the goal line stand in Knoxville this steamy Saturday night.

Tennessee's right guard swings outside the tackle looking for Taylor, who has literally been hiding behind his own defensive tackle,

reacting to running back Ford's every move. The guard can't find the man he is supposed to block—Nate Taylor, the "Ty Ty Termite."

Taylor comes at the ball carrier, his head up, his body square to the ground. He meets Ford solidly. His eyes are in the back's numbers. His helmet hits the ball. No back can hold the ball when that happens. A few inches off, or a split-second either way, and Tennessee might have kept possesssion.

The ball pops away from Ford. Pat McShea, from his right defensive end position—away from where the play is developing—is supposed to trail on such plays. He is supposed to go hard after the ball carrier, in hot pursuit.

But Pat McShea has failed to carry out his assignment. He has folded back into the play, and when Taylor forces Ford's fumble, there is McShea in the wrong place, at the right time. The ball dribbles toward him, and he outfights three orange jerseys for possession.

Georgia takes over on its one. A great play and a little luck and the Bulldogs are still holding on, 16-15. But 4:02 remains to play and they are backed deep against their own end zone.

"We've got to get the ball out of there," George Haffner says to assistant Charles Whittemore from the coaches' booth above the stadium. So many things could happen. A fumble. A blocked kick. Another safety would beat Georgia.

First, Haffner calls for an inside handoff to Walker. His heart goes to his throat when he sees the Volunteer defense penetrate. But Herschel instinctively veers just enough to avoid a solid tackle and gets past the line of scrimmage for a yard.

"We're going wide," Haffner says to Whittemore. "We've got to give Herschel some room to run."

Herschel Walker, the raw recruit from Wrightsville, playing in his first college game, before 95,000, takes the pitch six yards deep in his own end zone. He moves the ball four yards. Georgia is penalized for delay of game, but Herschel gets the call again, and this time he goes wide for three yards. No first down, but Walker has moved the ball out far enough for punter Broadway to have some room for the subsequent kick.

"That's when I knew Herschel Walker was something special," Haffner says now. "When you call on a freshman in that situation, before all those people, and you pitch the ball to him in his end zone, and he brings it out like he did, you know he can perform."

Broadway boomed away a punt for 47 yards, his best of the night and a key play in the game, and the Georgia defense held on. The clock ran out. The Bulldogs had won their opener, and Herschel Walker had made a smashing debut. Nothing would be the same again.

Haffner:

"We learned from the Tennessee game that Herschel still had a lot to learn, but we saw he was, in fact, an exceptional back who was certainly far enough advanced to play in our league. But I don't think anybody on our staff had any inkling of what was to come. Yet we realized we couldn't have beaten Tennessee without him."

Pace:

"Georgia was probably not that good a team the night they played us, but they grew, and they got better. That is what you have to do. That is why some games and some wins can mean so much. This meant so much to Georgia because it proved to itself it could come back and win a very tough game. That is something players need to learn in September. It comes in handy down the line."

What a way to start the season, I was thinking as the Georgia players and coaches shouted their way back to the dressing room. I remembered that opener in Knoxville in 1968. Without informing then-athletic director Joel Eaves at Georgia, Tennessee athletic director Bob Woodruff had installed Tartan Turf at Neyland Stadium, which was considered a controversial move at the time.

"We don't want to be guinea pigs," Eaves said, publicly chastising Woodruff for putting Georgia in the position to become the first visiting team to play on the new Tennessee rug. It wouldn't have made Eaves any madder if Woodruff had announced he was mining the field.

Tennessee came back late in that game and, on a controversial two-point conversion, tied a Georgia team that wound up undefeated during the regular season.

There would be so much ahead for this 1980 Georgia team, of course, and it would turn out Tennessee was probably overrated in its opener. But at least the first hurdle has been taken. Georgia led the Southeastern Conference race with its 1-0 record.

Frank Ros, the first alien ever to captain a Georgia football team, had talked about the pig

incident back in the spring. He had talked about the *togetherness* of this team. Erk Russell would mention it, too: "The team never really gave up," he said of the performance in Knoxville.

There was something special about this group. You could sense it in the last quarter-and-a-half in Knoxville. And, of course, there would be no more questions concerning No. 34, Herschel Walker.

After the game, I expected a mob for the dressing room radio show I do with Dooley. Sports information director Claude Felton escorted him from where the team was celebrating to a quiet interview room. Only a couple of sportswriters came with him.

I was really surprised. At the first break, I said to Vince, "Where is everybody?"

"With Herschel," he grinned.

Woerner, the Returner

Texas A&M would come to Athens in the sweltering September heat to open the Bulldogs' home season at Sanford Stadium. A 60,000-plus crowd would also come to see Herschel Walker. The state's sports sections had covered little else the week following the Tennessee game.

Vince Dooley was worried about the Aggies. Vince Dooley is always worried. But they had knocked over Ole Miss in their opener in Jackson the week before, and they were big.

The smoothness of Georgia's offense that was missing in Knoxville the week before blossomed against Texas A&M, an offense being run by George Haffner.

Buck Belue hit Amp Arnold for six yards and the first touchdown. They would connect again for a third, 19 yards. The Bulldogs, stunning the cheering crowd, were up 28-0 at the half.

Walker had a one-yard sneak for a first half touchdown. He would drive another one-yard for a second touchdown in the third quarter. And with 3:52 to go in the period, he gave the crowd what it had come to see—a 76-yard blast for his third touchdown of the day. The Aggies went down easily, 42-0. Georgia was 2-0 and rolling.

Next came Clemson. Another huge crowd was at Sanford Stadium, 61,800 strong. Herschel Walker. Herschel Walker. Herschel Walker. The name was on everybody's lips.

Singlehandedly, they were saying, he had won the Tennessee game. He had helped destroy A&M. Now, Clemson, a school that had wanted him so badly.

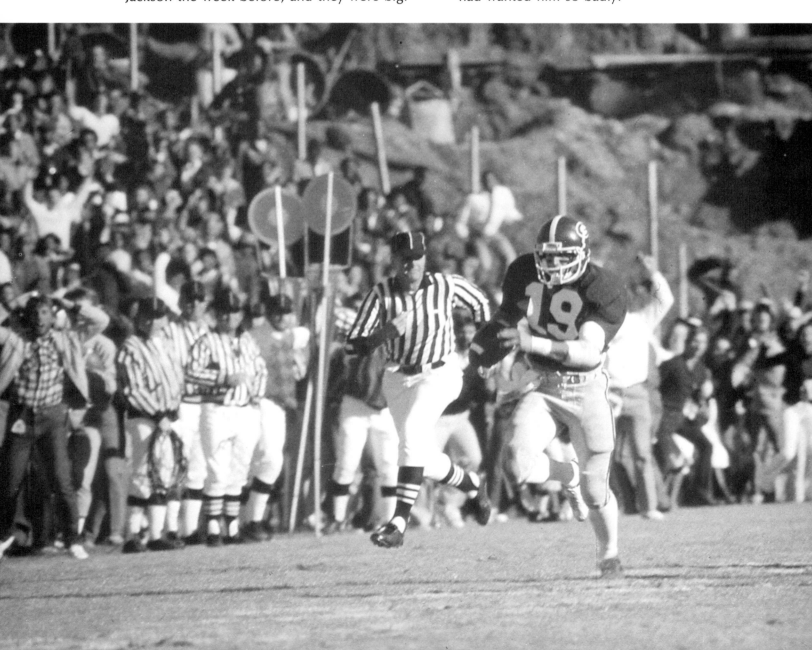

In the first half Herschel Walker would carry the ball only six times, and he would gain but 12 yards. Georgia would have NO first downs. Clemson would have 15. Georgia would have only 33 yards total offense. Clemson would have 239. But Georgia would lead, 14-10, thanks, not to Herschel Walker, but to a young man who was signed, sealed and delivered four years earlier to the Texas Longhorns. Some background:

Scott Woerner was a little boy when he lived in Baytown, Texas, and all he ever wanted to do was grow up and play football for Darrell Royal at the University of Texas. His father, John, was transferred by his company, Mathison Gas Products, to Jonesboro, Georgia, when Scott was in the fourth grade. Already, the youngster was a superb athlete.

There was no midget football program in Baytown, so Scott Woerner concentrated on track. Junior Olympics are popular in Texas, and Scott competed in meets almost every weekend. He still has a shoebox filled with ribbons.

He excelled in hurdling and jumping events and had fair speed for sprints. Those who know him best believe had he stayed away from football and concentrated on track, he would have been good enough in the decathlon to have made the Olympics.

But he did get involved in football and he played quarterback for Jonesboro High, coached by one of Georgia's best ends ever, Weyman Sellers, whose assistant was former Georgia quarterback Paul Gilbert.

That didn't matter to Scott Woerner. He still wanted to go to the University of Texas. He WOULD go to the University of Texas.

After his final high school game in Jonesboro, in 1976, Woerner went to see Texas play Arkansas. His Uncle Howard and Aunt Katherine, a member of the Texas faculty, live in Austin. She had contacted the athletic department about her talented nephew, and Texas had become well aware of his talents.

His relatives picked him up at the airport in Austin on Friday. Saturday, he visited with Royal. He told the Texas coaches he wanted to

Man on the move. The best Georgia punt returner since Charley Trippi? At least. Scott (The Returner) Woerner rambles against Clemson on a punt return for a touchdown. Later, he would set up another Bulldog score with a long return of an interception.

sign. They told him that when the signing date came he would have a scholarship. That was that.

Afterwards Woerner sat in the stands with his aunt and uncle and watched Texas defeat the rival Razorbacks. When the game was over Woerner kept his eyes on Darrell Royal. He would be playing for this man for the next four years.

Royal didn't leave the field after the game, however. He walked over to a podium on the 30-yard line and began speaking into a microphone. Scott Woerner couldn't believe his ears. Darrell Royal was saying he was quitting as head coach at the University of Texas. At that moment Woerner changed the commitment he had held for so long. He wouldn't go to Texas after all. A week later he attended the WSB radio Metro All-Star breakfast in Atlanta. He walked up to Georgia assistant Chip Wisdom and said he wanted to play football for Vince Dooley. Dooley signed him the next day at his home in Jonesboro.

"Georgia had been my second choice all along," Woerner says now. "I liked the school and I liked the coaches. I had simply grown up as a little boy thinking about nothing but Darrell Royal and Texas. The feeling never left me."

Scott Woerner is hardly outspoken, and never brash, but his feelings about college football are certainly worth hearing in a time when athletes are becoming more greedy and illegalities in recruiting are perhaps more widespread than ever:

"Another reason I was attracted to Texas," he explains, "was because Royal was so outspoken about illegal recruiting, and I have come to appreciate Vince Dooley the same way. Nobody ever offered me anything more than a scholarship at Georgia. I didn't want anything else, and I wouldn't have signed if they had even hinted anything else was available.

"I consider it an honor to play college football. My family doesn't have a lot of money, and I'm no saint, but all I wanted was an opportunity to play college football and get an education. That should be enough for a player."

Texas recruited Scott Woerner as a quarterback. Georgia recruited him as a football player. He began his career at Georgia as a running back with the freshmen. He pulled a muscle soon after arriving in Athens, however, and was standing on the sidelines

watching practice when Dooley wandered up to him.

"What do you think about defense?" he asked the freshman out of the blue.

"Okay," Woerner replied. Like I said, he is hardly outspoken.

Dooley took him to backfield coach Sam Mitchell and said, "Here's a defensive back for you."

There were a number of seniors on the defensive unit in 1977, and the opportunities for Woerner to play would be many. He also wanted a chance to run with the football. He wanted to return punts. He turned out to be the prototype for the ideal punt returner.

He concentrates and he is fearless. Few who have worn the Red and Black have had more guts than Scott Woerner. The closest of those who have played for Vince Dooley was Wayne Swinford. You could tell Swinford you would be behind him with a baseball bat, and if he fielded the punt, you would hit him with the bat. He would still catch anything within his reach. Woerner was the same way.

Against Georgia Tech in 1978, when he was a sophomore, he caught a punt the second a Tech defender's helmet struck his chin. The defender literally ran through him. But Woerner held onto the ball and drew a 15-yard interference penalty.

"It was worth it," he remembers. "We scored after that. The way I look at it, the 15-yard penalty meant a first down and a half that the offense didn't have to make."

His ability to concentrate is amazing. He can watch television or read a book with the entire room in an uproar. That concentration and his great hands enabled him to field punts and never lose control—or the ball. Only twice in his entire Georgia career did he fumble away a punt to the opposition.

Assistant coach Bill Lewis on his prize pupil, Scott Woerner:

"I think he could actually hear the footsteps bearing down on him when he was fielding a punt, but that is why he was so great. He never took his eyes off the ball. He could concentrate so well, he could *feel* what was going on around him.

"Something else that was important about him is that he wanted to return punts. It's tough to catch a football in punting situations because if you make a mistake, everybody in the house knows you have failed.

"That kind of pressure never bothered Woerner. He enjoys it. I've never seen an athlete with his positive attitude as a punt returner. He wasn't a finesse runner after he caught the ball, he was a slashing runner. He could break tackles."

It was the entire kicking game—and some heroics by Scott Woerner—that won the Clemson game for Georgia. The yardage totals were overwhelmingly in favor of the visitors, but Georgia was developing as the kind of team that could win—and would win—by being stable in every phase of the game. The Georgia specialty teams that handled and covered punts and kickoffs, were improving each week.

Georgia assistant John Kasay, who played on the early Dooley teams, is in charge of special teams. Kasay expects people to play for him as he played—flat out on every play. After Georgia defeated SMU in the 1967 Cotton Bowl, a defensive lineman for the Mustangs found the relentless offensive guard Kasay an opponent he'd like to forget. "That No. 66," he said, "must have been taking mean pills before the game. I've never seen anything like him on a football field." Kasay coaches the same way.

Georgia kicked off to Clemson, at 1:30 P.M., September 20. The sky was overcast, the temperature in the high 70s, and that awful humidity stood at 97 percent.

Homer Jordan, from Athens' Clarke Central High, started as the Clemson quarterback. The usual throng had followed the Tigers down from Clemson, a short, two-hour drive. Georgia-Clemson has become an intense rivalry. Two years earlier the Bulldogs had given Clemson its only loss of the season in Athens. In 1979 Clemson defeated Georgia in Death Valley.

The two schools had competed closely for the talents of Herschel Walker, as well. Clemson, recall, had been one of Walker's final three schools. The bumper stickers came out of Clemson soon after Georgia won the recruiting battle. They read, "Herschel Who?"

Jordan tried a pass on the first play from scrimmage. It went incomplete. Two running plays gained nine yards, and the Tigers had to punt.

Woerner was under the kick at his own 33. With Woerner, Georgia ran what is termed a "middle return." In front of the returner were three personal protectors of the ball carrier, Dale Williams and Mike Fisher on the wings and Bob Kelly in the middle. It was their assignment to form a wedge and try to open a seam up the middle to give Woerner his

chance to burst away from the onrushing tacklers.

Woerner has the ball and Kelly and Fisher and Williams have opened that seam. One defender has broken through, but Woerner is able to escape his grasp. He tears through the opening in the middle.

"I could hear what was going on around me as the ball was coming down," Woerner would recall. "I kept my eyes on the ball, but I could hear the popping in front of me. I knew there was a chance to break it. I could just sense it because of the good blocking."

The crowd is on its feet. The game is barely a minute-and-a-half old, and already there is an apparent big play.

Now, there is only one man between Woerner and six points, the Clemson kicker. Woerner is tearing down the field along the sidelines, in front of the Clemson bench. He makes an abrupt cutback across the field and glides untouched into the end zone. Georgia leads, 7-0.

Clemson takes the kickoff and moves down the field, only to miss a field goal attempt. Georgia takes over, but Georgia can't move. Womack gets four, but Belue is thrown for an eight-yard loss. Herschel Walker carries the ball for the first time. He is stacked in the middle of the line for no gain.

The Clemson players are leaping with raised fists. They have stopped Herschel Walker. Their fans are on their feet, too. "Herschel Who?!" they scream. Georgia must punt.

Jordan brings Clemson down the field once more. The Tigers move from their 40 to the Georgia 11. On second down Jordan passes incomplete. Clemson calls time. On third down Jordan aligns his team in a flanked-left formation. Georgia is in its goal line defense, which means an extra defensive lineman, Jack Lindsey, is in the game. The pass coverage is man-to-man.

Clemson starts the play with a man in motion. Safety Jeff Hipp rotates with him, as he is supposed to do. Scott Woerner, playing the left cornerback position, has the responsibility of covering the tight end, who might run a delayed route in such a situation.

The man in motion runs a post route over the middle in front of Hipp after the ball is snapped. The Clemson tight end does not delay. Woerner doubles with Hipp to cover the motion man. As the pass is thrown, Woerner cuts in front of the receiver, leaps into the air and comes down with the interception.

He is inside the end zone, but he thinks he has landed outside. He spots room to his right and heads downfield with the ball. He has 10 yards, 20, now 30. He is at midfield.

At the Clemson 40, he feels his legs tighten. The heat and the humidity are telling. Only a few minutes earlier he had raced 67 yards with the punt return. He keeps churning, but a Clemson player with sprinter's speed is closing in on him. At the Clemson two-yard line Woerner is caught, 100 yards from where he came down with the interception. Belue dives in for the touchdown, and Georgia has a 14-0 lead in the last minute of the first period.

There was a chance to put Clemson away on the next series of downs. Jordan fumbled on second down, and the Bulldogs recovered at the Clemson 24. On second down Belue passed to Amp Arnold for 22 yards to the two, but Arnold fumbled the ball back after being hit.

Mike Gasque replaced Jordan as quarterback for Clemson. He immediately took his team 98 yards for a touchdown. Georgia 14, Clemson 7. Before the half Clemson would get three more. The teams went into their dressing rooms at 14-10. Clemson had that incredible yardage advantage, but Georgia still had its lead.

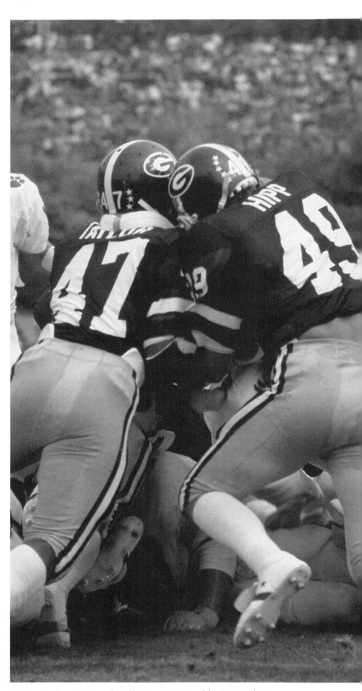

Dawg Defense. Dale Carver (left) halts a Tiger in his tracks; Nate Taylor (47) and Jeff Hipp (49) tackle in tandem.

I wondered what would happen in the second half. I didn't think the situation looked promising for Georgia, which had not been able to move the ball after the tremendous offensive showing the week before. And why couldn't Herschel break away?

The defense was tired. Jimmy Payne, the defensive tackle, was sprawled on the dressing room floor with his naked upper body quivering with fatigue. He couldn't even sit in on the defensive meeting with the rest of the team. I expected him to sit out the second half.

I underestimated Jimmy Payne. I underestimated the entire Georgia team. The Bulldog offense finally moved after the second half kickoff. Walker got 12, Walker got 8, Walker got 12 again before the drive fizzled at the Clemson 25. Rex Robinson hit a 42-yard field goal. Georgia, 17-10.

A Robert Miles interception of a Mike Gasque pass would afford Robinson another chance of three points in the third quarter. Robinson was perfect. Georgia, 20-10. Sanford Stadium was breathing easier. But not for long.

Clemson cut the lead to four with two field goals of its own. Time was winding down. Georgia, with seven minutes to go, has

More Dawg Defense. Mike Fisher makes your basic flat-on-your-back tackle.

95

possession on its own 28. Amp Arnold gets 13 on a reverse. Now, Herschel. Give the ball to Herschel. Keep the ball on the ground. Get the first downs. Eat at the clock.

Walker gets six. Walker gets 11. Another first down. But Ronnie Stewart is stopped for one. Belue loses three. Walker loses one. Less than four minutes to go. Georgia leads by four. Jim Broadway is in to punt.

Get the ball high and deep, the players are shouting to punter Jim Broadway. It's a good snap, but it can't be. It is. Broadway has fumbled the snap and Clemson has recovered

on the Georgia 41. I looked at the clock. Three minutes and 20 seconds left.

Gasque gains two to the 39. Then he is back to pass. The receiver runs into Scott Woerner's back, but the official sees it another way. The flag goes down and Woerner is charged with pass interference. Clemson has the ball, first down, on the Georgia 10. It is bleak. Gasque is back to pass again. He throws. Jeff Hipp comes down with the ball. The defense that was on the field so long, that was so tired, has held again. Herschel makes a run for a first down that is the final blow for Clemson. Clemson

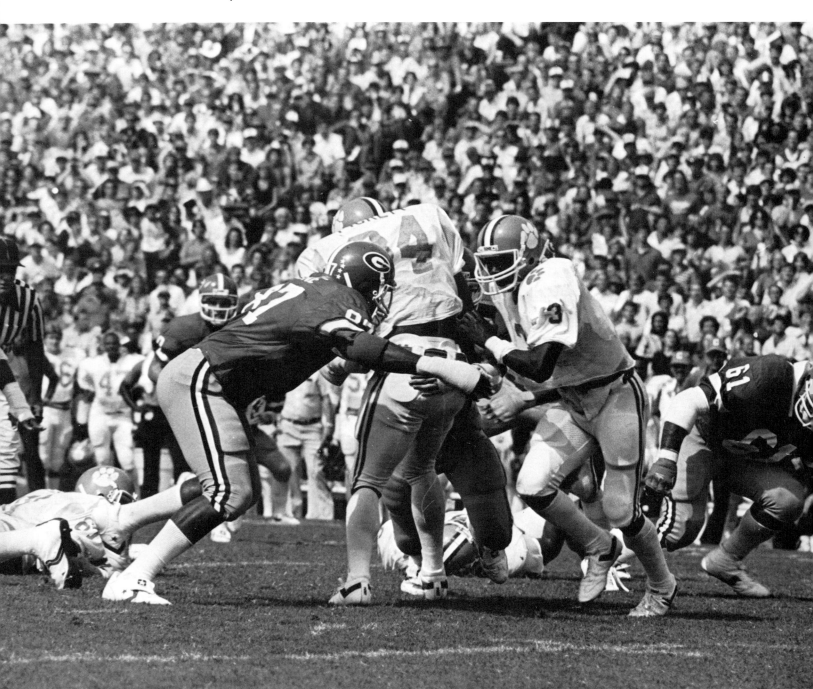

Jimmy Payne (87) and Eddie Weaver pay a visit to the Clemson backfield.

runs out of time outs. Belue falls on the ball. Georgia goes to 3-0 with a 20-16 victory and will move up in the polls with TCU, Ole Miss, and Vanderbilt headed to Athens before another road game is to come, against Kentucky in Lexington. Georgia fans are beginning to talk, beginning to wonder how far this team might go.

It will be favored against a weak TCU team. Ole Miss has to play between the hedges, Vanderbilt is weak again, and Kentucky is obviously no powerhouse.

What if . . . ? What if Georgia could win the next four and come home the first day of November against South Carolina and George Rogers undefeated? The last Georgia team to win its first seven was the 1971 team that went to 9-0 before falling to Auburn and Pat Sullivan.

The defense was bending, but not breaking. The momentum—and Herschel Walker—were there on offense. Imagine, 7-0 going into South Carolina.

There is nothing wrong with dreaming.

"Herschel Who?" The Clemson fans remembered the bitter loss to Georgia in the recruiting battle for Herschel Walker.

YEAH! YEAH! YEAH!

It could have been worse. It could have been much worse. Georgia is off to a sluggish start against what is obviously a weak team from Texas Christian University. Two minutes remain in the first period on this windy, overcast 27th day of September. Georgia is second down and three on the TCU 49.

Buck Belue gives the ball to Herschel Walker. He is loose. Moving one way, then another. Running over people. Forty-one yards downfield he is finally caught at the TCU eight.

But Herschel is not bouncing up as he

usually does. He is hurt. He limps off the field. It is his ankle. The team surrounds him as trainers and the team doctor examine the man who has made Georgia go the first three games of 1980.

It is too early to tell the extent of the injury until there is further examination, but Walker will not return to the lineup on this day. No matter, on *this* day. Walker's run has set up the first touchdown, and the Bulldog record will go to 4-0 with an eventual 34-3 victory.

But Ole Miss arrives in two weeks after an open date. Ole Miss, with its brilliant

Carnie Norris (36) rambled through the Rebels while Herschel Walker nursed an injured ankle.

quarterback, John Fourcade, won't be that easy. What if Herschel Walker still isn't ready?

The decision was made later to hold Herschel and his slightly-sprained ankle out of the Ole Miss game as much as possible. The Bulldogs would go with Carnie Norris. Maybe, just maybe, Norris would respond and Walker could rest the ankle at least part of the game.

Carnie Norris responded with his best game ever. His senior year in high school, 1978, he had been named South Carolina's back-of-the-year at Spartanburg High. So he signs with the University of Georgia, has a good freshman year, and then winds up playing behind Herschel Walker.

But his chance came against Ole Miss. The Rebels came into the game in Athens—bright and fair and 80 on October 11 —with a record of only 1-4, but the Rebels could score with the strong and swift Fourcade.

Georgia jumped to a quick, 17-0, lead. Carnie Norris was running up and down the field while Herschel Walker remained on the bench. Buck Belue found Amp Arnold in the end zone for a 34-yard pass. It looked like it would be easy.

Rarely is Georgia-Ole Miss easy. Just before the half Belue threw a careless interception the Rebels ran back for a touchdown. The score gave Ole Miss life. Fourcade put his team within three, 14-17, in the third period, and Rex Robinson had to kick a 43-yard field goal, and Belue had to sneak one yard for another touchdown following an Ole Miss fumble to put the Rebels out of reach. The game ended 28-21, Georgia went to 5-0, and Carnie Norris had 150 yards. Walker played briefly and appeared ready to return to the lineup the next weekend against Vanderbilt. Thank goodness. Had the injury been worse—had he been out for the season, or out for five or six games—I didn't want to think about it.

* * * *

By Thursday of each week Vince Dooley and his staff normally have completed preparations for the next game. Unfortunately for Vince Dooley, he can't take Thursday night off.

If there is not an Athens Touchdown Club meeting he must attend, then there is the weekly pep rally produced by Mike Castronis and the Georgia cheerleaders. Thursday before the Vanderbilt game, Dooley had to miss the pep rally, however, because his son, Derek, was playing for the City Youth Association

football championship. Derek's team would lose that night. The night was off to a rotten start. It would get worse, nearly tragically worse.

After the game, the Dooleys—Vince driving, Barbara in the front seat, Derek in the back, still in his football uniform—rode into downtown Athens to see the face of a bulldog that had been painted in the middle of the street at the intersection of College and Clayton. The bulldog-in-the-street idea had come from Castronis and the cheerleaders, who were led by Denise Cummins, who was also homecoming queen.

So impressed was he by the painting, Dooley turned around after driving past it and came back down College Avenue for a second look. He stopped at the light just short of the painted bulldog. The three Dooleys leaned toward the windshield to get a better look. Barbara saw what was about to happen a split second before the collision took place.

Police were chasing a traffic offender who ran the red light at College and Clayton and slammed into the rear of Dooley's new Lincoln. The impact of the collision was so strong the trunk of the Lincoln flew open and the spare tire was later found a block away at the site of the old downtown Varsity restaurant.

All three of the Dooleys were knocked unconscious. Vince suffered a broken nose, a busted lip that required 11 stitches, and a

After the wreck. Dooley on the sidelines for Vandy with a broken nose and 11 stitches in his lip.

FAR RIGHT: Thirty-five years later, the record falls. Herschel Walker runs through the Vanderbilt defense for 283 yards, breaking Charley Trippi's (RIGHT) 35-year-old Georgia record for single-game rushing yardage. Trippi's total was 239. BELOW: Vandy couldn't move on the Bulldog defense. To say the least.

concussion. Barbara was thrown into the dash. Her head shattered the windshield. Later examination would indicate she had 11 broken ribs, and doctors would have to remove her spleen. Derek, in the back seat, was not seriously injured. The driver of the other car was charged with drunken driving and running the red light.

I received a phone call from a neighbor, Joy Turnage, who had happened by the wreck scene. I was to make certain two of the other Dooley children, Denise and Daniel, would not be alarmed when they arrived home later and found their parents gone.

I left a note at the door of the Dooley house and headed to St. Mary's Hospital. Vince looked worse off than any of the three. His nose and mouth looked like he had tangled with a tire tool.

His doctor was a former Georgia linebacker, Happy Dicks, a neurosurgeon who had just moved to Athens to start his practice. He ordered Barbara and Derek to remain in the hospital. He also wanted Vince to stay. Vince wouldn't cooperate. He insisted a broken nose and a stitched lip were not enough to interrupt his routine. Also, he wanted to return home to be with his other children.

I called Deanna, the oldest of the Dooley children, who was in school at North Georgia College in Dahlonega. I wanted her to know her family was okay before she heard about the accident on the 11 o'clock news. Then I drove Vince home.

He was in obvious pain, but we talked. We talked about the wreck, and he even got around to talking about the upcoming game with Vanderbilt.

I knew Dooley would recover from the accident when he looked at me very seriously as he got out of my car and said, "You know, Vandy can really move the football. I'm really worried about their offense."

Actually, he was not all that well that night. He had to take heavy medication for the pain to get through the rest of the week. Although he was firmly in control during the Vandy game, he was drained by its end. Happy Dicks kept a close watch on his old coach during the ordeal and stayed within a few paces of him on the sidelines during the game. He also second-guessed himself later about allowing Dooley to go home the night of the wreck. Later he would tell Barbara, "I felt I should have kept him overnight, but how do you tell your coach he can't go home?"

Barbara Dooley missed the Vanderbilt game, of course, and also Kentucky the following weekend. She was also forced to leave the South Carolina game at the half. What she missed in Georgia-Vandy and Georgia-Kentucky was her husband's team rolling to big shutout victories.

I expected a rout against Vanderbilt. It was Homecoming Day, October 18, and Herschel Walker was back. And how he was back. On his first carry from scrimmage he broke for a touchdown on a 60-yard run. He would add a 48-yarder and a third touchdown run of 53 yards. He would total 283 yards to break Charley Trippi's 35-year-old single-game Georgia rushing record of 239.

Georgia crushed Vanderbilt, 41-0. Georgia was 6-0, and headed to Lexington. Georgia would be heavily favored on a cool October 25 evening, but I had to think of two years earlier, 1978, when the Bulldogs went against the Wildcats at night in Lexington. Georgia was off and running on a 5-1 season. That night, a star would be born.

* * * *

. . . Kentucky calls time to put more pressure on Robinson . . . and again for Georgia, the whole ball game coming down to this. Rex Robinson, outta Marietta, Georgia. Sixteen to fourteen, Kentucky, with eight seconds! The stadium's standing! Naw, some of 'em are upside down, but they're trying to stand. It's gonna be held just inside the nineteen! It's set down! He puts it up! It looks good! Watch it . . . watch it! YEAH! YEAH! YEAH!

Larry Munson. Classic Larry Munson. Vintage Larry Munson. Kentucky had put Georgia down 16-0 that night in Lexington two years earlier. But the Bulldogs had come back, back to that 16-14 with eight seconds when Rex Robinson kicked the 29-yard field goal to win it, 17-16.

Larry Munson and Rex Robinson. They were both so much a part of the 1980 story, too.

Everything Larry Munson says when he broadcasts a Georgia game, as he has done since he replaced the brilliant late Ed Thilenius in 1966 (Thilenius moved up to professional football broadcasting with the arrival that year of the Atlanta Falcons), comes through my headset down on the sidelines where I do reports for the Georgia broadcasts.

Sometimes I am so preoccupied with my own routine and my efforts to gather information to relay to Munson, I don't actually hear what he is saying. But there are times when the game is no longer in doubt, and I simply coast the sidelines and listen to this marvelous talent at work.

The only problem is that while Munson is good regardless of the circumstances of the game, he is something else again when the game is tight. When he's up, when the team is about to pull a game away from certain defeat, or when it is letting one slip away, when the excitement is there, Munson is at his best.

We do a pre-game radio show together, and before the South Carolina game in 1980 one of our guests was Francis Tarkenton, the former Georgia and NFL star, and now an ABC-TV personality. Before we went on the air Tarkenton said to Munson:

"Larry, I want to tell you. I've listened to a lot of announcers, but you are the best by far I

have ever heard. You know how to make the game interesting."

"I'm a homer," replied Munson.

"That's why they love you," Tarkenton replied.

Munson IS a homer. He is FOR Georgia. There IS bias in his voice, and it is there on purpose. Still, I know officials of other schools who have walked up to him and said, "I wish you called our games. You're the best I've ever heard."

He has become a folk hero in the state of Georgia. That call of Robinson's field goal in Lexington had done it. He was in constant demand as a speaker—second only to Dooley—during the following months. In late summer Dooley was speaking to a group of Atlanta-area alumni. Munson, also a part of the program, arrived late because of a television commitment. He was ushered down front and the crowd interrupted Dooley with a standing ovation for Munson.

Georgia had not expected a good season in 1978. And Georgia had not expected to come from behind that Saturday night in Lexington. But both happened, and Munson—with the power and the drama in his voice—recreated the thrilling moments that took place.

But it had taken some time—over a decade, as a matter of fact—for Munson to reach that pinnacle of respect and adoration with the Georgia fans. He had a contrasting style—a choppy, staccato delivery—to that of the golden-toned Athens-bred Thilenius who rarely, if ever, showed his own emotion during a Georgia game.

Second, the Georgia people never got to know Munson. He had been hired by John McHale of the new Atlanta Braves to team with Milo Hamilton on Braves broadcasts when the Milwaukee club moved south in 1966. Munson would not continue his then-current duties calling Vanderbilt football and basketball for station WSM in Nashville. When the Georgia broadcasting job opened in 1966, Munson applied and Joel Eaves hired him.

But Munson was having trouble coping with the ballooning ego of his fellow Braves broadcaster, Hamilton, and that rift finally led to Munson parting company with the club.

He promptly moved back to Nashville where he had a number of business interests, and the only time he was in Athens or around Georgia fans was on Friday nights before home games. He would slip into Athens and stick to himself

with his early-to-bed routine while the rest of the town was partying.

By mid-morning he would be at Sanford Stadium, but when he signed off with the final score he was out the door, dashing for his car to speed back to Nashville for commitments there. He met more cops in North Georgia than he did Bulldog alumni.

It was Dan Magill—wearer of the triple crown for Georgia (sports information director, secretary of the Bulldog Club and tennis coach)—who also had a great deal to do with Munson's rise in favor. And Magill, always in the press box, had never heard Munson do live play-by-play.

Magill first began to notice Munson's genius by putting together broadcast tapes of big moments for parties honoring championship teams. When he arrived at his office on Sunday mornings in the fall he would have tapes of current games brought over by L. H. and Hugh Christian of Athens station WRFC. Magill would then listen to Munson. He began to look forward to those sessions.

One Sunday, after a big win, he announced to Dooley: "I've listened to a lot of big league announcers, but Munson is the best I've ever heard."

Magill and his friend, the late Billy Joe Brown, began editing highlights of Georgia broadcasts in 1975, making them available to members of the Bulldog Club. Magill knew Georgia people would enjoy hearing moments like Robinson's kick against Kentucky over and over. He was right. Thousands of the tapes have been sold.

In 1978 Munson moved back to Atlanta to work for the Georgia Network, a radio news outlet and to host a sports call-in show for Channel 36. His Georgia Network sports reports are syndicated to more than 100 stations throughout the state. His day begins at 5 A.M. or earlier. Until his nightly television show was cancelled—due to other commitments by the station—he rarely returned home in the evening before his two children were in bed. Munson is an exceptional talent, but he is still pounding away at a rugged schedule and has not received the financial benefits of his success and popularity that he should have. He's 57 and still beating himself to death, driving to every nook and cranny of the state in a second-hand 1970 Chevy Malibu to make speeches.

But he is a professional. He works at his job.

He knows scores. He knows statistics. He knows history. He reads everything he can get his hands on—magazines, books, and newspapers—to keep current. He still takes his hometown newspaper, the *Minneapolis Tribune.*

What I like best about him is he is not a prima donna. There is no giant ego with which to contend when you deal with Larry Munson. There was, for instance, the little problem that came out of the opening game in 1980 with Tennessee.

When Herschel Walker scored his first touchdown, running over the Tennessee safety, Munson uttered what some of Georgia's less liberal listeners thought was too-emphatic a "God Almighty!" There were calls to radio stations that carried the game, and calls to athletic department officials in Athens.

"It just came out," he would tell me later when I informed him of the calls. He explained further:

"You have to understand how excited I was, too. Beating Tennessee in Knoxville is something that I'm not used to. You remember all those years I went there with Vanderbilt. I know how tough it is, and for a raw freshman to do what Herschel did, I just got carried away."

Munson became genuinely concerned about the reaction from the listeners.

"I've got to do something," he said to me a few days before the next broadcast, the Texas A&M game.

I suggested we take some time in the pregame broadcast to do whatever he wanted.

"You throw it to me," he said, "and I'll apologize."

That is exactly what he did. He said he was sorry. He said he hoped people would forgive him. Name one other big-time announcer who would have done that.

He was born in Minneapolis, son of Harry Munson of Swedish descent. He was introduced to sports and outdoor life by his father. They hunted, they fished, and they huddled by a radio, searching for the golden voice of Ted Husing, the great sportscasting pioneer.

A favorite story Munson uses today in his speeches concerns Husing's broadcast of a prize fight. Husing had placed a bet on one of the fighters, who got knocked cold in the first round. Startled, Husing blurted out, "Well, the dumb S.O.B. just got knocked out."

Instantly realizing what he had done, he

turned his head aside and yelled into the microphone, "You can't talk like that! We're on the air!"

After being discharged from the army in 1945, Munson heard a commercial literally begging for students for a radio announcing school.

"They promised placement within six months," he remembers. "In less time than that they had me a job in Devil's Lake, North Dakota. It was 37 degrees below zero the day I reported for work."

Six months later he answered an ad in a broadcasting magazine which called for an announcer to do Wyoming football in Cheyenne. Munson succeeded Curt Gowdy as sports director at KFBC. Gowdy was taking a Class AA baseball job in Oklahoma City. He advised Munson that if he wanted to make any money he should get into baseball.

Munson remembered Gowdy's advice. In 1947 he headed to Nashville to do play-by-play for the Nashville Vols of the old Southern Association, a Class AA league, for station WKDA. Later he made a deal to announce Vanderbilt basketball and also moved to 50,000-watt, clear channel WSM, famous for its broadcasts of the Grand Old Opry.

His first football broadcast, incidentally, got him the job in Cheyenne. The station had asked him to submit a tape of a previous game he had done. There was a problem. Munson had never broadcast a football game.

He faked it. He conjured a tape of a make-believe Ohio State-Minnesota game, complete with crowd noise he dubbed onto the tape, and was hired.

There would be plenty of moments for Munson's genius in 1980. Already there had been Herschel Walker's heroics and the captivating end to the Clemson game. Fortunately, for the Bulldogs, Munson had a breather in Lexington two years after the Robinson kick.

Scott Woerner's interception set up a first touchdown, Herschel Walker scoring from the two. In the second half Buck Belue would score from the three, then hit Amp Arnold on a 91-yard touchdown pass.

And Robinson would hurt the Wildcats again, not as dramatically as 1978, but with field goals of 50 and 47 yards to complete the Georgia scoring. The game ended 27-0.

The dream had come true. The Bulldogs, now ranked fourth nationally, would return to Athens at 7-0 to meet South Carolina and its Heisman-candidate running back, George Rogers.

At this point Georgia's critics were beginning to question the strength of the Bulldogs' schedule. Who had they beaten? Tennessee had proved no contender after opening losses to Georgia and Southern Cal. Texas A&M was getting pushed around, as was Clemson, TCU, Ole Miss, and Vanderbilt.

South Carolina, loser to Southern Cal in Los Angeles and conqueror of Michigan in Ann Arbor, would be the first test. But who would have thought a kid who nearly died from whooping cough, who had no chance to become an athlete, who almost flunked out of school, would emerge heroic from a game that brought national attention because of the matchup between the nation's premier running backs, George Rogers and Herschel Walker?

The name, again, is Rex Robinson. It keeps cropping up everytime the Bulldogs need it the most.

"...But the Train Had Done Run..."

South Carolina brought its best team ever to Athens on the first day of November. Can there be a prettier place to be on a perfect autumn Saturday? The crowd would be a whopping 62,200. The temperature at game time, 68 degrees, not a cloud in the sky.

Suddenly Georgia-South Carolina had attracted national attention. It would be televised across the nation, and everybody with a typewriter and a microphone would attempt to get a credential to cover the game. There had never been such a media demand for working press tickets at Sanford Stadium. Sports information director Claude Felton and his assistant, Greg McGarity, had to turn down more than 100 requests. There was simply no place to put another body.

It was almost as bad for ticket manager Virginia Whitehead. The game had long been sold out but her phone kept ringing. People were literally begging for tickets.

Georgia was ranked fourth in the country, with its perfect 7-0 record. And Georgia had Herschel Walker, the sensational freshman who, by now, was front page sports news across the country.

South Carolina was 6-1, rated 14th. That one loss was to Southern Cal in Los Angeles, and the Gamecocks had gone to Ann Arbor and upset Michigan before over 100,000. South Carolina had George Rogers, running back from Duluth, Georgia, who was the mid-season choice to wind up with the Heisman Trophy. Still, Walker was gaining in national support, and there was even speculation the battle might settle who would eventually win the trophy.

A week earlier, Dooley and I were driving to Atlanta where he was to speak to the Atlanta Touchdown Club. For the first time he mentioned Herschel Walker in connection with the Heisman. I said that you can never assume any great year will ever be duplicated. I suggested that if Walker continued his pace and deserved the trophy, Georgia should push hard for him to receive it. Dooley agreed, and, later, he and Felton worked toward that end.

When the game kicked off, however, I don't think the Heisman trophy was on anybody's mind, especially on the Georgia side of the field. Winning the game, remaining unbeaten, and moving still higher in the polls was. The individual who was probably least concerned was Herschel Walker.

"This game is between Georgia and South

RIGHT: Rex Robinson. A serious childhood disease, then problems in the classroom. The Georgia placekicker almost wasn't around for the 1980 season. BELOW: George Rogers. His face tells the story. His late fumble insured the narrow Georgia victory over South Carolina.

106

Carolina," he told me on Thursday. "It's not between me and George Rogers. Football is a team sport."

Later, when I asked him if he wouldn't want to win the Heisman one day, he said, "It would be nice, but I'm not certain what the trophy means. It's a little unfair because too much attention is given to one player. It's more important to honor a team. Maybe someday, I would appreciate winning it, but if I don't, it's not that important."

Already, the writers were calling him "Humble Herschel."

South Carolina's apparent weakness was a lack of a potent passing attack. With passing—AND George Rogers—the Gamecocks could have overwhelmed most opponents. But would Rogers three, four, five, and seven-yard the Bulldog defense to death?

On the pre-game show I can remember Larry Munson saying, "This one is so big! But do you realize the one next week in Jacksonville is even bigger!"

The season had reached its crucial point. South Carolina today, then Florida, then Auburn, then Georgia Tech. The Bulldogs were four games away from a perfect season, two—Florida and Auburn—away from another Southeastern Conference title.

* * * *

Georgia kicks off into the Carolina end zone: It will be Rogers versus Walker, just as everybody had figured. Read the play-by-play for the first half of the first quarter. It opens with Carolina on its own 20:

—Rogers for four to the 24. Rogers for 12 to the 36. Wright for two to the 39. Two passes fall incomplete. Carolina punts.

—Georgia takes over on its own 30. Walker for one to the 31. Walker for one to the 32. Belue passes to Arnold for 13 to the 45. First down. Walker for one to the 46. Walker for three to the 49. Belue passes incomplete. Georgia punts.

—Carolina takes over on its 35. Rogers for three to the 38. Rogers for six to the 44. Rogers for five to the 49. First down. Rogers for one to midfield. Wright for six to the Georgia 44. Rogers hit for a three-yard loss by Weaver. Carolina's punt is blocked by Pat McShea.

—Georgia's ball on the Carolina 40. Walker for seven to the 33. Walker for two to the 31. Walker for four to the 27. Walker for 16 to the

11. Walker for six to the five. Walker for one to the four. Walker loses one, back to the five. Robinson in to kick 22-yard field goal. He misses.

He WHAT? Rex Robinson had spoiled the Georgia fans with long field goal after long field goal. The crowd couldn't believe it when his chip shot sailed wide to the left. The miss was carelessness.

The ball was on the left hash mark, facing toward the railroad tracks. The wind was to Robinson's back. He has a natural tendency to kick to the right because he brings his head up at impact. He knew exactly where he should aim the ball, but he failed to adjust enough for the angle from which he had to kick. It drifted with the wind just outside the crossbar.

Georgia had been close to breaking out in front with Walker's running, only to have him stopped inside the five. Now, Rex Robinson, the brilliant placekicker, has failed from 22 yards.

"It's like hitting a bad golf shot," Robinson would explain later. "You can't let it get you down, or it will affect your next one."

The next attempt came in four minutes. Georgia, after a Carolina punt, moved down the field again, this time on a 41-yard pass from Belue to Lindsay Scott that put the Bulldogs first down at the Gamecocks' 40. Walker got five to the 35, and three more to the 32. But he lost eight on a bad pitch. Georgia was fourth and ten, back at the South Carolina 40. I was amazed to see Dooley wave Robinson on the field for a 57-yard field goal attempt.

There was still a trailing wind, and Robinson has that kind of range, but what if he missed it? South Carolina would take possession again in good field position on its own 40. Dooley seldom calls for the non-percentage play, which is one reason he has been so successful. This time he was playing a hunch. He knew Robinson wanted to make up for the easy one he missed.

He made the 57-yarder, with distance to spare, on the last play of the first quarter, and Georgia led, 3-0. Kicking coach Bill Hartman was not surprised from his perch in the press box. Before the game, he had told Robinson he would feel comfortable with his kicking from the 30, into the wind, and from the 40, with the wind to his back. Hartman's estimate was right on target.

Robinson, now a senior, had enjoyed a tremendous career at Georgia. The field goal to beat Kentucky was his most dramatic moment, of course, but he had come through in other clutch situations time after time. And he was such an unlikely hero. . . .

* * * *

Rex Robinson first started kicking when he was seven. His neighbor in Marietta was Bob Willis, the soccer coach at Paulding County High School. He introduced Rex to soccer.

Later, however, the youngster would switch to kicking footballs. In a vacant field next to his house he spent long hours practicing. He fashioned two pine cones to form a tee and was conscious, even then, of getting his kicks up in a hurry. Pro scouts say this ability to get the ball high will likely make him successful in the National Football League.

That vacant field soon became the focal point of Rex Robinson's life. When it got too dark to kick he would put down his football and pick up his telescope and look at stars. His parents always knew where to find him—even at 10 o'clock at night—in the field, either with a football or a telescope.

Those sessions in the field were responsible for his development as a kicker, but, in the beginning, they were also a means for passing time and amusing himself. His brother and sister were much older, and there were few playmates his age in the neighborhood. He grew up a quiet and withdrawn child, which probably resulted from his slow development physically. Learning to enjoy being by himself became an advantage for him later as a kicker, however. While the rest of the team practices, the lonely kicker is off to himself, working a great deal on his own.

During his varsity career at Georgia he averaged kicking at least 40 balls a day during spring and fall practices. Kicking coach Hartman has this practice routine for his kickers:

—First, five balls from the left hash mark on the 20-yard-line. Then, five from the right hash mark at the same distance.

—Drop back 10 yards and kick five more from each hash mark until the ball is on the 50, which is a field goal of 60 yards.

Often Robinson would make everything from inside 50 yards, and three of five from 50-to-60

Three more points. Rex Robinson (5) hits on a key field goal against South Carolina and Jim Broadway (3) offers a hug.

and even two of five from 60. He can also kick with his left foot. He hits the ball with the top of his foot, not with the side as do some soccer-style kickers. He connects right on his shoe laces, almost like a punter.

Something else. Robinson and the walk-on substitute kickers at Georgia, also know how to execute the famed Notre Dame backfield shift, devised by Knute Rockne. Hartman taught them during practice sessions.

The first months of Rex Robinson's life were difficult—and nearly tragic. When he was five months old, his sister brought home the whooping cough, and toddler Rex caught it. His lungs were so small they couldn't handle all the coughing pressure.

His face would turn blue during a coughing attack. His mother recalls handing him over to his father many times, thinking he was dead. His mother is a nurse. She administered her son ice baths during these frightening seizures and also installed an oxygen unit in the home to give the baby breathing assistance.

The pediatrician was afraid the baby might be retarded because there had been so little oxygen going to his brain during the coughing spells. Miraculously, however, this didn't happen. Rex Robinson escaped narrow brushes with death time after time.

The ordeal left him thin and frail until age nine, when his body began to mature. He became pudgy at 10, and he still has to watch his weight. He developed strength in his legs by constantly kicking and playing soccer through grade and high school.

As a freshman at Georgia he led the team in scoring with 45 points. As a sophomore he hit 74, and as a junior, 66. He would miss his first extra point attempt at Georgia, then hit 101 straight, second best in NCAA history.

But nothing has ever come easy for Noble Rexford Robinson. When Georgia went to Knoxville to open the 1980 season he almost wasn't along for the trip. There was the matter of his tendency to cut classes.

"I can't explain that," he says. "It's the one area of my life in which I haven't done my best."

Came the summer of 1980, Robinson had to attend summer school in order to become eligible for football in the fall.

"I think Coach Dooley had really lost faith in me," Robinson said. "He had good reason, I suppose."

Dooley most certainly had his doubts about his placekicker making it. He called Robinson into his office as summer school was about to begin. Included in the meeting were Hartman and team academic counselor Curt Fludd.

"Coach Dooley said he had run out of patience with me," Robinson recalled. "I didn't like what he was saying, but I knew he was right. I knew it was my fault. He told me that he was through worrying about whether I went to class or not, and that I had to prove I wanted to play in the fall. He said he was leaving it up to me. He said we had some walk-on kickers who might not be as good as me, but he was ready to go with them."

Dooley wasn't the only one on Robinson's case. Assistant coach John Kasay came down on him, too.

"You won't make it," Kasay challenged the young kicker. "You won't be around here in the fall."

"You can sometimes have this love-hate thing with Coach Kasay," Robinson says. "You hate what he demands of you, but you know it's for your own good. I learned something from him about mental toughness. He forced me to work harder. I'm glad he rode me like he did. Otherwise, I might not have made it."

Robinson made it. He was on the airplane, eligible to play, when the team left for Knoxville. He would set record after record in 1980. He would make All-America. He would also provide the eventual winning margin as Georgia and South Carolina continued their battle in Athens.

* * * *

Georgia, leading 3-0 on the Robinson 57-yarder, was holding Rogers and South Carolina. Midway through the second period the Bulldogs went on another long drive from their 20:

Belue passed to Herschel Walker for 12, to Lindsay Scott for 17 on a pass interference call, and then to Jimmy Womack for 31 to the South Carolina 31. Seven plays later, the Bulldogs were first down on the Gamecocks' four.

But, earlier, there had been a problem getting the ball over the goal line from down close. It would happen again. Walker was stopped for no gain, then he got three to the one, then he tried to go up the middle again, and the Carolina defense stopped him for nothing.

Georgia called time. Will Dooley call for another field goal attempt, or will he go, on fourth down, for the seven? Go for it, he says.

Rogers is set back on his heels by Frank Ros, Jeff Hipp, Dale Williams. Chris Welton (10) is there, too.

The pass play never gets off the ground. Belue is hit as he tries to throw, and the pass falls incomplete.

Carolina takes over on its one. Georgia has botched another opportunity to score. You get a feeling in a game like this, a feeling that says you're missing too many chances to put the other team away early, a feeling that says it will come back to haunt you later. The half ends with Georgia ahead, still, 3-0.

The Bulldogs received the second half kickoff. After two plays, they stood third and six on their own 24. A passing situation? George Haffner, in the press box, sent the word down to run play "22," which has also been called the "lead draw" in the Georgia playbook.

The offensive coaches had put the play in the attack early in fall practices. It is basically a deception play that, if executed correctly, could gain big yardage. When Herschel Walker came on the scene, the coaches felt the play's potential could be greatly increased with his exceptional speed.

Early in the season, however, it brought less than desired results, and the man who was most aware of the problem was assistant

Charles Whittemore. Like all varsity coaches, he has multiple responsibilities. He does more than coach receivers and flash the offensive signals to the quarterbacks from the sidelines on Saturday afternoons.

Georgia, as most teams do, scouts not only its opponents, but also itself. It is Whittemore's responsibility to scout the Bulldogs. At the conclusion of each game he compiles detailed statistics on the offense. He and the other offensive coaches grade the films, but Whittemore takes each play and charts its production, for the game just played, and also for the season.

At any point during the year he can look at his charts and tell what the results of a particular play have been. He can tell how many yards the play has been averaging. He can tell if it seems to be increasing or decreasing in yards gained.

If it is doing poorly, as "22" was early in the season, adjustments may be made to see if such corrective efforts will make it work better. If the negative trend continues, the play may be abandoned altogether. Whittemore and the other coaches felt "22" should be kept, and that it should produce more.

111

Late one Sunday night as he finished compiling his weekly stats, Whittemore said to Wayne McDuffie, John Kasay, Mike Cavan and George Haffner, " 'Twenty-two' isn't giving us much help."

The Georgia coaches decided perhaps they were delaying too much in giving the ball to the tailback, that perhaps the defense was recognizing the play and having time to recover.

They decided they would force the play to develop sooner, have the offensive line execute quicker and instruct the tailback to start sooner. Don't give the defense that extra split second to read and react.

Georgia numbers its positions on the offensive line even to the right and uneven to the left. "Two" means the point of offensive attack would be at right guard, "four" at right tackle, "six" at the tight end and "eight" anything wide.

The "20" series is the draw series which means that the tailback on "22" is to follow the right guard and the fullback downfield, provided there is running room. This same play to the left would be "23," follow the fullback and the left guard.

To run "22" the way it is drawn, the tailback takes a step to his left and then cuts back to his right and gets the ball from the quarterback who is dropping back. By this time the guard should have made his block on the penetrating defensive lineman in front of him, giving the tailback some daylight. If the fullback adds to the daylight with any kind of help on the linebacker, then the play should get desired results.

It is a big play concept, but not one designed to necessarily go all the way. A good 10-yard gain on a draw will often get the first down.

With Herschel Walker, however, enough daylight and anything can happen. Against South Carolina "22" was the big play of the game. Third period, Georgia at its own 24, third down and six.

When the play started, the right guard blocked his man to the inside and fullback Jimmy Womack shot through and knocked down the middle linebacker. Lindsay Scott got on the left cornerback quickly. Herschel blasted through the line in a flash, hit the sideline and outran the secondary 76 yards for a touchdown and a big 10-0 lead.

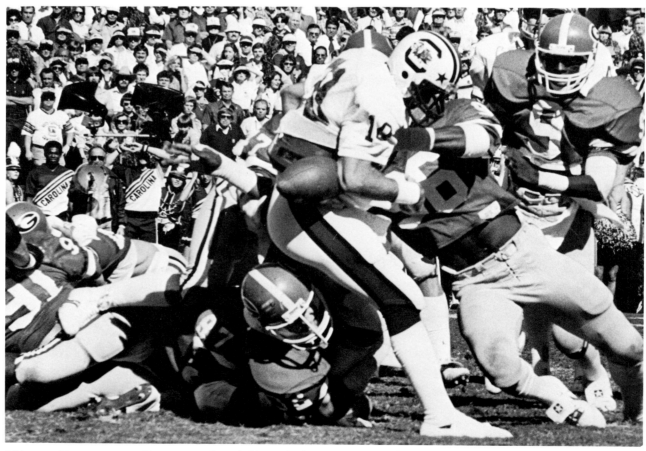

Erk's gang likes turnovers. They get one here led by Dale Carver (96), Tim Bobo (32), Jimmy Payne (87), Nate Taylor (47). Also on the scene Dale Williams (9) and Tim Crowe (91).

The South Carolina safety appeared to have the angle on Walker, but Herschel's afterburners can leave a lot of good athletes behind.

Hubert Mosely, a South Georgia pharmacist and one of those who believes that if you say your prayers every night and do right, when you die, you will go to Athens, explained it this way:

"That defensive back just knew he could get to Herschel on the sideline. He knew the spot where they would meet, but when he got there, the train had done run."

Rex Robinson came through again three minutes later—from 51 yards out and into a strong wind—and Georgia's lead was 13-0. But those missed opportunities—they would hurt.

Carolina kicked a field goal in the third period. The score went to 13-3. Late in the period it was Carl West, not Rogers, who finally got the Gamecocks a touchdown. Following a poor Georgia punt, he shook loose for 39 yards, and Carolina was back in the game, 13-10.

The two teams swapped possessions. South Carolina had gained field position at the Georgia 47 after the defense had tackled Belue for a 12-yard loss and another short punt.

Now the pressure was on the defense, which had held on all day. The nation was watching. Sanford Stadium was holding its breath. Here came South Carolina. Seven minutes, 20 seconds remain, and here comes George Rogers:

—It is Rogers for nine to the Georgia 38.

—Rogers for three to the Georgia 35. First down.

—Rogers for eight to the Georgia 27.

—Rogers for seven to the Georgia 20. Another first down. But Rogers is shaken up. He is obviously tired. It is late, he has carried the ball time after time. Rogers comes out of the game.

—Carolina has called time out. A replacement is in for Rogers.

—On first down, it is West for three to the Georgia 17. Rogers comes back into the game.

—Rogers is handed the ball. He heads right. Cornerback Scott Woerner has the best shot at him. Woerner rushes up to make a big hit, but Rogers has the moves, as well as the power. He fakes Woerner, who misses with a straight-ahead tackle. Instead, Woerner's headgear lands on Rogers' right arm, under which he is carrying the ball.

The ball has been loosened from Rogers hold

by the Woerner miss-hit. In the next second, defensive end Dale Carver renders a jolting blow to the big Carolina running back. The ball has come free! It is loose! And there to retrieve it at the Georgia 16 is defensive guard Tim Parks!

Georgia is saved. The Bulldogs, thanks to a roughing-the-kicker penalty, move again, eating up precious clock. Behind Walker, having a wonderful game before his first national audience, Georgia again moves to the South Carolina one, with time running out. But for the third time, the Gamecocks hold. The final score remains at 13-10.

"The game came down to one play," South Carolina coach Jim Carlen said afterwards. "That one play was George Rogers' fumble, and that was my fault. I shouldn't have played him at that particular time. He had just come out of the game, and he was exhausted. I take full responsibility for that turnover. George was just tired."

Freshman Herschel Walker clearly won the personal battle with Rogers. Walker finished with 219 yards and one touchdown. Rogers had 168 yards, no touchdowns, and that killing fumble.

"They both had great games," said Dooley, "and they both had great supporting casts."

There was other news after the game. Unbelievable news, as the scores came in. Mississippi State had knocked off No. 1 Alabama. And No. 2 UCLA would fall later in the day. That would mean Notre Dame, currently ranked third, would move to first, and Georgia would edge in right behind the Irish at No. 2, the highest-ranking ever for a Dooley team.

The beer was cold all over the state that Saturday night, but why did Larry Munson have to throw a damper on the party? Remember his words in the pre-game show:

This one is so big! But do you realize the one next week in Jacksonville is even bigger?

In Jacksonville, Georgia would meet Florida, off to a good start after a disastrous year in 1979. Georgia would carry an 8-0 record into the game, and that No. 2 national ranking.

The ghosts in the Gator Bowl are many. Anything could happen.

113

MIRACLE ON DUVAL STREET

The lights had been out in their room at Jacksonville's Ramada Inn for over an hour, but Buck Belue and Lindsay Scott weren't asleep. The challenge of the Florida game in the Gator Bowl would come with the daylight of November 8. They talked.

"We gotta hook up again," Belue, the quarterback, said to Scott, the receiver.

How Georgia had fought to put these two brilliant high schoolers on the same team, and both had had their moments in the past. But "Belue-to-Scott" had not materialized as had been expected.

Scott heard Belue's remark in the darkness and tried to remember the last time he had caught a touchdown pass. It had been a solid year.

"Buck," he said, "you realize I haven't caught a touchdown pass since the Florida game last year?"

Incredible. Lindsay Scott finished his thought.

"I've forgotten what it's like," he said. "I don't even remember what it's like to catch a touchdown pass."

It had all begun so brilliantly for Lindsay Scott his freshman season, 1978. He led the team in receiving with 36 catches for 484 yards and two touchdowns. He led the Southeastern

Conference in kickoff returns with a 26.5 average, and it was his 99-yard return of the second-half kickoff in Baton Rouge that led Georgia to an important win over LSU. *Football News* made Lindsay Scott a member of its Freshman All-America team at the end of the 1978 season.

As a sophomore, Scott had 34 catches for 512 yards and one touchdown, but the Bulldogs had a mediocre 6-5 season, and Lindsay Scott expected more of himself, and so did the Georgia fans. They kept waiting for all that talent to suddenly peak.

Suddenly it did. Unfortunately Scott's best game as a Bulldog came against his teammates. In the spring game of 1980, he caught eight passes for 142 yards and four touchdowns. This season—1980—would be his.

It took only a couple of weeks after that tremendous spring game performance for the world to start caving in on Lindsay Scott.

Final spring quarter exams were underway on campus, and academic counselor Curt Fludd was walking by Scott's room at McWhorter Hall, the athletic dormitory. Two football players stood outside Scott's door. Fludd sensed a problem.

The problem was inside Scott's room. Lindsay and his girlfriend, who was not

Joy in Jacksonville. Buck Belue (left) and Lindsay Scott celebrate their miracle.

supposed to be in the room, were having a lover's quarrel.

Fludd knocked on the door. He knocked again.

"He won't let me out!" the girl shouted to Fludd, who still could not convince Scott to open the door. He finally used his pass key to get inside. There, he confronted Scott, who demanded he leave the room. When Fludd refused, Scott pushed him down on the bed.

He was embarrassed, Scott would say later. The argument with his girl was enough, but then he was caught violating a dormitory rule. He lost control.

"The moment I pushed him, I was sorry," Scott would explain. "I hated myself for what I had done."

After the incident, Fludd's first move was a call to Scott's father in Jesup.

"Lindsay has put me in a position where I have no choice," Fludd said to Raymond Scott. "I have to report this to Coach Dooley."

Raymond Scott understood. Dooley returned to Athens two days later. He and Fludd met. The result was a decision to remove Lindsay Scott from scholarship for one year. If he remained in school and played football in the fall, he would have to pay his own way.

Scott took the decision maturely. He resolved to stay in shape and to play in the fall. For the moment, all was well again; then, near tragedy.

It is late summer, and Lindsay Scott, despite being minus his scholarship, is looking forward to opening practices and the coming 1980 season. His mind is drifting as he is driving south toward his hometown of Jesup on Georgia Highway 15, near Soperton, where former highway commissioner Jim Gillis paved almost everything, including paths to outhouses.

As he neared Tarrytown he slowed to observe the speed limit and eased through the little village, which doesn't even have a caution light. He began to resume speed again. Suddenly he lost control of his car. It spun wildly. The next thing Lindsay Scott knew he was in a hospital with a concussion and three dislocated bones in his foot.

His car was mangled. He had been thrown clear during the wreck. He was NOT wearing his seat belt. That may have been what saved his life.

One of the attending doctors had the bad news. He told Johnnie Mae Scott, Lindsay's mother, first. Her son would never play

football again because of the injuries from the accident.

She was so pleased Lindsay had lived through the wreck—she had seen the smashed vehicle—that she had no concern for his football future.

Johnnie Mae broke the news to her son.

"It hurt," Lindsay remembered. "It really hurt, but I told my mother, 'I've got to try. I've just got to try.'"

It was close to a miracle recovery. The foot began to heal. Pre-season practice was just around the corner, but Lindsay Scott was making remarkable progress. As the weeks passed and the opener against Tennessee came closer and closer, Scott got better and better. He was still a doubtful starter for the game in Knoxville, however.

The countdown began. Would he make it? He made it. Somehow, Lindsay Scott had recovered from the dorm incident, and an automobile accident. And he lined up as a starter against Tennessee on September 6 in Neyland Stadium.

The Georgia passing game was supposed to be its best in years in 1980, with Belue the fulltime quarterback, and with receivers like Amp Arnold and Norris Brown, and with Scott healthy again. Also, the new offensive coordinator George Haffner had arrived from Texas A&M with new plans and wrinkles.

But complicated offenses take time. Early in the 1980 season there were problems with the passing game. Lucky for Georgia the defense was holding strong, and Herschel Walker was a one-man running game. But when would Lindsay Scott break loose? It was bound to happen. It *had* to happen.

* * * *

The usual throng began arriving in and around Jacksonville on Thursday before the game. Georgia was now 8-0, ranked second nationally. Florida came in a surprising 6-1, with its freshman quarterback Wayne Peace. There was no question how the Gators would attack Georgia: They would spread people all over the Gator Bowl turf and fill the air.

The day was bright, warm and beautiful, with 68,529 in the stands. It took Herschel Walker less than two minutes to explode. With 13:09 still to go in the first quarter he took a pitch from Belue, headed right, found a hole, turned on the speed and dashed 72 yards. Georgia led 7-0. In the second quarter a pass from Belue to

Scott Woerner displays the emotion of the season. The Bulldog defense bags another turnover against Texas A&M.

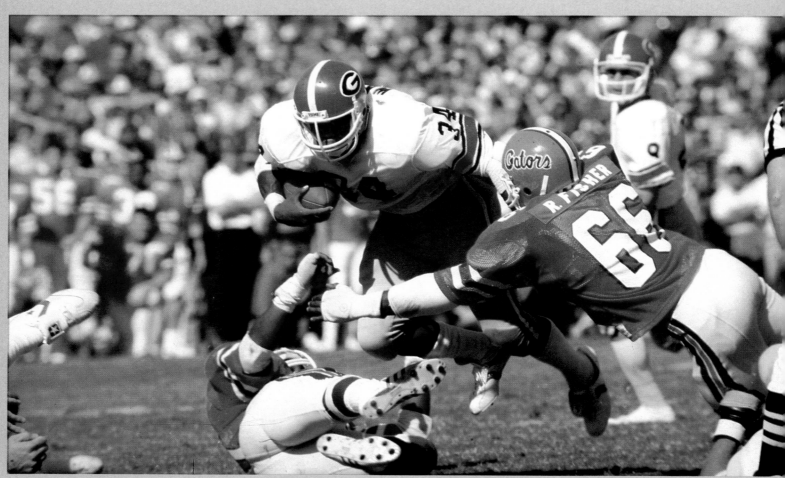

ABOVE: Woerner running for glory against Clemson. BELOW: Herschel gains on the Gators.

ABOVE: Jimmy Payne smothers a Yellow Jacket. BELOW: Belue and Amp Arnold run the reverse.

Charles Junior signals the officials his catch was good on the lush green of Sanford Stadium.

ABOVE: Amp Arnold is down with an injury in Jacksonville's Gator Bowl. LEFT: Cheerleader Scottie Johnston with a glad hand for a friend. RIGHT: Chris Welton (10) and Dale Carver (96) put the skids on Auburn's James Brooks.

LEFT: Trumpet salute to a grand ol' Dawg. RIGHT: Georgia's own UGA. BELOW: The party's over in Auburn and fans and players celebrate the winning of the 1980 Southeastern Conference championship.

Buck Belue prepares to launch a long one in Athens st Georgia Tech.

ABOVE: Study in concentration. Buck Belue calls signals against the Yellow Jackets. RIGHT: Herschel Walker dives through the powerful Notre Dame defense for his first touchdown in the Sugar Bowl.

PREVIOUS PAGE: Herschel Walker excites crowd with his 23-yard TD run in third quarter but nothing like the 65-yard dash in the final quarter to establish the all-time freshman rushing record. ABOVE: Pat McShea defends against another pass from Florida quarterback Wayne Peace.

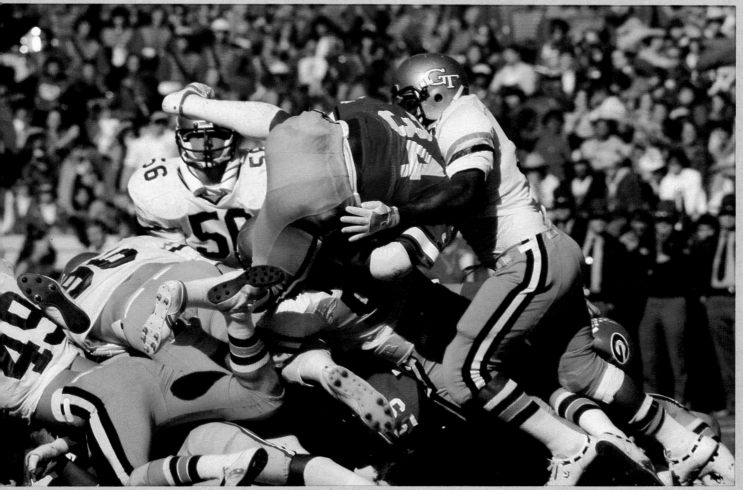

TOP LEFT: Nat Hudson (65) gives Herschel a hug after touchdown run against Florida. TOP RIGHT: The ever-concerned Dooley watches as Georgia squeezes past South Carolina. BOTTOM: Georgia Tech defender meets the rookie from Wrightsville. As usual, it's no match.

PREVIOUS SPREAD: The swarming Georgia defense hunkers down against Auburn, and rover Chris Welton leads the attack. ABOVE: Last grasp brings down a Yellow Jacket. RIGHT: Georgia offensive linemen Joe Happe (56), Hugh Nall (54), and Nat Hudson (65) prepare the way for Buck Belue and the Georgia offense. BELOW: From the talented pen of Jack Davis.

BONITO LE FLEUR
DAWGS 16 TENN 15
DAWGS 42 TEX.A&M 0
DAWGS 20 CLEMSON 16
DAWGS 34 TCU 3
DAWGS 28 OLE MISS 21
DAWGS 41 VANDY 0
DAWGS 27 KENTUCKY 0
DAWGS 13 S. CAROLINA 10
DAWGS 26 FLORIDA 21
DAWGS 31 AUBURN 21
S 38 GA TECH 20
BOWL
S 17 N.D. 10

PREVIOUS SPREAD: ''Glory! Glory!'' in the Sugar Bowl. Herschel Walker gives Georgia a lead after Notre Dame allows Bulldog kickoff to fall free. PREVIOUS PAGE: Jimmy Womack (25) sends a defender to the Superdome floor, allowing Walker to score his second and deciding touchdown against the Irish. LEFT: It's official. Georgia fan has Bulldogs' 12th victim recorded moments after the Sugar Bowl's end. ABOVE: ''Bulldog Terrortory'' from Jack Davis. BELOW: Tense moment in New Orleans.

Nothing could be finer. Herschel Walker gains key yardage in the squeaker against South Carolina.

LEFT: Miracle of miracles. Lindsay Scott at the end of the 93-yard touchdown pass-and-run that saved Georgia's unbeaten season against Florida. TOP LEFT: One last hurrah from the troops on the tracks. ABOVE: Why they call it the "Peach State."

ABOVE: Jeff Harper. We're No. 1! RIGHT: Tower of strength Jimmy Payne (87) gets in the way of the Auburn passing attack.

Vintage Herschel Walker: PREVIOUS PAGE: On the loose for 76 yards against South Carolina. ABOVE: The yardage piles up against Georgia Tech.

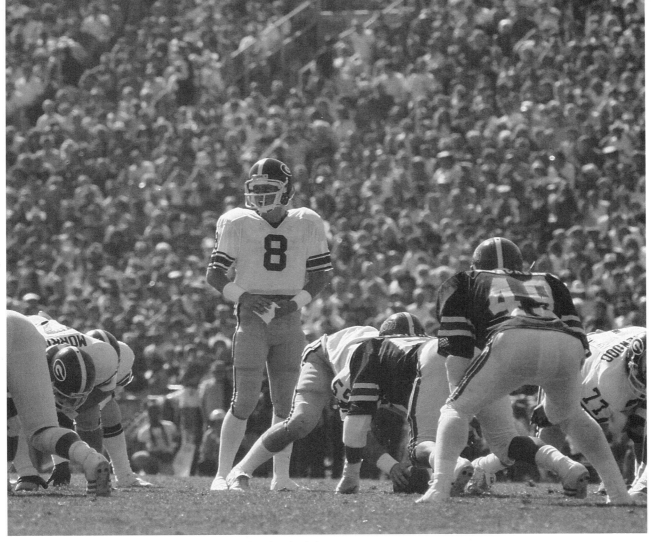

In command. Quarterback Buck Belue surveys the Florida defense.

Ronnie Stewart gave Georgia a 14-3 lead. But Peace hit Chris Collinsworth for a touchdown before the half and the Bulldogs went to their dressing rooms at a shaky 14-10.

It looked like a rout in the second half. Georgia came roaring down the field twice. But as was the case in the South Carolina game the week before, the Bulldogs had trouble getting the ball over the goal line. Georgia should have had 14 points and an easy afternoon. That rarely happens with Georgia-Florida. All Georgia got was two Rex Robinson field goals and six points. At 3:58 of the third period the Bulldogs were ahead 20-10.

Florida could explode at any minute. You could feel it on the sidelines. Florida did explode. Young Peace hit split end Tyrone Young for 54 yards to set up a touchdown. The Gators went for two. The Gators got two. Fourteen minutes, fourteen seconds remain in the game and the Georgia lead is 20-18.

And, suddenly, the Bulldogs can't move. Ten minutes earlier the thing looked like a breeze. Now it was a fight, a dead-even fight. The tension on the sideline was rising.

Florida gets the ball back and again Florida moves. With 6:52 showing, the Gators are fourth down at the Georgia 23. In comes kicker Brian Clark for the field goal. The field goal is good.

It can't be. It just can't be, but it is. The Bulldogs have come so far. They are ranked second nationally. Who knows what might happen? Notre Dame, ranked first, must still play Alabama in Birmingham and Southern Cal in Los Angeles. The Irish on this day, however, are struggling against Georgia Tech, with only one win all season, on Grant Field in Atlanta.

What a miserable thing to be happening to the Georgia dream. Six minutes and 52 seconds to go. The clock is moving. The Bulldogs aren't. Florida gets possession of the ball again. The Gators have the lead, 21-20. The Gators have the ball and time is running out.

The Bulldogs defense finally holds as the clock ticks down to less than two minutes. On the sidelines I watched the Georgia team. The players were drained and dejected. I don't think the Lord takes sides in a football game,

FOLLOWING SPREAD: Breaking away. Herschel is loose and on his way to an early touchdown against the Gators.

but I was encouraged to see some players praying. It is important, in such moments, to call upon every resource.

I walked past trainer Warren Morris, who was shaking his head in dismay when Florida punted the ball out on the Georgia eight-yard-line.

"That did it," he said. "They just put the nails in our coffin." Trainers are always pessimistic.

I looked at the scoreboard and listened to Larry Munson on my headset. "It'll take a miracle now," he screamed, breathlessly. "We've done it before, but I don't know if there is one left. But it's gotta be a miracle. Do the Dogs have it?"

Que sera, sera, I thought. I hope I'm around when a Georgia team goes all the way, I went on thinking, but I guess it was not meant to be this year.

On first down Belue lost a yard scrambling. Second and 11 on the Georgia seven. On second down Belue tried to hit Charles Junior on a sideline route. The pass fell incomplete. Third down, 11 and still on the Georgia seven.

Some of the crowd had begun to leave the Gator Bowl. Some of Georgia's most loyal supporters—not mentioning any names—were already on the street outside, headed for the parking lot.

It was over. Surely, it was over. On the Florida sidelines, they thought it was over. They were already celebrating. Even the Florida players on the field were celebrating. After the sideline pass from Belue to Junior went incomplete, the Gator defensive backs danced the "funky chicken."

Third down, 11 yards to go, at the Georgia seven. Florida leads, 21-20. A minute and a half to play:

In the antiquated Gator Bowl press box, high above the field, George Haffner, Georgia's offensive coordinator, is going crazy.

"We gotta have a possession pass! We gotta keep possession! Left 76, Charley! Left 76! Oh, my God! Somebody be there! Get the ball to somebody, Buck!"

In the booth with Haffner are fellow Georgia assistants Sam Mrvos, Steve Greer, and Chip Wisdom. Haffner calls the offensive plays. He sends them down to Charley Whittemore on the sidelines. Head Coach Vince Dooley makes the crucial calls on goal-line and kicking situations. The game is run by committee, with Dooley as chairman. Whittemore sends the plays to the quarterback with semaphore signals.

I can see Whittemore signaling Belue. With his left arm straight out, fist closed, Belue knows it is a left formation. He can see Whittemore touch his right knee for the code for "seven." Whittemore then touches his right hand behind his waist for the code for "six:" "Left 76" is the play.

In the huddle, Belue is calm. First, he calls the play:

"Left 76."

Then, he tries to encourage the troops:

"I don't have a lot to say. You know what we have to do. Let's do it."

The play is designed to gain a first down, a *possession play*. Get the first down, then another, and maybe the ball will be close enough for Rex Robinson to win it with a field goal. On the sidelines the Florida players are still dancing the "funky chicken."

Lindsay Scott jogs up to the line of scrimmage. He is the split end to the right side as the Bulldogs face the St. John's River.

Chuck Jones, the flanker, goes to the other side of the line, opposite Scott. The line is down. Belue cries out his signals. Georgia is desperate. The Florida end zone is 93 yards away. *It's gotta be a miracle.*

The ball is snapped. The offensive line breaks into pass blocking. Tight end Norris Brown leaves the line of scrimmage and cuts underneath the Florida coverage. He is the secondary receiver.

Lindsay Scott is the man Belue wants to hit. Lindsay runs his route perfectly. Fifteen yards deep, he curls to the inside. Florida has it played perfectly. Haffner had figured the Gators for a deep zone and a limited rush. He has figured they will give up something short, but they are covering the short routes, too.

Belue has dropped back into the end zone. He slides right, still looking for Scott. It appears, as he moves to his right, he may have room to run. The Florida defense reacts momentarily to that possibility. Nat Hudson, the Georgia right tackle, instinctively slides off his block and pivots to his left and blocks another charging Florida lineman headed at Belue.

Belue is motioning to Scott with his left hand. He cocks his right arm as he drifts forward to the line of scrimmage. Scott slides to the inside, just enough. He's open. For a split-second, he is open.

Belue throws the ball. It's a little high, but

Buck Belue is scrambling and directing his receiver Lindsay Scott. The pass play is "Left 76"

not for Lindsay Scott, who goes up, catches the ball, and tucks it under his left arm as he comes down. He is slightly off balance. His right arm goes to the ground, setting him in a sprinter's stance.

The Florida strong safety has reacted as he should have to the ball. He is in position to make the play, but he wants a more direct angle on Scott, so he attempts to stop suddenly. He slips and almost falls onto the grass.

That is the break. That is what Scott must have to get any more yardage than the pass has gained already. Chuck Jones has sprinted deep on a post route, and he has taken the other safety and the right cornerback with him.

Scott has turned and is headed for the sideline. Jones doesn't make a block, but what he does do is literally get in the way of the right cornerback and the safety who are now in pursuit of Scott. Jones has shielded them from the sideline, slowed them just for a second, thus reducing their angle on the man with the ball.

Scott would recall later:

"I was covered at first, but then I saw Buck motion for me to slide to my right. When he got the ball there, I knew I had a first down. I came out of the huddle thinking first down. I kept reminding myself to run a good route. I never concentrated more in my life. I was determined to run the best route I ever ran."

And after he caught the ball:

"The last thing in my mind was touchdown as I turned up the field. I saw there was some room, a little daylight, at least something to work with. I saw the strong safety slip, which was a good sign. He had the angle. Then I knew maybe I had a chance. My confidence came on strong. I felt I was in a situation in which I had to produce. I had to turn it on. I had to outrun the defense. It had given me just a little daylight, and I had to take advantage of it."

The race was on, and Lindsay Scott, only a few months away from a near-tragic auto accident, is leading. He is at the Georgia 40, then to midfield, and into Florida territory. The

154

Who's No. 1? Rex Robinson as the clock runs out in the Gator Bo

FAR LEFT: The Play. Scott has the reception. "I saw a little room, a little daylight," he would say later. LEFT: The Georgia receiver has outmaneuvered the Florida defense and is bound for the end zone. BELOW: The end of the line: 93 yards later, the greatest play in the history of Georgia football, Belue-to-Scott, November 8, 1980, Jacksonville's Gator Bowl, is completed and Georgia has ccme back in the closing moments for a 26-21 victory that will move the Bulldogs to No. 1 in the ratings.

stadium is coming apart. Larry Munson has fallen out of his chair in the Georgia broadcast booth. Vince Dooley is racing along the sidelines with his receiver, jumping and hollering and windmilling his arms. He looks like a third base coach waving home the winning run in the seventh game of the World Series.

With 1:03 showing on the scoreboard clock, Lindsay Scott wins the race. He crosses the goal line. *It's gonna take a miracle.* It IS a miracle. They will shout it all day and the next and the next: "God is a Bulldog!"

It is bedlam in the Georgia end zone. There is no more "funky chicken" on the Florida sidelines. The entire Georgia bench has emptied and is diving on Scott.

Dooley looked at me on the sideline and smiled. It was that half-grin of his, that broken smile, the one that suggests he's pleased, and delighted, but not totally shocked that it came off. It's his confidence smile. I never asked him, but I don't believe he ever gave up that Saturday afternoon in Jacksonville. I went over and gave him a big hug and made plans to give equal treatment to Buck and Lindsay.

The scoreboard shows the result of the Scott-to-Belue, 93-yard connection, the one they had talked about the night before in their room at the Ramada Inn:

GEORGIA 26—FLORIDA 21

Dooley quickly regained his composure. The scene in the end zone would draw a 15-yard penalty on the ensuing kickoff. Dooley began shouting for order and organization. Florida had thought the game was over, too. He ordered his team to go for a two-point conversion. A point-after kick would give Georgia only a six-point lead.

The Bulldogs missed the attempt at two. Florida would get the ball back, and with quarterback Peace's arm, there was still no Georgia lock.

But Mike Fisher, from Jacksonville, ended it with an interception of Peace in the closing seconds. Georgia could run out the clock. Belue took a couple of snaps and curled down in the Gator Bowl turf like a contented South Georgia bird dog.

Georgia had come back from the dead.

The post-game celebration would not end, for some, until Sunday morning. Only moments after the winning Georgia touchdown another miracle was announced: From Grant Field in Atlanta: Georgia Tech had tied Notre Dame, 3-3. *"God Is a Bulldog."*

The Bulldogs would be ranked No. 1 when the wire service polls were released the following week. For the first time in Vince Dooley's reign at Georgia, his team would be ranked the nation's best.

But how about that play! That unbelievable, incredible, amazing, stupendous, helluva, helluva, helluva play!

Lindsay Scott after he crossed the goal line:

"When I crossed over, it was the most satisfying moment of my life. It meant we preserved our ranking and we stayed undefeated. I felt the bottom had fallen out at one time on me, but now I was back.

"In the end zone it was like being in another world. I was being crushed, and the yelling was deafening, but I was filled with humility. I said it out loud: 'I'm the luckiest football player in the world today.' And I meant it."

The play, Belue's throw and Lindsay Scott's catch and subsequent run had everything—drama, electricity, turning sure defeat into victory. It was probably the play of the year in American sports. It will probably go down as the greatest play in the history of Georgia football.

There have been some other dramatic moments in the past, of course:

Lamar (Racehorse) Davis catching a pass at the final gun to beat Auburn. Trippi's 65-yard punt return in the Oil Bowl. Theron Sapp's one-yard plunge in 1957 at Grant Field to break the long, eight-game losing streak to Georgia Tech. There was the Richard Appleby end-around pass to Gene Washington in 1975 to beat Florida and put Georgia in the Cotton Bowl.

And the "flea-flicker" against Alabama in 1965 can never be forgotten. Kirby Moore, the quarterback, to end Pat Hodgson, who flips the ball to halfback Bob Taylor, who scores, ending an 87-yard touchdown play that whips Bear Bryant.

And many others from all eras.

The play that comes the closest to Belue-to-Scott is probably Fran Tarkenton-to-Bill Herron to defeat Auburn in 1959. Georgia's program had been down for a number of years, and Wally Butts needed a big season to turn the situation around again. Tarkenton hit Herron for 13 yards and a 14-13 victory over Auburn and the Southeastern Conference championship just before the seconds ticked away at Sanford Stadium.

But Tarkenton had the ball on the *Auburn 13*. Belue had the ball on his *own seven*. There was hope in Athens in 1959, reasonable hope. Nobody in his right mind expected what he saw in the Gator Bowl as the shadows fell on November 8, 1980.

There is little time to rest on the laurels of the Florida win, however, because Auburn is next. Win at Auburn and Georgia wins the conference title, a trip to the Sugar Bowl, and maintains its No. 1 ranking.

Auburn is waiting. Anxiously.

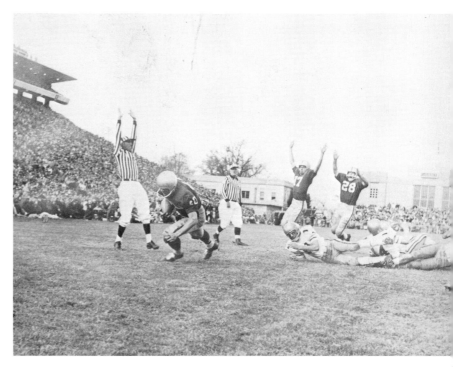

Moments to remember. BELOW: Fran Tarkenton (10) passes to Bill Herron (81) for 13 yards and a touchdown against Auburn in 1959. The score gave Georgia a dramatic, come-from-behind 14-13 victory and the Southeastern Conference title. RIGHT: And who can forget the "man who broke the drought," Theron Sapp, scoring here against Georgia Tech for a 7-0 Bulldog victory after eight straight losses to the Yellow Jackets.

Other moments. OPPOSITE PAGE: The famous "flea-flicker" play beat Alabama in the 1965 opener. Kirby Moore (14) passes to Pat Hodgson, who then laterals to Bob Taylor. Taylor scored, and a two-point conversion play whipped the Crimson Tide on national television, 18-17. ABOVE: Georgia trailed Florida 7-3 in the closing minutes in 1975 when Richard Appleby (84) faked an end-around play and then threw to flanker Gene Washington for an 80-yard touchdown play and a 10-7 win. Washington was mobbed in the end zone.

Into the Valley of Hate

Georgia and Auburn began playing football against one another in 1892 when Auburn whipped the Bulldogs, 12-0, at Piedmont Park in Atlanta. The series is the oldest rivalry in the Deep South.

The rivalry has always been deep. The rivalry has always been intense.

There were a couple of good one-liners being passed around between the two schools during the 1980 season.

FIRST GEORGIA MAN: "You realize, don't you, that there are earthquakes in California and Auburn University is located in Alabama?"

SECOND GEORGIA MAN: "I realize that."

FIRST GEORGIA MAN: "But do you know why?"

SECOND GEORGIA MAN: "No. Why?"

FIRST GEORGIA MAN: "California had first choice."

And what were they saying about Georgia down in the Loveliest Village?

FIRST AUBURN MAN: "Do you know what the Georgia fans holler when their *cheerleaders* run onto the field?"

SECOND AUBURN MAN: "What?"

FIRST AUBURN MAN: "'How 'bout THEM dawgs.'"

You get the picture. There are even

suggestions these days Georgia-Auburn has gone past Georgia-Georgia Tech in its intensity. I doubt that, but Auburn is a natural rival for the Bulldogs. The two schools recruit heavily against each other and, through the years the athletic personnel of the two schools have been closely intertwined. The late Ralph (Shug) Jordan coached under Wally Butts at Georgia before returning to Auburn to become head coach. When he left Athens he took a number of Butts' other assistants with him.

When Dooley left Auburn to succeed Johnny Griffith at Georgia in 1963 he hired several who had worn the Auburn Orange and Blue to coach for the Bulldogs. Now, Pat Dye, who played in one of Georgia's most memorable games—the 14-13 upset of Auburn in 1959—is the new Auburn head coach.

The teams used to play on a so-called neutral field, Memorial Stadium on Victory Drive in Columbus, a Georgia city, located only 40 miles from the Auburn campus.

Often there was more fighting in the stands than on the field. Jordan once noted that more people slipped into the game than bought tickets in the 28,000-seat stadium. It was so crowded that if you left your seat to go to the restroom, it would be occupied when you returned.

The parties for Georgia-Auburn began on Monday and Tuesday in those days. "I can remember during grade school and high school the week of the Georgia-Auburn game was nothing but one continuous fight," says Bill Hartman, Jr., the former Georgia player who now coaches the Bulldog kickers.

There have been some classic games:

In 1942 Georgia had probably its most talented team ever, led by Heisman Trophy winner Frank Sinkwich. But Monk Gafford and

Auburn ruined the Bulldogs' dream of a perfect season with a big upset. The year before, Georgia had won with no time left on the clock.

In 1957 a fumble inside the Auburn five-yard line kept Georgia from upsetting Auburn's national championship team. Then came the '59 game, one of the biggest in Georgia history.

It took Dooley two seasons to defeat his alma mater after he arrived in Athens. That first victory came in Auburn in 1966 and it clinched a Southeastern Conference title. The Bulldogs had to come from two touchdowns behind in the second half. Again, in 1968, Georgia whipped Auburn in Cliff Hare Stadium to clinch an SEC championship.

Both teams were undefeated when they met in Athens in 1971. Pat Sullivan and Terry Beasley would give Georgia its only loss in an 11-1 season with a 35-20 victory.

Then came 1978 and Georgia's ragamuffin team that had the audacity to contend for another conference title. All it had to do was go to Auburn and pick up one more victory. Even with its brilliant running back Willie McClendon, Georgia couldn't do it. The game ended in a 22-22 tie and Alabama finished the season with an outright SEC championship and a trip to the Sugar Bowl.

Even in 1979 when Georgia was having a frustrating season, the Bulldogs still weren't out of the running in the conference race and would have gone to the Sugar Bowl with a victory over Auburn in Athens. But, again, Auburn was the spoiler, 33-13.

In 1980—38 years after it ruined the 1942 Georgia team's chance at a national championship—Auburn had the opportunity to do it again. The week before, the Gator Bowl miracle and Georgia Tech's similarly miraculous tie with Notre Dame had sent Georgia to the top of both wire service polls. The Bulldogs could come to Auburn at 9-0. A victory would mean the conference championship, the trip to the Sugar Bowl, a hold on the No. 1 rating, and the opportunity—assuming victory over Georgia Tech two weeks later in Athens—to play somebody for the 1980 national championship. Auburn meant *everything*.

Meanwhile the Auburn football situation couldn't have been gloomier. It had been a lousy year. The Tigers were 4-5 and their head coach, Doug Barfield, was being roasted on the alumni spit. He was being attacked from every direction and, everyday, the state's newspapers were breaking another story concerning his impending dismissal.

Auburn had talent, because Auburn had running back James Brooks, who, in his own mind, was better than Herschel Walker. But the coaches had had trouble settling on a quarterback in 1980 and the offense had struggled.

As each week passed and the speculation concerning Barfield continued, the team had become more frustrated and its concentration had been directed away from the playing field. But every time Auburn lost a game, all season, the Georgia coaches were saying, "It doesn't

Georgia's Jimmy Payne introduces himself to Auburn quarterback.

mean a thing. When we get down there in November, they will be ready."

Coaches were, of course, athletes themselves. They know about pride and emotion, and they know how a team with good personnel can decide, suddenly, to play together. Maybe it's been a rotten season, but one afternoon all the things that have been going wrong can suddenly go right, and the result is spelled u-p-s-e-t.

The one Georgia coach who worried most about Auburn being prepared mentally for the Bulldogs was Steve Greer. He had played for Dooley but had coached seven seasons at Auburn before returning to Athens in 1979. He knew the absolute hate that builds for the game each year after having been at both schools. He was convinced, he would tell others, that Auburn *hates* Georgia more than Georgia *hates* Auburn. And this is just a game?

Maybe the Auburn emotion comes from the fact there are always a great many players from Georgia on the Auburn roster. Or maybe some of it even carries over from the time when Dooley left Auburn for Georgia. There was a great deal of jealousy from the Auburn staff concerning that move.

The Auburn staff was shocked when they heard Joel Eaves had picked the lowly Auburn freshman coach to take over the floundering Georgia program. Privately they laughed at the move. Nobody ever hired a freshman coach. Georgia did with Johnny Griffith, but that didn't work. Why on earth would Georgia try it again?

Greer had been assigned as the scout for the Auburn game because he was familiar with the Tigers' personnel, and he knew about this emotional thing. Dooley wanted Greer to try to communicate to the Georgia players what it would be like when they hit Jordan-Hare Stadium on Saturday, November 15.

"It will be emotional, more than you've seen in a long time," Greer told the players the week before the game. "It's big for Auburn. Auburn people probably dislike you as much as they dislike Alabama. That should tell you what they think of you. You can't win this game if you aren't emotionally as high as you can get. It will be that tough."

The weather was miserable. Dark and misty. It appeared that any minute the sky would open and dump rain all over the field and the 74,000 that had gathered to watch. A sea of umbrellas surrounded the field.

Dooley, too, appealed to his team before the

game. In the dressing room, he spoke softly, but firmly:

"Men, I don't have to tell you how big this is," he began. There was absolute quiet in the room. I knew that in a few minutes there would be bedlam. Dooley continued:

"They don't believe you're No. 1. Auburn doesn't think you *deserve* No. 1. They expect to show everybody that you are not as good as they are. You can't let up and win any championships.

"You remember last year. Surely, you remember last year. And you older players remember what it was like down here in '78 when they knocked us out of a championship with that tie. Let's pay 'em back."

Dooley paused a moment. The tension was building. He started talking again. Kickoff was just moments away:

"Now, they are probably going to do what they did in '78. They'll probably come out in orange jerseys. It doesn't matter, men, what kind of jerseys they wear. You can whip their ass in any color jerseys. Let's show 'em what a championship team is made of!"

He gave that sweeping motion with his right hand toward the door, and the team started forward, screaming, yelling, and pounding each other. Would they, in three hours, be just as excited?

Dooley's reference to the jerseys came from an Auburn trick in '78 where the team warmed up in blue jerseys, then came out in orange. Auburn considered the move effective psychologically and, just as Dooley had predicted, the coaching staff tried the same move again.

Early it appeared to be working. Auburn was a running team, with the power and speed of Brooks and its big offensive line. Georgia expected Auburn to come inside with the dive handoff, and then to come outside with Brooks on the pitch sweep. The two previous games Auburn had hurt Georgia with that attack. This year the Bulldogs were stouter and quicker inside on defense, but, boom, Auburn comes out passing. Early in the second period quarterback Charlie Thomas took his team 91 yards in nine plays. He passed to split end Byron Franklin the last 34 for the touchdown. At 11:05 of the second quarter, Auburn led, 7-0. The skies were still threatening.

It was apparent Georgia could move the ball too. Quarterback Buck Belue was having his best running game of the season. He brought the Bulldogs back after the Auburn touchdown

The title clincher in Auburn. A day for umbrellas.

with a drive to the Auburn 23 where Rex Robinson hit a field goal from 40 yards. Auburn, 7-3.

With less than five minutes in the half, Auburn still had that four-point lead. Then, the break. Then, somebody made a big play in a season of big plays.

Auburn lined up to punt. Alan Bollinger took a perfect snap and moved to kick the ball downfield. Here came Greg Bell. Greg Bell is from Birmingham. Auburn was a big game for him for a number of reasons.

He stations himself on the defensive right corner when the opposing team is kicking. Normally he blasts toward the kicker from the outside, hoping that he can anticipate the snap. If the kicker hesitates, or takes extra time or an extra step, he will have a chance of getting to the ball.

On a whim, Greg Bell changes his routine on the play. He attacks inside, and moves past the Auburn line of scrimmage. Nobody has touched him. Bollinger steps to kick. He meets the ball, and Bell, at the same time.

The thud of the collision could be heard all over Jordan-Hare Stadium. For a second, it appeared that Bell was balanced on the kicker's toe.

It is a beautiful sound, that thud. It is a beautiful sight, Bell flying through the air and blocking the kick. The Georgia sideline is screaming as Georgia's Freddie Gilbert picks up the loose ball and sprints 27 yards into the end zone. Robinson's point makes the score, 10-7. It is still so close, but it is also apparent that Georgia, after a slow start, is untracked now.

Another big play will take place just before the half.

There are only a few seconds to go before the halftime intermission. Georgia is on the Auburn one, but it has no timeouts. The crowd is screaming. The coaches are screaming. The players are screaming. The only cool head belongs to Buck Belue.

Quickly he pulls his team together on the line for a desperate try at one more play. The ball is snapped with one second on the clock. Belue lobs a high pass and under it runs tight end Norris Brown. Touchdown, Georgia. The score is 17-7 at halftime.

The breaks are going Georgia's way. That touchdown at the buzzer was a huge one. Ten-point lead to what would have been a three-point lead. And wouldn't that score also cut down on the Auburn emotion? And that's not all. Georgia will get an added benefit

165

Norris Brown has Buck Belue's touchdown pass on the last play of the first half to give Georgia a 17-7 lead over the Tigers. Such a moment is to be savored.

because of Auburn assistant coach Paul Davis who was incensed that the referee had stopped the clock after a fumble on the play before Georgia scored. Had the official not stopped the clock, Belue probably would not have had time to get the pass off to Brown.

Davis made what was a fatal mistake. Before Rex Robinson kicked the extra point, he walked onto the field to complain to an official. The official threw his flag, and Auburn was penalized 15 yards at the start of the second half.

Robinson put the ball down on the Auburn 45 to kick off the second half. His onside kick bounced perfectly, squibbing a few yards, and then bouncing high in the air. Will Forts of Georgia leaped and came down with the free football at the Auburn 33. A few plays later, Belue dived over from the one. Georgia led, 24-7.

Auburn came back with two fourth quarter touchdowns, but Georgia was never threatened after that. And Herschel Walker gave Auburn a taste of his magic before it was over. He took a pitch and started running one way. Seemingly trapped, he turned around, ran back the other way completely across the field and wound up in the end zone. He ran maybe 40 yards, but he got credit for only the 18 between the line of scrimmage and the Auburn goal.

For the fourth time in his career, Vince Dooley had won a Southeastern Conference title. Remember Knoxville, I was thinking. Remember when it was getting so late in the third quarter and Tennessee had a 15 point lead. Who would have guessed Georgia would have even gotten past that first hurdle?

The Bulldogs finished the conference race with a perfect 6-0 record. Interestingly, all four of Dooley's conference titles at Georgia were clinched in Auburn, where he played and coached for 12 years.

The Sugar Bowl berth is secure now; and later word comes that Notre Dame will be the opponent. The Irish will lose to Southern Cal to end the prospect of the game being a showdown for the national title, but Georgia-Notre Dame has all the makings of a classic.

Also, at 10-0, the Bulldogs will hold to their No. 1 rating for at least two weeks, and it looks promising to hold that position until at least January 1. Georgia Tech will be visiting Athens for the regular season finale, and Georgia Tech has only a win over Memphis State and that tie with Notre Dame in an otherwise miserable first season for new head coach Bill Curry.

The happy flock that left Auburn that foggy Saturday night and headed back across the Chattahoochee and out of what must be the worst football traffic jam in the country was clearly thinking national championship now that the conference title was secure. What nobody was thinking, however—fans, players, assistants—was that all those sick Auburn fans who hated Georgia so much that gray Saturday would be united two weeks later in trying to recruit Vince Dooley to return to Jordan-Hare Stadium for good.

****

It took forever for the day of the Georgia Tech game, November 29, to finally arrive. The entire week before I was in knots. It couldn't happen, could it? Georgia Tech, 1-8-1, couldn't beat undefeated Georgia, 10-0, and ranked first in the country.

The mere thought of it was frightening. The only comfort I could take in worrying about such a situation was that there would always be somebody worrying more than me—Vince Dooley.

I worried about the Georgia players. They were No. 1. They were undefeated. They were SEC champions. You won't find an athlete anywhere that plays quite as well when he's fat and sassy as he does when he's hungry. And if Georgia Tech could tie Notre Dame, with all its talent, was it not conceivable Georgia Tech could, with a tremendous surge of emotion, be ready for Georgia?

I have always maintained Georgia Tech has a psychological advantage over Georgia each year

because Tech, although it will soon begin to play an Atlantic Coast Conference schedule, has not competed in a conference for many seasons. Georgia's conference finish is already settled after the Auburn game each year, however, and the Bulldogs are in position to suffer an emotional letdown.

Dooley, however, has never failed at getting his team ready emotionally for the Yellow Jackets. Annually, no matter the records of the two teams, he calls it "the biggest game of all. We have to live with it an entire year."

Dooley also has the best series record of any coach ever to have taken part in the Tech-Georgia rivalry. He has only four losses in 17 years.

Dooley is a thinker. He considers every angle. He didn't want his team to stumble this last step toward a perfect regular season. He came up with a classic. Dooley invited Harvey Hill, a retired Atlanta lawyer and banker, over to talk to his team about Georgia Tech the week before the Yellow Jackets came to town.

Harvey Hill, in his early seventies, played on the 1927 Georgia team that was headed to the Rose Bowl before it was upset in the rain and mud of Grant Field in Atlanta.

Imagine the scene: Harvey Hill, his voice quivering with emotion, lecturing the youngsters who are hanging on his every word:

"We should have won that game against Georgia Tech," he began. "We were upset, and we had to live with it the rest of our lives. It bothers me today. I'll never forgive, nor will I forget."

He is pounding his fist into his hands as he talks:

"I don't want what happened to us, to happen to you. You've got to be ready for those &&%%$#! You've GOT to be ready. I want you to give it back to them! You are No. 1, and you MUST STAY NO. 1! Make 'em pay!"

He was on the verge of tears as he repeatedly reminded the 1980 Georgia team, "You are going to have to live with this the rest of your lives. Don't let them ruin your season."

I don't know if Harvey Hill's speech had a bearing on the outcome of the game or not, but I do know Vince Dooley never worked harder for a Georgia Tech game.

At Sanford Stadium before kickoff on a bright late autumn Saturday, I looked across the field at Bill Curry the new Tech head coach. He was an all-American center in his

167

See you later, Yellow Jackets. Herschel Walker leaves Tech defenders in his dust on a brilliant 65-yard run that breaks Tony Dorsett's record for yardage gained as a freshman.

first game against a Vince Dooley team. That was in 1964. Curry's Tech team lost, 7-0, in Dooley's first year at Georgia.

Now here is Curry back as the Tech head coach, and he is wearing a Super Bowl ring even. You wonder how people find their allegiances. I've known Bill Curry for a long time. His father, Red, went to Georgia and as a student handed out equipment to Georgia athletes. Now here is his son leading the Gold and White.

All my worrying had been for nothing. Georgia was ready. Tech had its moments, too, behind the passing of Mike Kelley, but the Yellow Jackets could never get closer than 10 points after Georgia had moved to a 17-0 halftime lead.

Late in the game the question was, would Herschel Walker get enough yards to break the single-season rushing record held by Tony Dorsett. He got the yards. And more. In the middle of the fourth period he broke into the open and led 11 Georgia Tech defenders into the end zone, finishing a 65-yard run that accounted for the final 38-20 score.

Walker's total for the season: 1,616 yards. Georgia's record for the season: 11-0. Georgia is the only major college team in America with a perfect record.

There will be trauma ahead, of course. The Dooley-Auburn affair, described in detail in Chapter 3 of Book I, will surface. But, no matter. What a season it has been—from the stolen pig party in the spring to 11 straight Saturdays of victory in the autumn.

Dooley, of course, eventually turned down a huge contract from Auburn, which prompted my favorite bumper sticker of the season: "Some People Wouldn't Go to Auburn for a Million Bucks."

The heavy recruiting season follows the Georgia Tech game. The players get time off. Suddenly, Christmas comes and Christmas goes. The team reunites in Athens, and on December 28 it departs for New Orleans and the Sugar Bowl.

One more time. One more time and Georgia has its first national collegiate football championship.

Remember Dooley's words on the eve of the meeting with Notre Dame. They fit again here:

Somehow, someway, we've got to do it one more time.

Tell
Jimmy the Greek
To Stuff It

"We're gonna send you back to Georgia, just like we did Jimmy Carter."
—Notre Dame fan to Georgia fan on Bourbon Street.

"I hate those turkeys. Let's kill 'em."
—Georgia player on the sideline during the 1981 Sugar Bowl.

Twenty-four more hours. That is all that is left. Georgia, the nation's top-ranked collegiate football team, will play Notre Dame, once-beaten and once-tied, in the 1981 Sugar Bowl game, inside the mammoth Louisiana Superdome.

If Georgia wins the game, it will become the national champion. After 89 years of football the Bulldogs still don't have a national championship. Notre Dame could decorate a room with them.

It is New Year's Eve. Frank Broyles, former Arkansas coach and now ABC football broadcaster, is talking with Georgia coach Vince Dooley at the Fairmont Hotel in New Orleans where the Georgia team is having lunch.

"They're big, Vince, you know," says Broyles.

He sounds like he is trying to warn Dooley.

"They're strong, too," Broyles continues.

Dooley is shaking his head.

"But the main thing," Broyles goes on, "is they are quick. Notre Dame is a lot quicker than people realize. When you see a big team, you expect it to be slow. But you can be fooled. This team is very big, but it is quick. They can move."

Broyles IS trying to warn Dooley. As I listened, I wondered, was Notre Dame so big

and quick that Georgia wouldn't have a chance? Would there be that much difference between the teams? Between midwestern college football and the football we play in the southeast? Could there be that much difference between the abilities of the drawling boys from Valdosta, Jesup, and Ty Ty and the fast-talkers from Moeller High in Cincinnati?

I awakened in my room at the Fairmont the next morning at 4:30. I wondered if Dooley were awake. It would make me feel better to know he was worried, too. Then I wondered if Herschel Walker were sleeping soundly. Let Dooley and me stay awake. Herschel is the one who needs his rest.

I knew I would never get back to sleep. I decided to jog through the nearby French Quarter. It is five o'clock in the morning, the first bright day of 1981, and there are still revelers from the incredible Sea of Red the night before. It is five o'clock in the morning, and you can still hear the screams:

"HOW 'BOUT THEM DAWGS!"

The morning drags on. Then it is time for the pre-game meal. The players come and go, and I watch each face, looking for a positive sign that they are ready to play. My friends will ask me the inevitable question that is asked a million times before a game like this:

"Are they ready?"

Who knows? The coaches never know. They may have a hunch, a vibe, but it is impossible to predict how a team will play.

Out in the lobby the fans are stirring. The emotion—the awful tension—is building.

"How do you feel?" somebody asks me.

"Great," I reply, "but I don't count."

The team is eating in the Emerald Room. Dooley is standing outside the door with his funeral face. He always goes into a game with his funeral face. Smiles follow victory. They never precede battle.

"How do you feel?" I asked him. I couldn't believe I had actually asked that. The nervousness of the moment was getting to everybody.

Dooley shrugged his shoulders.

"Are they ready?" I blurted out.

He looked away into the distance and never gave me an answer. Still, I felt better by having said something. I was tired of being in knots, and that little exercise made me feel that I was closer—like the team—to kickoff. It was important to get on with it.

I am ready to get out of this crowded lobby scene. I want to be on the buses, headed for

the Superdome. If I am this keyed up and anxious, I think to myself, how does the team feel?

I go back to room 471 and explain once again to my daughter, Camille, why she can't be on the sideline like her brother, Kent. They won't let little girls on the sidelines. Try explaining that.

Now the team is in the lobby. Another sea of red has formed. The team makes its way through the yelling, screaming mob. The fans believe.

We are in the buses, and the buses are rolling. The police escort turns on its sirens. The world knows of our mission. The sirens say it: The game will be played soon. The sirens get you in the mood.

The team bus I am in is silent throughout the ride.

They go to their dressing stalls in the quarters normally used by the New Orleans Saints. That is my first sign to start worrying again. Georgia is the home team, but the home team at the Superdome, the Saints, had an awful year in 1980. Why couldn't Georgia have dressed on the other side of the building? The host team should have its choice, and Georgia is the host team.

Quit worrying, I say to myself. Things like dressing quarters don't determine outcomes of ball games. Whatever will be, will be.

But I still look for signs as I watch the players put on their pads. There is no laughter, no raised voices. This is a ritual, one they have gone through many times in their lives, even as little boys. Their thoughts are private, but I catch myself wanting to know if they feel they can win.

The team is dressed and the specialists and quarterbacks and receivers take the field. I walked out ahead with Erk Russell and Chip Wisdom, who wanted to see the Notre Dame placekicker, Harry Oliver. In the films, they had noticed he kicks with a low trajectory. If that is true, there might be a chance to block one and give Georgia a big break, perhaps at a critical time.

"He got that one up pretty good," Erk said before Widsom joined him.

Oliver kicked again.

"Now, that's more like it," Erk went on. "Kick it low. That's right. Give us a chance at it."

Oliver kicked again. This time, the ball rose quickly again! But there was an inconsistency that gave the two Georgia coaches some hope for a block.

They watched the Notre Dame punter, Blair Kiel. Kiel is also the Irish quarterback.

"Maybe he'll get tired late in the game," Russell said.

He gets tired, he takes an extra second to punt, and maybe Georgia could block that, too.

You look for everything, every angle. That started me worrying again. What had Notre Dame seen? Was there some weakness evident in our films? Have we more weaknesses than they do? If so, have they spotted them? Is there something drastic that is going to happen because they have expertly figured out a plan of attack?

The seats are filling up. It is obviously a Georgia crowd. The Georgia fans have stormed into New Orleans, just like they did in 1976.

Why did I have to think of '76? That could have been a national championship too. Georgia met top-ranked Pittsburgh in this very Superdome five years earlier in the Sugar Bowl.

Georgia had been emotionally ready to play that day. The problem was Pittsburgh was far ahead of the Bulldogs physically. The Panthers not only had Tony Dorsett, they also had quarterback Matt Cavanaugh and a passing attack. Erk was ready to stop Dorsett, but it was Cavanaugh who hurt Georgia with his passing, thus opening the running game.

And Pitt had done a number on the Bulldog offense. Ray Goff, the Georgia quarterback, had stormed through the Southeastern Conference with his option running. But he was not a passer. Pittsburgh knew this. The Panthers' big linebackers shut down the option game, and Georgia was finished, 27-3.

I remembered how depressed Dooley had been when the game was over. He does not often show emotion, but he was down after Pitt whipped his Southeastern Conference champions so soundly.

I looked at Dooley standing under the goal posts. He was showing no emotion. I looked down at the end zone where I was standing. The word *GEORGIA* was painted on the carpeted floor. I looked toward the other end of the field where Notre Dame was about to finish its pre-game warmup.

Would it be like 1976? Did Dan Devine, the Notre Dame coach, have more players, more balance than Dooley? That was the case in '76 with Johnny Majors' great team. Would the outcome be the same?

I thought of the other teams Dooley had brought to New Orleans. What's wrong with me? Why am I being so negative all of a sudden around a team that has been so positive about itself all season?

What do they know? They're kids.

Dooley was 0-4 with Georgia in New Orleans going into the 1981 Sugar Bowl. His 1968 team lost in the Sugar Bowl to Arkansas in old Tulane Stadium. Two other teams had lost regular season games to Tulane. Dooley's father was from New Orleans, and it remains one of his favorite cities. But he has simply never had much luck here.

On New Year's Day 1947, he had hitchhiked to New Orleans from Mobile with a boyhood friend. Georgia and Charley Trippi were playing North Carolina and Charlie (Choo-Choo) Justice. Trippi was Dooley's hero. The youngster naively expected somebody to befriend him and give him a ticket to the game.

He sat outside the gates on a curb and visualized what was happening by interpreting the roar of the crowd inside. He looked up and there stood a New Orleans policeman who had noticed the forlorn youngster.

"One of these days," he told the cop, "I'm going to come back and get inside that stadium."

After the 1968 loss to Arkansas Dooley would retell that story and add, ". . . but when I looked out on the field and tried to figure out how I would explain to the alumni why we were playing so poorly, I thought to myself, 'Coming back here was a terrible mistake.'"

Maybe it would be different this time. Maybe there was something to the law of averages. And this time Georgia was bringing Herschel Walker to town. And even Frank Broyles, so concerned about Notre Dame's size and quickness, had also pointed out to Dooley, "You can beat them in more ways than they can beat you."

If Notre Dame stops Herschel, then Buck Belue could pass them silly. Georgia would be like Pitt in 1976. I felt a little better.

Dooley led his team back to the locker room, past the elevator where a few minutes earlier President Jimmy Carter, in office for three more weeks, had been lifted to his box where he would watch the team he pulled against as a student at Georgia Tech.

"Hey, Jimmy," a fan had cried out. "How 'bout them Dawgs!"

"Yes," the president replied, "how 'bout them Dawgs!"

Back in the dressing room there would be no fiery pre-game speeches. The preparation was over. You need not appeal for emotion

from a team that is playing for the national championship. It was the little things, the possible edges, that were being discussed.

Dooley was pacing about. He had noticed the heat on the field. That meant conditioning would be a factor. Dooley said to Erk Russell, "Let's use as many as we can and try to keep 'em fresh late in the game."

He lit a cigarette. Dooley quit cigarettes years ago and went to a pipe. Then it was cigars. Then he quit smoking altogether. Why a cigarette now?

I didn't have to ask that question. He was calming his own nerves. I watched him. He only puffed. He didn't inhale.

Scott Woerner walked into the coaches' room to ask Bill Lewis about the Notre Dame punter. Was there anything he should know?

I looked at the posters around the room, most of which had been displayed by Claude McBride, the team chaplain. One poster included the letters, *G.A.T.I.A.*

G.A.T.A. is a key acronym in the Georgia football program, thanks to Erk Russell. In

How 'bout THIS dawg?

1965, the first time Dooley took a Georgia team to Grant Field to play Georgia Tech, Russell noticed that nearly everything he saw in the dressing quarters was stencilled, "G.T.A.A." for *Georgia Tech Athletic Association.*

Russell is always searching for a symbol that can be graphically translated into some inspirational message, so he told his underdog team that day, "Men, let's move one of those letters in front of that *T*, and get after their ass." Georgia did, and Georgia won, and Georgia never plays a game without that code on a blackboard or a poster.

G.A.T.I.A. was taking license with the familiar phrase, now changed to *Get after their IRISH ass.*

The kickoff is moments away. I remember the scene so vividly:

The coaches keep streaming in and out of the rest room. Nervousness prevails. Outside, the crowd is roaring and the Georgia players are encouraging one another. The managers and the trainers clasp hands and wish each other luck.

George Haffner wishes everybody luck and heads for the press box with Wisdom, Steve Greer, Wayne McDuffie, Rusty Russell and Sam Mrvos, where he will call plays. John Kasay tells Charley Whittemore, "At times like these, I wish I still chewed tobacco."

Erk tries to reach Wisdom on his two-way radio. A manager puts black smear below the eyes of Dale Williams to reduce the glare of the Superdome lights.

Erk is still trying to reach Wisdom on his radio. Equipment managers Howard Beavers and Ray McEwen help Dooley suit up his Motorola radio system so he can talk with Haffner.

From the john I hear a loud noise. Someone is throwing up.

Vince says to his players: "Men, it is a little warm out there, which is good for us. Go like hell, but get your hand up and let us know when you are tired."

A minute or so later the officials come to the door and ask for the captains. Vince calls Frank Ros and interlocks his arm with the big linebacker's. "We'll take the ball," he says to his captain, who did not shave the morning of the game. His one-day-old beard is dark and heavy, like a week's growth.

The captains leave. The rest of the team cheers and surges toward the door. Dooley halts them and says, "Five minutes more. Sit back down for a little while."

Erk still can't get Wisdom to answer and seems concerned. Maybe he wants to ask him how he feels, which is exactly what Mike Cavan asks Charley Whittemore.

"Nervous," Whittemore says, "the most ever."

"Can we win?" Cavan presses. "Can we win, Charley? Tell me something. You always make me feel good."

Kasay cuts in, "I know we can."

"It's a sin to want something as bad as I want this," Bill Lewis sighs. Whittemore is trying to contact Haffner without success.

"Look, Charley," Cavan says. "If you don't get him and we get the kickoff, just run '58 halfback pass' on the first play."

Everybody laughs which seems to relieve the tension.

"Fifty-eight halfback pass" would call for Herschel Walker to throw a halfback pass on the first play of the game.

At one o'clock the voice of the soloist singing the national anthem enters the room. Rex Robinson sings *sotto voce* along with her.

Soon afterwards, Dooley says calmly, "Okay, men, let's go."

The players yell and burst forward. Erk slams the palm of his hand on Eddie Weaver's shoulder pads. "Everything you've got to give, Eddie. That's all I want."

Walking down the tunnel toward the exit to the field, I am in stride with defensive back Steve Kelley. Even in his football shoes and with his shoulder pads on, I feel bigger. I am taller, for sure, and I think how disadvantaged Georgia is to play giant Notre Dame with small athletes like Steve Kelley.

When he and his brother Bob teamed up to recover the unfielded Irish kickoff following Rex Robinson's kick in the first quarter—one of the most important events of a treasured game—it made me realize that as long as college football is played there will always be some Davids who will slay some Goliaths.

The players queue up in the portal leading to the field and the Georgia fans are hanging over the rail and screaming at the top of their lungs.

There is jumping and movement and anxiety as the team waits to burst through the sign painted by Suzanne Hemphill.

I spot Pepper Rodgers, fired as Georgia Tech's coach after the 1979 season. He is working the game as a broadcaster for the Atlanta ABC affiliate, WSB.

Pepper shouts to me, "Good Luck."

I believe he meant it. An early riser, Pepper

174

had finished his jog down Canal Street and was reading the *Times-Picayune* at 6:30 when I discovered him in the Fairmont lobby two days before the game.

Pepper said, "I've always wanted to come to the Sugar Bowl with the nation's No. 1 team and here I am."

Georgia always regarded Pepper Rodgers as a good football coach. We never took him for granted. We respected him.

He was honest, but it does not always pay to be too honest in your comments when you coach college football. A lot of alumni, most often your own, may take offense at what you say.

I'll never forget what Dee Andros told the Athens Touchdown Club in September of 1974. He had brought his Oregon State team to Atlanta to try to adjust to the late summer heat and humidity before playing Georgia. I asked him to come to Athens a few days before the game to speak to the club. Andros coached against Rodgers when the latter was at UCLA.

Little Steve Kelly. A David against the Notre Dame Goliaths.

Now Rodgers was about to open his first season at Tech. Andros said to the Athens club: "Pepper Rodgers will make Vince Dooley a better football coach."

He was right, and here we are about to kick off the 1981 Sugar Bowl and Pepper Rodgers is wishing us luck. And meaning it.

There are strange twists in this business.

Notre Dame takes the field first, then Georgia blasts through the banner with all index fingers pointed upwards. There is whooping and hollering and wild emotion. I walk quickly behind Dooley to the Georgia sideline without any display of emotion. I don't want to be spotted from the stands doing something foolish.

But now I am in the midst of the team. I feel shielded from the crowd. I am whooping and hollering and jumping up and down too. I want to be a part of this national championship effort and I want to join in.

Both teams advance to the center of the field where the Sugar Bowl trophy is painted and watch the drama of the coin tossing unfold.

The Irish win the toss and take the ball.

Moments later Rex Robinson is kicking the ball down the field. It is high, it descends lazily. It is floating. Most of Rex's kicks are different. They boom downfield, and carry deep into the end zone. I am attracted to the ball's peculiar flight. It will give Georgia's coverage team plenty of time to get to the Notre Dame ballcarrier.

But there is no Notre Dame ballcarrier. The two deep men have let the ball fall between them. But, no harm done. They down the ball and the officials bring it out to the 20.

First down, 10 for Notre Dame. This is it.

* * * *

The word Georgia had was Notre Dame couldn't pass and the Irish passing game had, in fact, been weak during the 9-1-1 season. Georgia came into the game averaging 132 passing yards per game. Notre Dame had only 83.

But the word was out on Georgia, too: You could move the ball against Georgia in the air. Tennessee had done it. Florida had done it. Auburn had done it. Georgia Tech had done it. Now it was Notre Dame, spreading out like Florida, that was attacking the Georgia defense through the air.

Quarterback Blair Kiel passes on first down. The freshman throws incomplete. On second

down, however, he hits halfback Phil Carter for 22 yards and a first down. The Irish move to the Georgia 33 before they are faced with a fourth down. In comes kicker Harry Oliver. He is perfect from 50 yards. Notre Dame has scored on its first possession.

Scott Woerner returns the Irish kickoff to the Georgia 22. No surprises. Buck Belue hands the ball to Herschel Walker. He has two yards. Second down, eight. Belue gives the ball to Herschel again. The big back rolls through the Notre Dame defense for seven yards, but the Bulldogs are caught for holding. Herschel has been thrown out of bounds.

Mike Cavan, who watches Herschel's every move, noticed the problem first.

"Herschel's hurt!" he screamed to trainer Warren Morris. A pall came over the sidelines immediately. The second offensive snap for Georgia, and Herschel Walker is hurt. Carnie Norris goes in for Walker, who has taken himself out of the game with the injury.

When he arrived on the Georgia sideline, Herschel seemed more puzzled than anything else.

He said, in muffled tones over his mouthpiece, "I think it's just a bruise." That comforted players who had crowded around him. They passed the word that it didn't look bad.

Butch Mulherin, the team doctor and a former Georgia player, calmly went into action. He found the problem—a dislocated left shoulder—but it wasn't easy. Walker is so muscular, he had to search for the exact spot of the injury. The doctor popped the bone back into place. Herschel flinched slightly but showed no other expression of pain. Even in the 12th game of the season he wasn't familiar with pain. He had had few injuries as a high school athlete. In the TCU game, recall, a defender fell on his foot after a big gain and left the Georgia tailback with an ankle sprain.

Two weeks later, against Ole Miss, he was unsure of himself. He was afraid to cut on the ankle, afraid of what might happen.

"If he has another injury," Mulherin had explained, "he'll come back quicker. He won't be as uncertain, because he will have had experience with an injury. He'll know what to expect of himself."

Herschel would be back in the Sugar Bowl game the next time Georgia got possession.

The Bulldogs had to punt after the holding penalty lost 11 yards. Notre Dame has the ball again in great field position, on the Georgia 41.

The Irish advance the ball to the Bulldog 26, but the Georgia defense holds again. In comes Oliver for another field goal try.

"Be low," Wisdom says over the two-way radio, which finally worked, to Erk Russell on the field.

"Be there, Terry," says Russell. "Be there, Freddie." Terry Hoage and Freddie Gilbert are lined up inside and will attempt to block the kick. Maybe, if Oliver's trajectory is low, they will get to the ball.

Georgia had practiced long and hard on blocking a Notre Dame kick. Wisdom and Russell had devised a terrific plan: The two "kamikazies," Hoage and Gilbert, would jump on Frank Ros' back and spring from that position in an attempt to get a hand on the ball. That technique had worked in 1969 when Wisdom played for Dooley.

But the plan had to be scrapped—Hoage and Gilbert were killing Frank Ros. They kept kicking him in the posterior. They would line up four yards behind the ball and come fast and hard. As they leaped, they would often catch Ros in the seat of the pants with their shoes. Ros nearly missed the game with a bruised rear and a pulled hamstring muscle.

Wisdom stopped the practice routine and told Hoage and Gilbert to figure out with the down linemen how they could get the job done. That is known in the trade as "not overcoaching."

As the ball was about to be snapped for the second Notre Dame field goal try, Hoage said to Ros in the defensive huddle, "Just cut the center's legs. Keep him low. Don't let him come up."

Ros did just that, and Gilbert and Hoage hurdled the entire line of scrimmage with split-second timing. Hoage got the ball, and Georgia recovered at the Notre Dame 49.

A break like that had awakened the Bulldogs in Knoxville and again in Auburn. On the sideline you could sense a change coming. Notre Dame had dominated early, but Georgia had pulled off a big play. The pendulum was swinging.

Scott Zettek and Bob Crable, the giant Notre Dame defenders, managed to keep the Bulldogs out of the end zone, but Robinson tied the game with a 46-yard field goal. The score is 3-3.

Now Robinson is about to kick off again. Up goes the ball—with that high arc. It's another floater, but Georgia will be down the field to cover it.

A rest for the weary. Injured Herschel Walker carrie the ball 36 times against the Irish despite dislocating shoulder on his second run of the gam

Something incredible has happened! The ball has dropped between the two receivers for a second straight time and it is bouncing free!

Georgia's coverage team is quickly downfield and all over the ball. Bob Kelly has made the recovery at the Notre Dame one. So suddenly the game has turned completely around. The ball had bounced Georgia's way, but this had been an opportunist team all season, one that would exploit such fortune. All season this team seemed to sniff out opportunities and then capitalize swiftly and confidently.

The Georgia sideline is bedlam.

Herschel Walker heads into the game, but drops his mouthpiece. He reaches for it and kicks it away. He hesitates, and reaches for it again, and drops it again before he finally gets a good grip.

Well, I thought, there is something Herschel Walker CAN'T do: He has a hard time picking up a mouthpiece on artificial turf.

Two plays later Herschel dives over the big, quick Notre Dame linemen for the touchdown. His dislocated shoulder didn't seem to be bothering him. Robinson hits the extra point and Georgia has a 10-3 lead.

A minute later the Bulldogs get—or *make*—another break. A Notre Dame ball carrier is hit, fumbles, and Chris Welton has the ball for Georgia at the Irish 22.

Walker off tackle and out of bounds for 12 to the 10. Walker sweeps left and out of bounds for seven. Walker sweeps right, and into the end zone from the three. Brilliant running and blocking. Robinson is true again, and Georgia has a 17-3 lead at 13:49 of the second period.

The Georgia sideline began to bubble with confidence. Get one more and Notre Dame is in big trouble.

If Dooley was confident, he didn't show it. Quite the contrary, as a matter of fact. He was scowling at his team for looking at the giant television screens above the Superdome floor.

"Quit looking up there!" Dooley shouted. "The game is out here!"

Notre Dame is moving again, this time behind quarterback Jeff Courey, who has replaced Kiel. Courey scrambles for 20 yards to the Georgia 36. The Irish move to fourth down and three at the Bulldog 13. Devine calls time. The Irish will go for the touchdown. Courey

Jumping for Joy in Sugar Bowl. Woerner (19), Hoage (14), McShea (41), Payne (87), and Hipp (49).

rolls and throws to Pete Holohan in the corner of the end zone, but Scott Woerner leaps high to intercept and returns out to the Georgia 19. Another Notre Dame drive is thwarted.

Once more the Georgia sideline is thinking: Get into the dressing room at the half with a 21-point lead.

Georgia is rolling again behind Herschel Walker, who breaks up the middle for 23 yards to the Notre Dame 44. But Belue is not able to get anything passing. He is being rushed and hounded by the Notre Dame defense, and the drive ends.

There will be one more chance at adding points. Late in the second period Woerner will break away after fielding a punt and return 14 yards to the Notre Dame 46. But what followed was becoming the typical Georgia offensive possession against the menacing Irish defense:

——— First down: Belue rolls right, trying to pass and is dropped for a four-yard loss.

——— Second down: Belue throws short to Walker, incomplete.

——— Third down: Belue throws to Norris Brown, incomplete, almost intercepted.

——— Fourth down: Mark Malkiewicz punts.

At halftime, Georgia still led 17-3.

In the locker room it was, simply, "Don't let up." Football teams often say little at halftime. The coaches meet and decide what's working and what isn't. They speak in "x" 's and "o" 's.

This time, however, there seems to be encouragement of the players from the coaches:

"You can't let up!" John Kasay is saying to the offensive linemen. "Dammit! You can't let up!"

George Haffner is explaining what pass plays he wants to run in the second half. So far Georgia has not been able to complete a single pass, so fierce has been the defensive rush.

"You gotta hold 'em out there!" Haffner says. "You gotta give Buck more time!"

Steve Greer reminds his defensive linemen they have to go after the quarterback.

"Go after him! Put him on the ground!"

I wished the game was over, right then and there. I wondered if Notre Dame would agree to call it off. I was worried they might get the momentum back. Our defense was tiring.

Georgia has recovered a free ball on the Notre Dame one after kicking off and will take the lead for good moments later.

Dooley is talking to his team. It is almost time to return to the field:

"Listen, men," he begins. "Be smart. Let them make the mistakes. If they want to fight, don't fight back, unless it's legal. Reach down in your heart on every play. Reach deep. This is the biggest 30 minutes of your life. Let's go."

The team surged toward the door again. The offense would get the ball as the second half began. Move it and make something happen, I thought. Get to them early and make them have to come back from far down in the fourth quarter.

It is quickly obvious it will not be easy for Georgia in the second half.

Georgia can't go anywhere. Notre Dame is pounding Belue every time he tries to pass. Walker can't do it all. Notre Dame, behind Kiel's passing, moves in for a touchdown. At the end of the third period the Irish have cut the lead to 17-10. It could have been closer. Oliver barely missed a field goal in the period.

As the quarter ends, junior varsity coach Doc Ayers, who assists Dick Copas with sideline control, asks me if I know any scores from other bowl games.

"The only score I know, Doc," I said, "is this one. And it ain't enough."

At 10:56 to go, Georgia dodges another bullet. Greg Bell dives in from a corner and gets a fraction of another field-goal attempt that goes wide. The sideline is relieved again. If only the offense can move the ball.

Wishful thinking. Belue is sacked for a five-yard loss trying to pass. Walker gets four, but then is stopped for no gain. Georgia punts again.

The Irish defense is almost *stalking* Belue, closing in for the kill. He has yet to complete a pass. He is frustrated. Walker is battering away, but it is not enough. Damn! For one, stinking, first down! The clock is Georgia's only chance.

It will come down to a two-point conversion play, I figure. The Irish will get another touchdown, the score will be 17-16, and they will go for two. Will we hold them? The clock is ticking, ticking, ticking.

Then, another break. Mike Fisher has

LEFT: The Approach. Rex Robinson for three points against the Irish. ABOVE: Belue. Dejected, but he never lost his poise, nor the game.

intercepted a Kiel pass at the Notre Dame 37. This may be the clincher! Even if we get only six or seven yards, Robinson can hit the field goal and that will be the cushion to kill the clock.

The clock winds down to 8:18. Robinson hits it good from 48 yards out. It's far enough, but the ball misses right. We have to fight off the Irish again.

Georgia holds. But, again, Georgia can't move. The ball is punted back to Notre Dame, first down at the Irish 43. Five minutes and 10 seconds remain.

I position myself close to Erk Russell. I am hoping he will say something, anything that will give me confidence we can hold them. As the defense starts to go back onto the field, Russell puts his arm around linebacker Frank Ros, the Georgia captain, and says, "Frank, you've got five minutes left in your life. Have you got anything left?"

That gives me a sinking feeling. Erk seemed unsure.

"Coach," Ros answers, "you know we can hold 'em."

——— First down at the Notre Dame 43: Carter goes at right end for seven yards.

——— Second down, three, at the 50: Kiel wants to pass. He is sacked by Eddie Weaver for a four-yard loss.

——— Third down, seven, at the Notre Dame 46: Kiel passes for six yards.

——— Fourth down, one at the Georgia 46: Kiel passes. Scott Woerner intercepts at the Georgia 34.

Two minutes, 56 seconds remain. The confidence is coming back now. The sideline has erupted with emotion again, except for Dooley. He is calm as ever.

Erk Russell is on one knee, saying to nobody in particular: "We've got to have this. Oh, goodness, we've got to have it."

LEFT: Happiness is an interception for Georgia's Mike Fisher. ABOVE: Herschel can pass, but Notre Dame will remember he pushed for two TDs and 150 yards.

185

For the everlasting record, the last two minutes and 50 seconds, the last *beautiful* two minutes and 50 seconds:

———— First down, ten, at the Georgia 34: Belue runs right, out of bounds for six yards.

———— Second down, four at the Georgia 40: Walker at left guard gains one. Time out, Notre Dame. 2:42.

———— Third down, three at the Georgia 41: Belue rolls left for six yards. First Down.

———— First down, ten, at the Georgia 47: Walker at right tackle, no gain. Time out, Notre Dame. 2:16.

———— Second down, ten, at the Georgia 47: Walker sweeps left for three yards.

———— Third down, seven, at the 50: Belue rolls right, passes to Amp Arnold for his first completion of the day and seven yards. 2:05. First down.

———— First down, ten at the Notre Dame 43: Notre Dame is penalized five yards for offsides.

———— First down, five, from the Notre Dame 38: Walker runs right, then cuts back left for nine yards. First down. 1:28.

———— First down, ten, from the Notre Dame 29: Walker sweeps right for five yards.

———— Second down, five at the Notre Dame 24: Georgia is penalized five yards for delay of game.

———— Second down, ten, from the Notre Dame 29: Belue falls on the ball for loss of one. Time out, Notre Dame. :37.

———— Third down, 11, from the Notre Dame 30: Belue rolls left for four yards.

———— Fourth down, seven, from the Notre Dame 26: The clock runs out to end the game.

When Georgia had to do it, Georgia did it. It held Notre Dame time and again. And the offense, stopped all day, finally moved in those last, precious two minutes. When Belue hit Arnold, out with an injury since the Florida game, I said to team doctor Marion Hubert and business manager Kermit Perry on the sidelines, "That may be the greatest pass in Georgia history." If we were to have just one completion all day, that was the time to get it.

That pass play sealed it. Notre Dame was running out of time and time-outs. And Belue, harrassed all day, was moving his team. He could have singlehandedly lost the Sugar Bowl game for Georgia, had he thrown the ball away at the wrong time, had he forced a pass, had he thrown it into a crowd under all that pressure.

But he didn't make a mistake, not a single one. He never lost his poise. Years later, when people look at the statistics of the game, they will wrongfully conclude Buck Belue had a bad day.

He did not. If he plays another thousand games in his life, he will never have a better opportunity to crack than he did in New Orleans, New Year's Day 1981. Forget the statistics, except these: Buck Belue—no interceptions, no fumbles, no mistakes.

Herschel Walker would be named the game's most valuable player. How could he not win? He took 34 snaps after dislocating his shoulder, and gained 150 yards for the day, most of it right into the teeth of the Irish defense.

More incredible than that, he didn't fumble, despite his injury. He took the hardest licks the Irish could hand out. They wanted a shot at the freshman sensation, and they swung from their heels. Herschel took it, and gave some back.

There would be detractors of this team, of course. "Them Dawgs are dawgs," wrote one columnist. "Georgia was lucky," said others.

Georgia didn't convince the world its 12-0 record was good enough for the No. 1-ranking because it excelled in areas where most fans and would-be football experts carrying typewriters and tape recorders never look.

Georgia was a complete team. Dooley: "The 1980 Georgia team had more balance and was more of a complete team than any we've had at Georgia."

Georgia didn't make mistakes. It took away the football 44 times in the 11 regular season games, on 20 fumbles and 24 interceptions. It lost the ball via fumble or interception only 21 times, a two-to-one ratio. Georgia committed only 53 penalties for 469 yards.

And Georgia had, perhaps, the best kicking and specialty team in the country. Consider:

—Only four punts were returned against Georgia in 1980. Only *four*. Tennessee had two for 12 and four yards; Auburn had one for four; and Tech had one for two yards. Georgia punted 65 times in 1980. The average return was for 0.3 yards.

—At one point in the season, Georgia kicked 47 straight times without a single return.

—There were no missed extra points by Rex Robinson.

—There were no penalties called on the Georgia kicking game throughout 12 games.

Notre Dame, of course, won the statistics battle in the Sugar Bowl. The total yardage was 328-127, in favor of the Irish. But look at these statistics: Mistakes: Notre Dame—one fumble,

two balls not fielded on the kickoff, one of which Georgia recovered, and three interceptions. Georgia—none.

On the field, the Georgia crowd was taking the place apart. In the dressing room the team cheered endlessly.

There was Vince Dooley hugging every player. The half-nude, sweaty bodies left him dirty, grimy, and disheveled, but he wore a victory smile that was wider than Jimmy Carter's smile in 1976, the year Carter and Pittsburgh were No. 1.

There were tears, laughter, rejoicing and uncontrolled glee as Dooley raised a hand to signal that it was time to say thanks. It took a few minutes, but finally the team became quiet and the players reached for the hands of teammates. The head coach asked guard Nat Hudson to do the honors.

Every player was on bended knee and the circle of hands was unbroken. It was still. It was quiet, except for the screams of the Georgia fans who had gathered outside the locker room door about 20 paces away, waiting to touch their heroes.

Hudson prayed briefly, giving thanks for the strength to prevail and for assistance in helping the team reach its season's goals.

I am usually off to the side when the team conducts its post-game prayer, but suddenly I was caught in the middle, and Dale Carver reached for my right hand and manager Tim Chipman grabbed my left. There was a warm, electrifying feeling as Hudson prayed. You could sense the humility and appreciation.

At "Amen," the team cheered again and index fingers were raised again in still another salute to its lofty position.

Quiet returned as Dooley raised his hand. "I told you before the game," he said, punching the air with a closed right fist, "that you had more character and unity than any team I've been around and that I loved you. I'm gonna tell you again—you have more character and unity than any team I've ever been around and I love you!"

He then headed for the interview room, hugging each assistant. Brent Musberger, the CBS announcer, entered the dressing room and the players began to shout to him, "Tell Jimmy the Greek to stuff it," one said. "Tell him who's No. 1. Tell him where Georgia is. Tell him how many Notre Dame lost. Tell him who is undefeated and untied." They were referring to oddsmaker Jimmy the Greek's comments that the Irish were far superior to Georgia.

Musberger smiled and said, "They probably wouldn't appreciate my reasons, but I was pulling for Georgia."

He wanted to do a show about the road to the Sugar Bowl and the Super Bowl, featuring Georgia and the Atlanta Falcons. A Notre Dame win would have spoiled that script. The Greek, incidentally, probably should be forgiven. He didn't know how to measure the Bulldog's heart.

So let the doubters doubt. They will be forgotten. What the 1980 Georgia football team did will not.

It won 11 regular season games. It defeated Notre Dame in the Sugar Bowl, 17-10. And it was voted the No. 1 team in America.

And I keep a newspaper clipping in my wallet to prove it.

Epilogue

It is over now, Georgia's shining hour. The awards, the trophies, the parties are over. Life in and around Athens has returned to normal until Tennessee comes to town in September.

That is, life has returned to normal for most of us. But not, I am afraid, for Herschel Walker.

There has never been a story such as the Herschel Walker story in 1980. Frank Sinkwich didn't break in like this freshman from Wrightsville. Charley Trippi didn't either. And in more recent times, O.J. Simpson had two years of junior college behind him when he burst onto the scene and Herschel surpassed Tony Dorsett's freshman performance with his 1,616 yards in 1980. The only one who was a blockbusting hero from beginning to end was Ozark Ike, and he played in the funny papers.

But there is more than statistics to this story, and this effort would not be complete without a look at the young man—where he has been and where he is going—who gave us all so much in 1980.

I have never met a youngster quite like him. He was covered by the press like he was the president. Every move he made was news. He was in the news whether he wanted to be or not.

Soon after the Sugar Bowl the rumors began: Herschel had received an offer of $2 million from the Canadian Football League to leave Georgia. Then there was the plan by Georgia alumni to counter that by giving Herschel his own insurance agency. Alumni mean well. The NCAA had Herschel Walker out of the insurance business in no time.

Everywhere he went, even to class, he was the center of attention, a walking press conference.

He has never ceased to amaze me. In this day and time of the greedy, bragging, brash athlete, 19-year-old Herschel Walker, son of hard-working parents from Wrightsville, Georgia, continues his humble routine. I would bet anything it is sincere.

I fully expected him to finally throw up his hands in disgust after the Super Bowl. There

were times I could see the fatigue in his eyes as more and more interviews came his way. But still, he held on. His ability to handle attention and pressure is absolutely amazing. I expected him to suddenly scream out, "Leave me alone!" But he never did.

The question becomes, where does he go from here? Is there a breaking point? Will he change? I don't pretend to know the answer, and neither does he.

Before I speculate on his future, let me tell you a few things more about Herschel Walker, NOT the football star, but Herschel Walker, the boy-man from the house on the hill, up the dirt drive, across the railroad tracks.

He sleeps only a few hours a night.

"A lot of things happen when you are sleeping," he says. "I don't want to miss anything. Something exciting might happen, and I would hate to sleep through it."

He eats only one meal a day—supper. He doesn't like steak.

His magnificent physique is natural. He rarely lifts weights.

He's a loner. That started back in Wrightsville when he would sit off on a little hill by the railroad tracks and think for hours at the time.

"I'd think about life," he says.

So life, according to Herschel Walker, philosopher:

193

Herschel. "Someday I reckon they will know I'm not only here for the show. . . ."

—"Fancy clothes aren't important. My mother always worries about me being a sloppy dresser. There's no need to worry about things like that."

—"Growing up in a small town is great. You can mature faster and get out on your own. In a small town you don't have as many people telling you what to do and what not to do. You can see for yourself. You can learn right from wrong a lot faster."

—"I pray often during a game, but not to win. I pray I'll be guided and both teams will be watched over."

—"The biggest problem in the world is people don't trust their fellow man."

And, a few more questions for Herschel Walker:

—What would you do if you had a million dollars?

"I'd put it in the bank and pretend I didn't have it."

—Your father gave you a gun when you were younger, but you never liked to hunt. Why?

"I just didn't like to kill little animals. I don't think it is good to take another life, even if it's an animal's."

—You have talked about becoming an FBI agent. What if you had to use your gun?

"In that case, I would be doing my duty, and you have to do your duty. It is not my duty to go kill little animals."

Then there is Herschel Walker the poet. He has written poetry since his high school days. He still writes, often late at night at the dormitory study room while the rest of the campus sleeps. Read his innermost thoughts:

ABOVE: Everybody wants *something* from Herschel. RIGHT: Poetry used by permission.

194

May God Bless the World

*The World has problems, but He sees them
  through,*
Someone may do wrong, but He still loves you.
In time of illness and in time of joy,
God loves you more than a child loves a toy.
He gave His only Son, to see that we do well,
I will love for my Father to run my life,
I do not want to go to Hell.
*Hell will be very hot and hot weather I do not
  like,*
*We cannot wait too late to ask God to take us
  back.*
*He has given us so much, from us not even a
  thank-you.*
We have to face life; He is true
No one can do as He can do.
*God is the way, I'll like to meet Him, I hope
  you do, too.*
*May God bless the World, and may He bless
  you too.*

They Do Not Know

I wish they could see
The real person in me
Someday I reckon they will know
I'm not only here for the show
I have one Man Upstairs, I always pray,
They do not know, but they will see one day.

Thank You

It's something I like to say to you.
So I'll say it so true.
It is hard to say,
But give me time, I will find a way.
You've been a brother to me,
*It is more than what I thought people would
  be.*
*Please remember me when it is time for you to
  leave,*
I know I will remember you, keep in touch too.
For all you have done, Thank You.

Let the Day Go On

When I leave for just a little while,
Please do not hate me or shed tears,
*Please do not hug your sorrow through the
  years,*
And for my sake and in my name
Live on and do all things the same.
Forget about your sad time or empty days,
Fill each waking hour in useful ways.
Reach out your hand in comfort and in cheer,
In return I will always be near.
And never, never be afraid for that day.
I love you in a special way.

Remember Me

The hurt has hit now with all its force,
I sit here alone thinking of you, of course.
Without you my world is small,
And without you, I cannot do nothing at all.
*In the past few weeks, you I have really
  missed.*
Remember me and please remember this:
I'll always love you, no matter where you go,
If you hate me, please do not let me know,
Remember I love you, I care about you too.
*I pray we could be together, I really want to be
  with you.*

I Can Not Say No

It may be hard, but maybe one day I'll see,
The world is not what it used to be.
It starts with a tear in your eye,
Next, you cannot say goodbye.
You leave and say it is forever,
You know deep inside you can never.
*But the time comes when you think it won't
  last,*
*You just look for the good days, while the bad
  days pass.*
*The good days pass very fast, the bad days go
  very slow.*
I think the people realize now, I cannot say no.
It may not be good but it's not so bad,
Maybe it's something I picked up from my Dad.

He can't say "no." It's a problem, a real problem. It will get worse as his fame and fortune spread.

Herschel Walker has said he has no intention of leaving the University of Georgia until he has completed the work for his degree in criminal justice and his four years of football eligibility. He finished his first quarter of classwork with a 3.2 average.

I don't know. I don't think it is the lure of Canadian Football League cash that would cause him to leave. I think it might be the demand on his time, the continued invasion of his privacy. He is a private person.

He might do something totally unexpected. He might quit football altogether and apply to the FBI, or join the Marines.

Everybody wants a piece of Herschel Walker. They want to be with him, they want to have their picture made with him, they want something that belongs to him, they want to touch him. He has no freedom.

The requests for interviews from the national media continue. They will become an avalanche when he returns to summer practice. He has an unlisted telephone number. Still, he and his roommate, Barry Young, have to leave the phone off the hook to get any peace, or sleep.

He felt "pushed" during the final days of the battle to recruit him. He thought of escaping to Southern Cal. He may soon be thinking "escape" again.

Sadly, he is naive if he thinks that is possible. Not as long as Herschel Walker continues to play the sport of football will he be able to hide from the hordes that will flock to him.

Oh, for others to have his humility.

"The older players looked after me this year," he would say to reporters after the Sugar Bowl. "I was able to play well because I got a lot of help."

He always spoke in terms of his team. He signed autographs, "May God bless you." He never reads his press clippings. His scores of high school trophies and medals are prominently displayed in his Wrightsville home, but that is because his mother and father made the effort to do so. Herschel never even bothered to so much as unpack a trophy.

A lot of people were disturbed when Herschel Walker didn't win the Heisman Trophy his freshman year. But not Herschel Walker.

"I guess it would be nice to win it some day if the team does well," he says.

And that smile. It breaks across his face like morning. We can all learn from this marvelous, talented young man.

But let us not fault him when, and if, he does prove human. If he leaves us, let us send him away with our good wishes and our thanks for all he did, and not scowl at what, if anything, he left undone.

And if he carries a football long enough, he will surely fumble it at some point. Let us know patience at that time.

His mother, Christine Walker, says it best: "Herschel is just different."

He is, indeed. There have been times I thought we were all simply dreaming him. And I leave this endeavor with one more piece of Herschel Walker news. It didn't make the headlines, but it should have:

In the first quarter of his college experience, Herschel Junior Walker of Wrightsville, Georgia, not only became a national celebrity, led his football team to the national championship, made all-American, set a new record for yardage gained by a freshman, was interviewed by everybody who ever wore a working press ticket, but he also found time to compile a 3.2 average, just missing the dean's list.

Give him some room to breathe, and God only knows what he will eventually accomplish.

LEFT: On Campus. Will he ever find an escape?   ABOVE: John Terrell (right) registered for a winter quarter course in 1981, making him the only Georgia man who can boast that he "went to school with Sinkwich, Trippi and Herschel."

BOOK III

GEORGIA ◆ 17 | T 3 | :00 | QTR | BALL 0
NOTRE DAME 10 | O 0 / R 0 | | 4 | DOWN 0 / TO GO 0

The Numbers

1980 RESULTS (12-0)

September 6	Georgia 16	Tennessee 15	Knoxville 95,288
September 13	Georgia 42	Texas A&M 0	Athens 60,150
September 20	Georgia 20	Clemson 16	Athens 61,800
September 27	Georgia 34	TCU 3	Athens 59,200
October 11	Georgia 28	Ole Miss 21	Athens 60,300
October 18	Georgia 41	Vanderbilt 0	Athens 59,300
October 25	Georgia 27	Kentucky 0	Lexington 57,353
November 1	Georgia 13	S. Carolina 10	Athens 62,200
November 8	Georgia 26	Florida 21	Jacksonville 68,528
November 15	Georgia 31	Auburn 21	Auburn 74,009
November 29	Georgia 38	Ga. Tech 20	Athens 62,800

SUGAR BOWL

January 1	Georgia 17	Notre Dame 10	New Orleans 77,895

FINAL 1980 SEC STANDINGS

School	SEC Games	Pct.	All Games
Georgia	6-0-0	1.000	11-0-0
Miss. State	5-1-0	.833	9-2-0
Alabama	5-1-0	.833	9-2-0
LSU	4-2-0	.667	7-4-0
Florida	4-2-0	.667	7-4-0
Tennessee	3-3-0	.500	5-6-0
Ole Miss	2-4-0	.333	3-8-0
Kentucky	1-5-0	.167	3-8-0
Auburn	0-6-0	.000	5-6-0
Vanderbilt	0-6-0	.000	2-9-0

FINAL 1980 NATIONAL RATINGS

Associated Press
1. GEORGIA (58½) (12-0)................... 1251
2. Pitt (3½) (11-1)........................ 1187
3. Oklahoma (10-2)........................... 1100
4. Michigan (10-2)............................ 1033
5. Florida St. (1) (10-2)..................... 970
6. Alabama (10-2)............................ 928
7. Nebraska (10-2)........................... 879
8. Penn St. (10-2)........................... 797
9. Notre Dame (9-2-1)........................ 699
10. North Carolina (11-1)..................... 665
11. Southern Cal (8-2-1)...................... 610
12. Brigham Young (12-1)...................... 584
13. UCLA (9-2)............................... 502
14. Baylor (10-2)............................ 494
15. Ohio St. (9-3)........................... 389
16. Washington (9-3)......................... 253
17. Purdue (9-3)............................. 198
18. Miami, Fla. (9-3)........................ 192
19. Mississippi St. (9-3).................... 159
20. SMU (8-4)................................. 98

United Press International
1. GEORGIA (36) (12-0)....................... 596
2. Pitt (3) (11-1)........................... 543
3. Oklahoma (10-2)........................... 495
4. Michigan (1) (10-2)....................... 430
5. Florida St. (10-2)........................ 423
6. Alabama (10-2)............................ 419
7. Nebraska (10-2)........................... 354
8. Penn St. (10-2)........................... 328
9. North Carolina (11-1)..................... 232
10. Notre Dame (9-2-1)....................... 211
11. Brigham Young (12-1)..................... 167
12. Southern Cal (8-2-1)..................... 136
13. Baylor (10-2)............................ 116
14. UCLA (9-2).............................. 114
15. Ohio St. (9-3).......................... 70
16. Purdue (9-3)............................ 62
17. Washington (9-3)........................ 50
18. Miami, Fla. (9-3)....................... 14
19. Florida (8-4).......................... 13
20. SMU (8-4).............................. 8

GEORGIA at TENNESSEE

September 6 at Knoxville, Tenn.

GEORGIA	0	0	9	7	16
TENN.	0	9	6	0	15

UT—Safety-Belue fumble-recovered by Georgia in endzone 12:20-2nd Q
UT—Olszewski, 4-yd. run (Duncan PAT) 9:00-2nd Q
UT—Miller, 36-yd. pass from Olszewski (run failed) 4:02-3rd Q
GA—Safety-Punt downed by Tennessee in endzone 3:19-3rd Q
GA—Walker, 16-yd. run (Robinson PAT) 1:03-3rd Q
GA—Walker, 9-yd. run (Robinson PAT) 11:16-4th Q

Attendance: 95,288.

Weather: Temperature 87; Wind variable; Cloudy.

FINAL TEAM STATISTICS

	Tennessee	Georgia
First Downs	14	13
Rushes—Yardage (Net)	124	140
Passing Yardage (Net)	186	100
Return Yardage (Net)	78	66
Passes—Att.-Comp.-Int.	15-20-0	6-11-0
Total Offense—Yards	310	240
Punts (Number-Average)	6-245-40.8	9-328-36.4
Fumbles—Lost	5-4	4-2
Penalties—Yards	4-40	10-60

FINAL INDIVIDUAL STATISTICS

Tennessee

Rushing	Att.	Gain	Lost	Net	TD	Long
Daniels	12	28	0	28	0	4
Berry	5	30	0	30	0	12
Olszewski	9	29	17	12	1	10
Ford	15	59	5	54	0	16

Passing	Att.	Comp.	Int.	Yds	TD	Long
Olszewski	20	15	0	186	1	36

Pass Receiving	No.	Yds.	TD	Long
Gault	4	74	0	32
Ford	3	4	0	5
Daniels	2	5	0	3
Miller	2	52	1	36
Berry	2	12	0	8
Hancock	2	39	0	22

Punting	No.	Yds.	Avg.	Long
Warren	6	245	40.8	68

Georgia

Rushing	Att.	Gain	Lost	Net	TD	Long
Belue	15	39	40	–1	0	12
Womack	4	14	0	14	0	6
McMickens	4	8	5	3	0	7
Brown	1	0	0	0	0	0
Norris	8	40	4	36	0	16
McCarthy	1	3	0	3	0	3
Walker	24	90	6	84	2	16
Stewart	1	1	0	1	0	1

Passing	Att.	Comp.	Int.	Yds	TD	Long
Belue	11	6	0	100	0	27

Pass Receiving	No.	Yds.	TD	Long
Brown	2	46	0	27
Walker	1	9	0	9
Arnold	2	21	0	13
Scott	1	24	0	24

Punting	No.	Yds.	Avg.	Long
Broadway	9	328	36.4	51

TEX. A&M at GEORGIA

September 13

GEORGIA	7	21	14	0	42
TEX. A&M	0	0	0	0	0

GA—Arnold, 6-yd. pass from Belue (Robinson PAT) 10:34-1st Q
GA—Walker, 1-yd. run (Robinson PAT) 13:53-2nd Q
GA—Arnold, 19-yd. pass from Belue (Robinson PAT) 3:09-2nd Q
GA—Jones, 24-yd. pass from Paulk (Robinson PAT) :07-2nd Q
GA—Walker, 1-yd. run (Robinson PAT) 9:09-3rd Q
GA—Walker, 76-yd. run (Robinson PAT) 3:52-3rd Q

Attendance: 60,150.

Weather: Temperature 86; Wind, none; Warm and hazy.

FINAL TEAM STATISTICS

	Texas A&M	Georgia
First Downs	14	14
Rushes—Yardage (Net)	48-155	49-207
Passing Yardage (Net)	119	210
Return Yardage (Net)	0	132
Passes—Att.-Comp.-Int.	24-12-3	18-9-0
Total Offense—Yards	274	417
Punts (Number-Average)	11-414-37.6	9-369-41.0
Fumbles—Lost	4-3	3-1
Penalties—Yards	3-21	3-21

FINAL INDIVIDUAL STATISTICS

Texas A&M

Rushing	Att.	Gain	Lost	Net	TD	Long
Hector	15	89	2	87	0	18
Sanders	11	40	2	38	0	7
Mosley	14	39	20	19	0	10
Hill	6	13	0	13	0	4
Beal	2	6	8	−2	0	6

Passing	Att.	Comp.	Int.	Yds.	TD	Long
Mosley	19	9	2	62	0	22
Beal	5	3	1	57	0	41

Pass Receiving	No.	Yds.	TD	Long
Whitwell	2	49	0	41
Hector	2	7	0	4
Flinn	1	−1	0	−1
Sanders	2	−4	0	−2
Lewis	2	19	0	13
Scott	3	49	0	22

Punting	No.	Yds.	Avg.	Long
Stuard	11	414	37.6	60

Georgia

Rushing	Att.	Gain	Lost	Net	TD	Long
Walker	21	147	2	145	3	76
Young	6	23	0	23	0	7
Womack	3	18	0	18	0	14
McCarthy	3	11	1	10	0	8
Norris	6	10	1	9	0	5
Belue	2	5	0	5	0	5
Paulk	2	5	0	5	0	3
Stewart	1	1	0	1	0	1
D. Jones	2	1	1	0	0	1
Arnold	3	0	9	−9	0	0

Passing	Att.	Comp.	Int.	Yds.	TD	Long
Belue	13	6	0	147	2	53
Paulk	5	3	0	63	1	24

Pass Receiving	No.	Yds.	TD	Long
Arnold	3	52	2	27
N. Brown	1	53	0	53
Scott	2	42	0	29
Stargell	1	24	0	24
Junior	1	23	0	23
C. Jones	1	23	1	23

Punting	No.	Yds.	Avg.	Long
Broadway	9	369	41.0	55

CLEMSON at Georgia

September 20

GEORGIA	14	0	6	0	20
CLEMSON	0	10	3	3	16

GA—Woerner, 67-yd. punt return (Robinson PAT) 13:28-1st Q
GA—Belue, 1-yd. run (Robinson PAT) :12-1st Q
CL—Gasque, 1-yd. run after fumble (Ariri PAT) 6:44 2nd-Q
CL—Ariri, 21-yd. FG :34-2nd Q
GA—Robinson, 42-yd. FG 11:05-3rd Q
GA—Robinson, 27-yd. FG 7:53-3rd Q
CL—Ariri, 45-yd. FG 2:17-3rd Q
CL—Ariri, 25-yd. FG 6:49-4th Q

Attendance: 61,800.

Weather: Temperature 75; Wind S.E. 6 mph; Overcast

FINAL TEAM STATISTICS

	Clemson	Georgia
First Downs	26	10
Rushes—Yardage (Net)	63-204	41-126
Passing Yardage (Net)	147	31
Return Yardage (Net)	1	183
Passes—Att.-Comp.-Int.	27-13-3	7-2-0
Total Offense—Yards	351	157
Punts (Number-Average)	2-87-43.5	4-159-39.7
Fumbles—Lost	4-1	4-2
Penalties—Yards	4-40	7-97

FINAL INDIVIDUAL STATISTICS

Clemson

Rushing	Att.	Gain	Lost	Net	TD	Long
Pickett	12	77	2	75	0	24
McSwain	13	54	1	53	0	19
Austin	12	39	0	39	0	12
Gasque	9	27	1	26	1	9
McCall	7	11	0	11	0	4
Caldwell	1	4	0	4	0	4
Pope	1	0	0	0	0	0
Jordan	8	7	11	−4	0	4

Passing	Att.	Comp.	Int.	Yds.	TD	Long
Jordan	11	5	1	50	0	18
Gasque	16	8	2	97	0	30

Pass Receiving	No.	Yds.	TD	Long
Tuttle	8	92	0	30
Gaillard	2	25	0	15
McCall	1	18	0	18
Pickett	1	7	0	7
Magwood	1	5	0	5

Punting	No.	Yds.	Avg.	Long
Sims	1	44	44.0	44
Hendley	1	43	43.0	43

Georgia

Rushing	Att.	Gain	Lost	Net	TD	Long
Walker	23	125	4	121	0	20
Arnold	1	13	0	13	0	13
Womack	4	12	0	12	0	4
Stewart	1	1	0	1	0	1
Belue	11	14	21	−7	1	9
Broadway	1	0	14	−14	0	−14

Passing	Att.	Comp.	Int.	Yds.	TD	Long
Belue	7	2	0	31	0	24

Pass Receiving	No.	Yds.	TD	Long
Arnold	1	24	0	24
Walker	1	7	0	7

Punting	No.	Yds.	Avg.	Long
Broadway	4	159	39.7	45

T.C.U. at Georgia

September 27

GEORGIA	7	13	0	14	34
TCU	0	3	0	0	3

GA—Stewart, 4-yd. pass from Belue (Robinson PAT) :15-1st Q
GA—Robinson, 31-yd. FG 10:22-2nd Q
GA—Robinson, 36-yd. FG 6:07-2nd Q
TCU—Porter, 46-yd. FG 3:20-2nd Q
GA—Jones, 28-yd. pass from Belue (Robinson PAT) :12-2nd Q
GA—Stewart, 7-yd. run (Robinson PAT) 14:54-4th Q
GA—Young, 5-yd. run (Robinson PAT) 13:48-4th Q

Attendance: 59,200.

Weather: Temperature 73; Wind NNE 12-18 mph; Partly sunny.

FINAL TEAM STATISTICS

	TCU	Georgia
First Downs	7	17
Rushes—Yardage (Net)	36- −10	67-334
Passing Yardage (Net)	109	60
Return Yardage (Net)	19	125
Passes—Att. -Comp. -Int.	26-10-2	18-6-2
Total Offense—Yards	99	394
Punts (Number-Average)	11-460-41.9	9-293-32.6
Fumbles—Lost	5-3	3-1
Penalties—Yards	2-20	5-35

FINAL INDIVIDUAL STATISTICS

TCU

Rushing	Att.	Gain	Lost	Net	TD	Long
Morris	4	23	0	23	0	13
Gilbert	6	16	0	16	0	5
Bates	4	10	7	3	0	4
Wright	2	1	0	1	0	1
Stamp	5	2	25	−23	0	1
Haney	15	21	51	−30	0	5

Passing	Att.	Comp.	Int.	Yds.	TD	Long
Haney	20	8	2	91	0	20
Stamp	6	2	0	18	0	10

Pass Receiving	No.	Yds.	TD	Long
Stewart	5	73	0	20
Bates	3	33	0	13
Morris	1	3	0	3
Wright	1	0	0	0

Punting	No.	Yds.	Avg.	Long
Talley	11	460	41.9	57

Georgia

Rushing	Att.	Gain	Lost	Net	TD	Long
Young	19	86	3	83	1	21
Walker	9	69	0	69	0	41
Stewart	6	40	0	40	1	9
Womack	9	40	0	40	0	11
Norris	6	35	0	35	0	13
D. Jones	3	29	0	29	0	12
Belue	8	35	16	19	0	13
Clark	2	9	0	9	0	6
Simmons	2	8	0	8	0	5
McCarthy	2	3	0	3	0	2
Paulk	1	0	1	−1	0	−1

Passing	Att.	Comp.	Int.	Yds.	TD	Long
Belue	14	6	1	60	2	28
Paulk	3	0	1	0	0	0
D. Jones	1	0	0	0	0	0

Pass Receiving	No.	Yds.	TD	Long
C. Jones	1	28	1	28
Arnold	2	13	0	7
N. Brown	1	10	0	10
Walker	1	5	0	5
Stewart	1	4	1	4

Punting	No.	Yds.	Avg.	Long
Broadway	9	291	32.6	55

OLE MISS at GEORGIA

October 11

GEORGIA	3	14	0	11	28
OLE MISS	0	7	7	7	21

GA—Robinson, 27-yd. FG 0:00-1st Q
GA—Arnold, 34-yd. pass from Belue (Robinson PAT) 9:40-2nd Q
GA—Norris, 1-yd. run (Robinson PAT) 0:44-2nd Q
OM—Otis, 32-yd. interception return (Gatlin PAT) 0:09-2nd Q
OM—Fourcade, 1-yd. run (Gatlin PAT) 7:57-2nd Q
GA—Robinson, 43-yd. FG 14:45-4th Q
GA—Belue, 1-yd. run (Junior pass from Belue) 6:02-4th Q
OM—Toler, 13-yd. pass from Fourcade (Gatlin PAT) 1:42-4th Q

Attendance: 60,300.

Weather: Temperature 80; Wind NW 7-12 mph; Clear.

FINAL TEAM STATISTICS

	Ole Miss	Georgia
First Downs	19	16
Rushes—Yardage (Net)	42-148	55-283
Passing Yardage (Net)	181	88
Return Yardage (Net)	32	124
Passes—Att.-Comp.-Int.	35-18-3	11-5-1
Total Offense—Yards	329	371
Punts (Number-Average)	5-204-41.0	3-106-35.3
Fumbles—Lost	2-2	2-1
Penalties—Yards	4-30	5-45

FINAL INDIVIDUAL STATISTICS

Ole Miss

Rushing	Att.	Gain	Lost	Net	TD	Long
Hooper	14	49	0	49	0	11
Thornton	6	42	0	42	0	16
Fourcade	12	87	46	41	1	36
Thomas	9	17	2	15	0	5
Lane	1	1	0	1	0	1

Passing	Att.	Comp.	Int.	Yds.	TD	Long
Fourcade	33	16	3	162	1	27
Lane	2	2	0	19	0	11

Pass Receiving	No.	Yds.	TD	Long
Tyler	3	51	0	27
Toler	3	50	1	20
English	3	39	0	17
Hooper	3	8	0	5
Thornton	2	12	0	8
Thomas	2	–3	0	–1
Wise	2	24	0	18

Punting	No.	Yds.	Avg.	Long
Graham	5	204	40.8	46

Georgia

Rushing	Att.	Gain	Lost	Net	TD	Long
Norris	15	150	0	150	1	41
Stewart	10	48	0	48	0	9
Walker	11	50	6	44	0	25
Womack	4	19	0	19	0	13
Arnold	2	22	7	15	0	22
Young	3	9	0	9	0	6
Belue	9	21	20	1	1	11
D. Jones	1	0	3	–3	0	–3

Passing	Att.	Comp.	Int.	Yds.	TD	Long
Belue	11	5	1	88	1	34

Pass Receiving	No.	Yds.	TD	Long
Arnold	2	51	1	34
N. Brown	1	19	0	19
Stewart	1	14	0	14
Walker	1	4	0	4

Punting	No.	Yds.	Avg.	Long
Malkiewicz	3	106	35.3	37

VANDERBILT at GEORGIA

October 18

GEORGIA	10	14	3	14	41
VANDY	0	0	0	0	0

GA—Walker, 60-yd. run (Robinson PAT) 13:46-1st Q
GA—Robinson, 30-yd. FG 7:44-1st Q
GA—Walker, 48-yd. run (Robinson PAT) 9:29-2nd Q
GA—N. Brown, 58-yd. pass from Belue (Robinson PAT) 6:50-2nd Q
GA—Robinson, 41-yd. FG 0:00-3rd Q
GA—Walker, 53-yd. run (Robinson PAT) 12:06-4th Q
GA—Simon, 1-yd. run (Robinson PAT) 5:01-4th Q

Attendance: 59,300

Weather: Temperature 73; Wind SSW 8 mph; Overcast.

FINAL TEAM STATISTICS

	Vanderbilt	Georgia
First Downs	16	22
Rushes—Yardage (Net)	54-164	48-331
Passing Yardage (Net)	64	214
Return Yardage (Net)	0	74
Passes—Att.-Comp.-Int.	20-6-3	17-13-0
Total Offense—Yards	228	545
Punts (Number-Average)	9-420-46.6	3-101-33.6
Fumbles—Lost	4-1	1-1
Penalties—Yards	5-43	5-45

FINAL INDIVIDUAL STATISTICS

Vanderbilt

Rushing	Att.	Gain	Lost	Net	TD	Long
High	14	58	0	58	0	10
Potter	16	53	1	52	0	13
Jordan	5	23	0	23	0	9
C. Edwards	9	21	7	14	0	9
J. Williams	3	13	0	13	0	9
Taylor	7	18	14	4	0	9

Passing	Att.	Comp.	Int.	Yds.	TD	Long
Taylor	19	6	3	64	0	17
K. Edwards	1	0	0	0	0	0

Pass Receiving	No.	Yds.	TD	Long
C. Edwards	2	24	0	13
Smith	1	17	0	17
Roach	1	13	0	13
Buggs	2	10	0	7

Punting	No.	Yds.	Avg.	Long
Arnold	9	420	46.6	60

Georgia

Rushing	Att.	Gain	Lost	Net	TD	Long
Walker	23	292	9	283	3	60
Norris	3	16	0	16	0	11
Womack	8	12	0	12	0	5
Paulk	5	12	0	12	0	7
Arnold	2	11	3	8	0	11
McCarthy	2	7	0	7	0	4
Young	1	3	0	3	0	3
Simon	3	4	1	3	1	3
Belue	6	7	20	–13	0	4

Passing	Att.	Comp.	Int.	Yds.	TD	Long
Belue	11	7	0	139	1	58
Paulk	6	6	0	75	0	23

Pass Receiving	No.	Yds.	TD	Long
N. Brown	1	58	1	58
Scott	4	46	0	22
Arnold	3	41	0	17
Junior	2	26	0	14
C. Jones	1	23	0	23
Kay	1	11	0	11
Buckler	1	9	0	9

Punting	No.	Yds.	Avg.	Long
Malkiewicz	3	101	33.6	50

207

GEORGIA at KENTUCKY

October 25 at Lexington, Ky.

GEORGIA	7	6	7	7	27
KENTUCKY	0	0	0	0	0

GA—Walker, 2-yd. run (Robinson PAT) 2:02-1st Q
GA—Robinson, 50-yd. FG 6:14-2nd Q
GA—Robinson, 47-yd. FG 1:03-2nd Q
GA—Belue, 3-yd. run (Robinson PAT) 6:06-3rd Q
GA—Arnold, 91-yd. pass from Belue (Robinson PAT) 13:25-4th Q

Attendance: 57,353.

Weather: Temperature 43; Wind W 17 mph; Cloudy.

FINAL TEAM STATISTICS

	Kentucky	Georgia
First Downs	18	18
Rushes—Yardage (Net)	37-76	56-171
Passing Yardage (Net)	219	228
Return Yardage (Net)	40	62
Passes—Att.-Comp.-Int.	31-15-4	20-10-1
Total Offense—Yards	295	399
Punts (Number-Average)	4-172-43.0	2-72-36.0
Fumbles—Lost	1-1	4-1
Penalties—Yards	2-29	2-10

FINAL INDIVIDUAL STATISTICS

Kentucky

Rushing	Att.	Gain	Lost	Net	TD	Long
Jenkins	2	6	0	6	0	5
Brooks	10	25	4	21	0	8
Parks	8	26	0	26	0	9
Francis	3	4	0	4	0	3
Jackson	8	29	0	29	0	11
Abraham	1	1	0	1	0	1
McCrimmon	5	13	24	−11	0	8

Passing	Att.	Comp.	Int.	Yds.	TD	Long
Jenkins	8	3	2	48	0	30
McCrimmon	23	12	2	171	0	24

Pass Receiving	No.	Yds.	TD	Long
Watson	7	112	0	30
Wimberly	3	43	0	18
Brooks	5	64	0	20

Punting	No.	Yds.	Avg.	Long
Poulton	3	120	40	47
Jenkins	1	52	52	52

Georgia

Rushing	Att.	Gain	Lost	Net	TD	Long
Belue	8	14	28	−14	1	9
Walker	31	135	4	131	1	18
Womack	5	22	0	22	0	9
Stewart	1	4	0	4	0	4
Simon	7	23	0	23	0	6
McCarthy	1	4	0	4	0	4
Paulk	2	3	0	3	0	3
C. Jones	1	0	2	−2	0	−2

Passing	Att.	Comp.	Int.	Yds.	TD	Long
Belue	20	10	1	228	1	91

Pass Receiving	No.	Yds.	TD	Long
Scott	2	25	0	18
Arnold	4	127	1	91
Womack	2	28	0	18
N. Brown	1	12	0	12
C. Jones	1	36	0	36

Punting	No.	Yds.	Avg.	Long
Malkiewicz	2	72	36	37

SOUTH CAROLINA at GEORGIA

November 1

GEORGIA	3	0	10	0	13
S. CAROLINA	0	0	10	0	10

GA—Robinson, 57-yd. FG 0:00-1st Q
GA—Walker, 76-yd. run (Robinson PAT) 14:14-3rd Q
GA—Robinson, 51-yd. FG 11:21-3rd Q
SC—Leopard, 45-yd. FG 8:01-3rd Q
SC—West, 39-yd. run (Leopard PAT) 3:24-3rd Q

Attendance: 62,200.

Weather: Temperature 68; Wind NW 10 mph; Clear.

FINAL TEAM STATISTICS

	South Carolina	Georgia
First Downs	15	18
Rushes—Yardage (Net)	50-263	56-206
Passing Yardage (Net)	25	179
Return Yardage (Net)	0	54
Passes—Att.-Comp.-Int.	13-2-1	18-10-0
Total Offense—Yards	288	385
Punts (Number-Average)	8-287-35.8	6-172-28.6
Fumbles—Lost	2-1	1-0
Penalties—Yards	2-20	2-27

FINAL INDIVIDUAL STATISTICS

South Carolina

Rushing	Att.	Gain	Lost	Net	TD	Long
Rogers	35	174	6	168	0	16
West	4	51	0	51	1	39
Harper	5	26	0	26	0	14
Wright	5	16	0	16	0	6
Reeves	1	2	0	2	0	2

Passing	Att.	Comp.	Int.	Yds.	TD	Long
Harper	13	2	1	25	0	17

Pass Receiving	No.	Yds.	TD	Long
Gillespie	1	17	0	17
Smith	1	8	0	8

Punting	No.	Yds.	Avg.	Long
Norman	7	300	42.8	60
Team	1	0	0.0	0

Georgia

Rushing	Att.	Gain	Lost	Net	TD	Long
Walker	43	225	6	219	1	76
Womack	4	29	0	29	0	22
Stewart	1	1	0	1	0	1
Belue	8	6	49	−43	0	5

Passing	Att.	Comp.	Int.	Yds.	TD	Long
Belue	18	10	0	179	0	41

Pass Receiving	No.	Yds.	TD	Long
Scott	2	56	0	41
Womack	2	39	0	31
N. Brown	2	34	0	26
Arnold	2	25	0	13
Kay	1	13	0	13
Walker	1	12	0	12

Punting	No.	Yds.	Avg.	Long
Malkiewicz	5	156	31.2	35
Team	1	16	16.0	16

GEORGIA at FLORIDA

November 8 at Jacksonville, Fla.

GEORGIA	7	7	6	6	26
FLORIDA	3	7	0	11	21

GA—Walker, 72-yd. run (Robinson PAT) 13:09-1st Q
UF—Clark, 40-yd. FG 7:07-1st Q
GA—Stewart, 13-yd. pass from Belue (Robinson PAT) 13:39-2nd Q
UF—Collinsworth, 9-yd. pass from Peace (Clark PAT) 7:10-2nd Q
GA—Robinson, 24-yd. FG 9:38-3rd Q
GA—Robinson, 20-yd. FG 3:58-3rd Q
UF—Jones, 11-yd. run (Young pass from Peace) 14:14-4th Q
UF—Clark, 40-yd. FG 6:52-4th Q
GA—Scott, 93-yd. pass from Belue (Belue pass failed) 1:03-4th Q

Attendance: 68,528.

Weather: Temperature 74; Wind SW 10-12 mph; Sunny.

FINAL TEAM STATISTICS

	Florida	Georgia
First Downs	20	17
Rushes—Yardage (Net)	42-123	53-286
Passing Yardage (Net)	286	145
Return Yardage (Net)	24	29
Passes—Att.-Comp.-Int.	37-20-2	16-7-2
Total Offense—Yards	409	431
Punts (Number-Average)	7-246-35.1	5-231-46.2
Fumbles—Lost	2-1	3-2
Penalties—Yards	8-99	5-45

FINAL INDIVIDUAL STATISTICS

Florida

Rushing	Att.	Gain	Lost	Net	TD	Long
Peace	12	38	25	13	0	8
Jones	22	89	0	89	1	12
Davis	3	8	0	8	0	5
Collins-worth	2	12	2	10	0	12
Williams	3	3	0	3	0	2

Passing	Att.	Comp.	Int.	Yds.	TD	Long
Peace	37	20	2	282	1	54

Pass Receiving	No.	Yds.	TD	Long
Collinsworth	3	29	1	13
S. Jackson	3	23	0	12
Young	10	183	0	54
Jones	2	17	0	15
Garrett	2	30	0	15

Punting	No.	Yds.	Avg.	Long
Dickert	7	246	35.1	39

Georgia

Rushing	Att.	Gain	Lost	Net	TD	Long
Belue	9	33	7	26	0	15
Walker	37	245	7	238	1	72
Norris	1	4	0	4	0	4
Womack	5	18	0	18	0	7
Brown	1	0	0	0	0	0

Passing	Att.	Comp.	Int.	Yds.	TD	Long
Belue	16	7	2	145	2	93

Pass Receiving	No.	Yds.	TD	Long
Arnold	1	3	0	0
Scott	2	114	1	93
Kay	1	9	0	—
Stewart	1	13	1	—
Jones	1	4	0	—
Walker	1	2	0	—

Punting	No.	Yds.	Avg.	Long
Malkiewicz	5	231	46.2	57

GEORGIA at AUBURN

November 15 at Auburn, Ala.

GEORGIA	0	17	14	0	31
AUBURN	0	7	0	14	21

AU—Franklin, 34-yd. pass from Thomas (Del Greco PAT) 11:05-2nd Q
GA—Robinson, 40-yd. FG 7:01-2nd Q
GA—Gilbert, 27-yd. return after Bell blocked punt (Robinson PAT) 4:32-2nd Q
GA—Brown, 1-yd. pass from Belue (Robinson PAT) 0:00-2nd Q
GA—Belue, 1-yd. run (Robinson PAT) 12:31-3rd Q
GA—Walker, 18-yd. run (Robinson PAT) 5:44-3rd Q
AU—Brooks, 1-yd. run (Sullivan to West PAT) 13:05-4th Q
AU—Franklin, 22-yd. pass from Thomas (Run Failed) 9:18-4th Q

Attendance: 74,009.

Weather: Temperature 68; Wind SW 5 mph; Threatening rain.

FINAL TEAM STATISTICS

	Auburn	Georgia
First Downs	20	20
Rushes—Yardage (Net)	45-186	53-240
Passing Yardage (Net)	164	99
Return Yardage (Net)	0	64
Passes—Att.-Comp.-Int.	21-12-1	19-10-1
Total Offense—Yards	350	339
Punts (Number-Average)	6-201-33.5	6-231-38.5
Fumbles—Lost	1-1	3-0
Penalties—Yards	5-68	4-40

FINAL INDIVIDUAL STATISTICS

Auburn

Rushing	Att.	Gain	Lost	Net	TD	Long
Sullivan	3	12	0	12	0	8
Brooks	21	90	5	85	1	12
Willis	4	15	0	15	0	6
Dejarnette	5	19	0	19	0	7
Peoples	12	55	0	55	0	8

Passing	Att.	Comp.	Int.	Yds.	TD	Long
Sullivan	17	6	1	86	0	19
Thomas	3	3	0	72	2	34
Bollinger	1	1	0	6	0	6

Pass Receiving	No.	Yds.	TD	Long
Franklin	7	120	2	34
Davis	1	19	0	0
Brooks	1	5	0	5
Peoples	1	5	0	5
Clanton	1	6	0	6
Edwards	1	9	0	9

Punting	No.	Yds.	Avg.	Long
Bollinger	6	201	33.5	50

Georgia

Rushing	Att.	Gain	Lost	Net	TD	Long
Belue	9	84	7	77	1	26
Walker	27	84	7	77	1	18
Womack	3	10	0	10	0	4
Norris	10	79	2	77	0	45
Stewart	3	8	0	8	0	4
Scott	1	0	9	–9	0	–9

Passing	Att.	Comp.	Int.	Yds.	TD	Long
Belue	19	10	1	99	1	19

Pass Receiving	No.	Yds.	TD	Long
Scott	4	38	0	15
C. Jones	2	28	0	15
Brown	2	6	1	5
Womack	1	8	0	8
Kay	1	19	0	19

Punting	No.	Yds.	Avg.	Long
Malkiewicz	6	231	38.5	50

GEORGIA TECH at GEORGIA

November 29

GEORGIA	10	7	14	7	38
GA. TECH	0	0	14	6	20

GA—Robinson, 57-yd. FG 6:39-1st Q
GA—Walker, 1-yd. run (Robinson PAT) 1:37-1st Q
GA—Stewart, 5-yd. pass from Belue (Robinson PAT) 4:16-2nd Q
GT—Chadwick, 15-yd. pass from Kelley (Smith PAT) 11:42-3rd Q
GA—Walker, 23-yd. run (Robinson PAT) 11:23-3rd Q
GT—Allen, 4-yd. run (Smith PAT) 6:19-3rd Q
GA—Belue, 1-yd. run (Robinson PAT) 13:24-4th Q
GT—Henderson, 5-yd. pass from Kelley (kick failed) 9:51-4th Q
GA—Walker, 65-yd. run (Robinson PAT) 9:30-4th Q

Attendance: 62,800.

Weather: Temperature 51; Wind W 18 mph; Clear and cool.

FINAL TEAM STATISTICS

	Georgia Tech	Georgia
First Downs	21	24
Rushes—Yardage (Net)	29-119	58-323
Passing Yardage (Net)	333	98
Return Yardage (Net)	–2	35
Passes—Att.-Comp.-Int.	46-27-2	17-8-3
Total Offense—Yards	452	421
Punts (Number-Average)	5-179-35.8	2-82-41.0
Fumbles—Lost	2-2	3-0
Penalties—Yards	6-50	5-44

FINAL INDIVIDUAL STATISTICS

Georgia Tech

Rushing	Att.	Gain	Lost	Net	TD	Long
Allen	14	98	0	98	1	46
Cone	9	30	5	25	0	8
Wood	2	5	0	5	0	5
Kelley	4	4	13	–9	0	4

Passing	Att.	Comp.	Int.	Yds.	TD	Long
Kelley	46	27	2	333	2	30

Pass Receiving	No.	Yds.	TD	Long
Heggs	5	105	0	30
Rank	3	57	0	21
Cone	4	41	0	15
Etheridge	4	38	0	14
Allen	3	35	0	25
Chadwick	4	33	1	16
Bryant	2	12	0	7
Keisler	1	7	0	7
Henderson	1	5	1	5

Punting	No.	Yds.	Avg.	Long
Pierce	5	179	35.8	57

Georgia

Rushing	Att.	Gain	Lost	Net	TD	Long
Walker	25	212	7	205	3	65
Norris	7	27	1	26	0	8
Simon	6	26	2	24	0	12
C. Jones	1	16	0	16	0	16
Paulk	3	16	0	16	0	9
Womack	5	15	0	15	0	5
Belue	10	33	20	13	1	7
Stewart	1	8	0	8	0	8

Passing	Att.	Comp.	Int.	Yds.	TD	Long
Belue	16	8	3	98	1	31
Paulk	1	0	0	0	0	0

Pass Receiving	No.	Yds.	TD	Long
Walker	1	31	0	31
Scott	2	29	0	11
C. Jones	2	15	0	8
N. Brown	1	15	0	15
Stewart	2	8	1	5

Punting	No.	Yds.	Avg.	Long
Malkiewicz	2	82	41.0	44

SUGAR BOWL — GEORGIA versus NOTRE DAME

January 1, 1981 at New Orleans

GEORGIA	10	7	0	0	17
N. DAME	3	0	7	0	10

ND—Oliver, 50-yd. FG 10:41-1st Q
GA—Robinson, 46-yd. FG 1:45-1st Q
GA—Walker, 1-yd. run (Robinson PAT) 1:04-1st Q
GA—Walker, 3-yd. run (Robinson PAT) 13:49-2nd Q
ND—Carter, 1-yd. run (Oliver PAT) :54-3rd Q

Attendance: 77,895.

FINAL TEAM STATISTICS

	Notre Dame	Georgia
First Downs	17	10
Rushes—Yardage (Net)	50-190	52-120
Passing Yardage (Net)	138	7
Return Yardage (Net)	2	44
Passes—Att.-Comp.-Int.	28-14-3	13-1-0
Total Offense—Yards	328	127
Punts (Number-Average)	5-210-42.0	11-424-38.5
Fumbles—Lost	1-1	0-0
Penalties—Yards	8-69	6-32

FINAL INDIVIDUAL STATISTICS

Notre Dame

Rushing	Att.	Gain	Lost	Net	TD	Long
Carter	27	110	1	109	1	16
Kiel	10	38	11	27	0	12
Sweeney	1	2	0	2	0	2
Courey	5	40	0	40	0	20
J. Stone	6	16	4	12	0	6
Buchanan	1	0	0	0	0	0

Passing	Att.	Comp.	Int.	Yds.	TD	Long
Kiel	27	14	2	138	0	22
Courey	1	0	1	0	0	0

Pass Receiving	No.	Yds.	TD	Long
Carter	2	24	0	22
Masztak	2	22	0	16
Hunter	3	29	0	16
Holohan	4	44	0	14
Buchanan	1	5	0	5
Vehr	2	14	0	8

Punting	No.	Yds.	Avg.	Long
Kiel	5	210	46.0	42

Georgia

Rushing	Att.	Gain	Lost	Net	TD	Long
Walker	36	153	3	150	2	23
Norris	2	2	0	2	0	2
Belue	13	24	58	−34	0	6
Womack	1	2	0	2	0	2

Passing	Att.	Comp.	Int.	Yds.	TD	Long
Belue	12	1	0	7	0	7
Walker	1	0	0	0	0	0

Pass Receiving	No.	Yds.	TD	Long
Arnold	1	7	0	7

Punting	No.	Yds.	Avg.	Long
Malkiewicz	11	424	38.5	59

1980 Georgia's

First Row, Left-right: Chuck Jones, Mark Malkiewicz, Jim Broadway, Richard Singleton, Rex Robinson, Mark McKay, Gary Cantrell, Head Coach Vince Dooley, Buck Belue, Dale Williams, Chris Welton, Matt Simon, John Lastinger, Pat Douglas. 2nd Row: Terry Hoage, Jeff Paulk, Tommy Lewis, Daryll Jones, Charlie Dean, Scott Woerner, Greg Bell, David Painter, Steve Kelly, Lindsay Scott, Jimmy Womack, Jeff Lott, Donnie McMickens. 3rd Row: Melvin Simmons, Bob Kelly, Scott Williams, Mike Fisher, Tim Bobo, Ronnie Stewart, Herschel Walker, Mitch Mullis, Carnie Norris, Ed Guthrie, Barry Young, Pat McShea. 4th Row: Will Forts, Keith Middleton, Frederick Lamar, Mike Jones, Chris McCarthy, Nate Taylor, Frank Ros, Jeff Hipp, Stan Dooley, Charles Smith, Tommy Nix.

Champions

5th Row: Dan Leusenring, Hugh Nall, Wayne Radloff, Joe Happe, George Kesler, Larry Cage, Jack Lindsey, Tommy Thurson, Eddie Weaver. 6th Row: Harold Malloy, Mike Weaver, Scott Campbell, Todd Milton, Nat Hudson, Jeff Harper, Tim Reynolds, Joel Steber, Joe Douglas, Jay McAlister. 7th Row: Keith Cannon, Kevin Jackson, Tim Case, Marty Ballard, Guy McIntyre, Jimmy Harper, Tim Morrison, Jim Blakewood, Winford Hood, Mac Thompson, Roy Curtis. 8th Row: Charles Junior, Lon Buckler, Amp Arnold, Robert Miles, Clarence Kay, James Brown, Guy Stargell, Jimmy Payne, Norris Brown, Eric Jarvis. 9th Row: Freddie Gilbert, Tim Crowe, Dan Marlow, Warren Gray, Joe Creamons, Keith Bouchillon, Dale Carver, Keith Hall, Tim Parks, Landy Ewings.

VINCE DOOLEY
Game by Game Before 1980

1964 (7-3-1)
Capt.: Barry Wilson, DE

3	Alabama	31
7	Vanderbilt	0
7	South Carolina	7
19	Clemson	7
14	Florida State	17
21	Kentucky	7
24	North Carolina	8
14	Florida	7
7	Auburn	14
7	Georgia Tech	0

Sun Bowl

7	Texas Tech	0

1965 (6-4-0)
Capt.: Doug McFalls, DB

18	Alabama	17
24	Vanderbilt	10
15	Michigan	7
23	Clemson	9
3	Florida State	10
10	Kentucky	28
47	North Carolina	35
10	Florida	14
19	Auburn	21
17	Georgia Tech	7

1966 (10-1-0)
Capt.: George Patton, T

20	Miss. State	17
43	VMI	7
7	South Carolina	0
9	Ole Miss	3
6	Miami	7
27	Kentucky	15
28	North Carolina	3
27	Florida	10
21	Auburn	13
23	Georgia Tech	14

Cotton Bowl

24	S.M.U.	9

1967 (7-4-0)
Capt.: Kirby Moore, QB

30	Miss. State	0
24	Clemson	17
21	South Carolina	0
20	Ole Miss	29
56	VMI	6
31	Kentucky	7
14	Houston	15
16	Florida	17
17	Auburn	0
21	Georgia Tech	14

Liberty Bowl

7	N. C. State	14

1968 (8-1-2)
Capt.: Bill Stanfill, T

17	Tennessee	17
31	Clemson	13
21	South Carolina	20
21	Ole Miss	7
32	Vanderbilt	6
35	Kentucky	14
10	Houston	10
51	Florida	0
17	Auburn	3
47	Georgia Tech	8

Sugar Bowl

2	Arkansas	16

1969 (5-5-1)
Capt.: Steve Greer, DG

35	Tulane	0
30	Clemson	0
41	South Carolina	16
17	Ole Miss	25
40	Vanderbilt	8
30	Kentucky	0
3	Tennessee	17
13	Florida	13
3	Auburn	16
0	Georgia Tech	6

Sun Bowl

6	Nebraska	45

1970 (5-5-0)
Capt.: Tommy Lyons, C

14	Tulane	17
38	Clemson	0
6	Miss. State	7
21	Ole Miss	31
37	Vanderbilt	3
19	Kentucky	3
52	South Carolina	34
17	Florida	24
31	Auburn	17
7	Georgia Tech	17

1971 (11-1-0)
Capt.: Royce Smith, OG

56	Oregon State	25
17	Tulane	7
28	Clemson	0
35	Miss. State	7
38	Ole Miss	7
24	Vanderbilt	0
34	Kentucky	0
24	South Carolina	0
49	Florida	7
20	Auburn	35
28	Georgia Tech	24

Gator Bowl

7	North Carolina	3

1972 (7-4-0)
Capt.: Robert Honeycutt, FB

4	Baylor	14
13	Tulane	24
28	N. C. State	22
7	Alabama	25
14	Ole Miss	13
28	Vanderbilt	3
13	Kentucky	7
0	Tennessee	14
10	Florida	7
10	Auburn	27
27	Georgia Tech	7

1973 (7-4-1)
Capt.: Bob Burns, FB

7	Pittsburgh	7
31	Clemson	14
31	N. C. State	12
14	Alabama	28
20	Ole Miss	0
14	Vanderbilt	18
7	Kentucky	12
35	Tennessee	31
10	Florida	11
28	Auburn	14
10	Georgia Tech	3

Peach Bowl

17	Maryland	16

1974 (6-6-0)
Capt.: Keith Harris, LB

48	Oregon State	35
14	Miss. State	38
52	South Carolina	14
24	Clemson	28
49	Ole Miss	0
38	Vanderbilt	31
24	Kentucky	20
24	Houston	31
17	Florida	16
13	Auburn	17
14	Georgia Tech	34

Tangerine Bowl

10	Miami (Ohio)	21

1975 (9-3-0)
Capt.: Glynn Harrison, RB

9	Pittsburgh	19
28	Miss. State	6
28	South Carolina	20
35	Clemson	7
13	Ole Miss	28
47	Vanderbilt	3
21	Kentucky	13
28	Richmond	24
10	Florida	7
28	Auburn	13
42	Georgia Tech	26

Cotton Bowl

10	Arkansas	31

1976 (10-2-0)
Capt.: Ray Goff, QB

36	California	24
41	Clemson	0
20	South Carolina	12
21	Alabama	0
17	Ole Miss	21
45	Vanderbilt	0
31	Kentucky	7
31	Cincinnati	17
41	Florida	27
28	Auburn	0
13	Georgia Tech	10

Sugar Bowl

3	Pittsburgh	27

1977 (5-6-0)
Capt.: Ben Zambiasi, LB

27	Oregon	16
6	Clemson	7
15	South Carolina	13
10	Alabama	18
14	Ole Miss	13
24	Vanderbilt	13
0	Kentucky	33
23	Richmond	7
17	Florida	22
14	Auburn	33
7	Georgia Tech	16

1978 (9-2-1)
Capt.: Willie McClendon, TB

16	Baylor	14
12	Clemson	0
10	South Carolina	27
42	Ole Miss	3
24	L.S.U.	17
31	Vanderbilt	10
17	Kentucky	16
41	V.M.I.	3
24	Florida	22
22	Auburn	22
29	Georgia Tech	28

Bluebonnet Bowl

22	Stanford	25

1979 (6-5)
Capt.: Gordon Terry, DE

21	Wake Forest	22
7	Clemson	12
20	South Carolina	27
24	Ole Miss	21
21	L.S.U.	14
31	Vanderbilt	10
20	Kentucky	6
0	Virginia	31
33	Florida	10
13	Auburn	33
16	Georgia Tech	3

GEORGIA SUGAR BOWL ROSTER

No.	Name	Pos.	Cl.	Ht.	Wt.	Birthdate	Hometown	High School
82	Anthony Arnold	FLK	Sr.	6-0	170	12-18-58	Athens, GA	Cedar Shoals
20	Greg Bell	CB	Sr.	5-11	185	1-27-59	Birmingham, AL	Banks
8	Buck Belue	QB	Jr.	6-1	185	12-12-59	Valdosta, GA	Valdosta
77	Jim Blakewood	OG	Jr.	6-2	230	9-8-60	Savannah, GA	Benedictine
32	Tim Bobo	DE	So.	6-2	205	4-29-60	Smyrna, GA	Campbell
95	Keith Bouchillon	DE	Sr.	6-2	206	11-25-58	Birmingham, AL	Mountain Brook
3	Jim Broadway	P	So.	5-10	170	4-24-60	Eustis, FL	Eustis
88	Norris Brown	TE	So.	6-3	215	7-10-61	Laurens, SC	Laurens
81	Lon Buckler	FLK	So.	5-11	187	7-19-60	Atlanta, GA	Avondale
63	Scott Campbell	OG	So.	6-4	235	8-16-61	Medford, NJ	Shawnee
7	Gary Cantrell	ROV	Fr.	6-1	190	10-10-62	Atlanta, GA	West Fulton
96	Dale Carver	DE	So.	6-2	215	3-5-61	Melbourne, FL	Palm Bay
72	Tim Case	OT	So.	6-4	245	1-8-61	Tifton, GA	Tift County
26	Stan Charping	PK	So.	5-9	190	3-4-59	Augusta, GA	Putnam County
94	Joe Creamons	DG	Jr.	6-2	240	6-6-59	Eustis, FL	Eustis
91	Tim Crowe	DG	So.	6-1	232	9-12-60	Stone Mtn., GA	Stone Mountain
50	Stan Dooley	DE	Fr.	6-2	193	1-12-62	Toccoa, GA	Stephens County
99	Landy Ewings	DG	Fr.	6-2	245	6-8-61	Tifton, GA	Tift County
31	Mike Fisher	CB	Sr.	6-0	180	1-25-58	Jacksonville, FL	Bolles
42	Will Forts	LB	So.	6-0	205	4-4-60	Fayetteville, GA	Fayette County
90	Freddie Gilbert	DE	Fr.	6-4	213	4-8-62	Griffin, GA	Griffin
68	Warren Gray	OG	Fr.	6-3	239	8-15-62	Fayetteville, GA	Fayette County
97	Keith Hall	DE	Jr.	6-1	190	1-14-60	Moultrie, GA	Moultrie
56	Joe Happe	C	Jr.	6-3	240	6-23-58	Jenkinton, Pa.	William Penn
66	Jeff Harper	OT	Sr.	6-2	240	10-27-57	Macon, GA	Monroe Academy
75	Jimmy Harper	OT	Fr.	6-5	284	11-5-61	Eastman, GA	Dodge County
49	Jeff Hipp	SAF	Sr.	6-3	195	1-30-58	W. Columbia, SC	Brookland-Cayce
14	Terry Hoage	ROV	Fr.	6-3	196	4-11-62	Huntsville, TX	Huntsville
78	Winford Hood	OT	Fr.	6-3	259	3-29-62	Atlanta, GA	Therrell
65	Nat Hudson	OT	Sr.	6-3	260	10-11-57	Rome, GA	West Rome
71	Kevin Jackson	DG	So.	6-2	255	6-2-61	Cartersville, GA	Cartersville
1	Chuck Jones	FLK	So.	6-0	198	8-27-61	Valdosta, GA	Lowndes
17	Daryll Jones	QB	Fr.	6-1	192	3-23-62	Columbus, GA	Carver
45	Mike Jones	LB	Fr.	6-1	192	2-18-62	Lincolnton, GA	Lincoln County
80	Charles Junior	SE	So.	6-0	178	3-4-61	Waycross, GA	Waycross
84	Clarence Kay	TE	Fr.	6-3	215	7-30-61	Seneca, SC	Seneca
29	Bob Kelly	SAF	Sr.	5-11	176	7-19-57	Savannah, GA	Benedictine
23	Steve Kelly	SAF	Jr.	5-9	178	3-16-59	Savannah, GA	Benedictine
57	George Kesler	C	Sr.	6-1	205	1-18-59	Athens, GA	Clarke Central
12	John Lastinger	QB	So.	6-2	190	2-27-61	Valdosta, GA	Valdosta
53	Dan Leusenring	OG	So.	6-2	248	9-12-60	Pittstown, NJ	N. Huntington
59	Jack Lindsey	DT	So.	6-2	238	3-3-60	Lithonia, GA	Southwest-Dekalb
2	Mark Malkiewicz	P	Sr.	6-2	203	12-4-57	Atlanta, GA	Marist
92	Dan Marlow	DE	So.	6-3	215	3-5-61	Marietta, GA	Marietta
46	Chris McCarthy	FB	So.	5-11	202	6-12-60	Savannah, GA	Benedictine
74	Guy McIntyre	TE	So.	6-3	235	2-17-61	Thomasville, GA	Thomasville
27	Donnie McMickens	TB	Sr.	5-11	200	3-24-59	Canton, GA	Cherokee
41	Pat McShea	DE	Sr.	6-2	211	1-19-59	Anderson, SC	Hanna
43	Keith Middleton	LB	Sr.	6-1	217	6-14-59	Valdosta, GA	Valdosta
83	Robert Miles	DE	Sr.	6-4	225	11-14-58	Montgomery, AL	St. Jude
64	Todd Milton	OG	Fr.	6-1	238	2-3-62	Albany, GA	Deerfield-Windsor
76	Tim Morrison	OG	Sr.	6-3	260	12-10-58	Live Oak, FL	Suwanee
54	Hugh Nall	C	Sr.	6-0	235	1-18-59	Thomaston, GA	R. E. Lee
52	Tommy Nix	C	Sr.	6-1	200	7-23-58	Columbus, GA	Hardaway
36	Carnie Norris	TB	So.	5-9	190	1-1-61	Spartanburg, SC	Spartanburg
22	David Painter	SE	So.	6-2	180	7-31-60	Dalton, GA	Dalton
98	Tim Parks	DG	Sr.	6-3	245	12-17-57	Chamblee, GA	Chamblee
15	Jeff Paulk	QB	So.	6-1	190	5-28-60	Marietta, GA	Wheeler
87	Jimmy Payne	DT	So.	6-4	243	2-9-60	Athens, GA	Cedar Shoals
55	Wayne Radloff	C	So.	6-5	230	5-17-61	Winter Park, FL	Winter Park
5	Rex Robinson	PK	Sr.	6-0	215	3-17-59	Marietta, GA	Marietta
48	Frank Ros	LB	Sr.	6-1	218	3-1-59	Greenville, SC	Eastside
24	Lindsay Scott	SE	Jr.	6-1	190	12-6-60	Jesup, GA	Wayne County
28	Melvin Simmons	TB	Fr.	6-0	185	3-25-61	Williston, Fla.	Williston
11	Matt Simon	TB	Jr.	6-0	190	9-5-59	Statesboro, GA	Statesboro
86	Guy Stargell	TE	So.	6-0	215	2-8-60	Fayetteville, GA	Fayette County
33	Ronnie Stewart	FB	Jr.	5-10	202	5-18-59	Tampa, FL	King
47	Nate Taylor	LB	So.	5-11	198	1-3-61	Tifton, GA	Tift County
60	Tommy Thurson	LB	Fr.	6-2	207	11-16-62	Jacksonville, FL	Bishop Kenny
34	Herschel Walker	TB	Fr.	6-1	218	3-3-62	Wrightsville, GA	Johnson County
61	Eddie Weaver	DG	Jr.	6-0	270	4-25-60	Haines City, FL	Haines City
10	Chris Welton	ROV	Sr.	6-1	200	1-19-59	Atlanta, GA	Peachtree
9	Dale Williams	CB	Jr.	6-0	168	9-21-59	Columbus, GA	Hardaway
19	Scott Woerner	CB	Sr.	6-0	195	12-18-59	Jonesboro, GA	Jonesboro
25	Jimmy Womack	FB	Sr.	5-9	200	1-1-59	Warner Robins, GA	Warner Robins
38	Barry Young	FB	Fr.	6-1	210	4-30-62	Swainsboro, GA	Swainsboro

THE COACHES

First row, left to right: Bill Hartman, Doc Avers, Erk Russell, Vince Dooley, George Haffner, Steve Greer, Wayne McDuffie.

Back row, left to right: John Kasay, Bill Lewis, Charles Whittemore, Chip Wisdom, Mike Cavan, Rusty Russell.

INDIVIDUAL STATISTICS*

RUSHING	G	Att.	Yds.	Avg.	Gm. Avg.	TD	LG
Walker, tb	11	274	1616	5.9	146.9	15	76 AM/SC
Norris, tb	9	56	353	6.3	39.2	1	45 AU
Womack, fb	11	49	209	4.3	19.0	0	22 SC
Young, tb-fb	5	29	118	4.1	23.6	1	21 TC
Stewart, fb	10	25	112	4.5	11.2	1	9 TC
Belue, qb	11	95	63	0.7	5.7	5	26 AU
Simon, tb	3	16	50	3.1	16.7	1	12 GT
Paulk, qb	5	13	35	2.7	7.0	0	9 GT
Arnold, flk	9	8	27	3.4	3.0	0	22 OM
McCarthy, fb	11	9	27	3.0	2.5	0	8 AM
D. Jones, qb	3	6	26	4.3	8.7	0	12 TC
C. Jones, flk	9	2	14	7.0	1.6	0	16 GT
Clark, tb	1	2	9	4.5	9.0	0	6 TC
Simmons, tb	3	2	8	4.0	2.7	0	5 TC
McMickens, tb	10	4	3	0.8	0.3	0	7 UT
N. Brown, te	11	2	0	0.0	0.0	0	O UT/FL
Scott, se	11	1	–9	0.0	0.0	0	–9 AU
Broadway, p	11	1	–14	0.0	0.0	0	–14 CL
GEORGIA	11	594	2647	4.5	240.6	24	76 AM/SC
Opponents	11	487	1540	3.2	140.0	7	46 GT

PASSING	G	Att.	Cmp.	Int.	Pct.	Yds.	TD	LG
Belue, qb	11	156	77	9	.494	1314	11	93 FL
Paulk, qb	6	15	9	1	.600	138	1	24 AM
D. Jones, qb	3	1	0	0	.000	0	0	0 TC
GEORGIA	11	172	86	10	.500	1452	12	93 FL
Opponents	11	300	150	24	.500	1829	7	54 FL

RECEIVING	G	CGT	Yds.	Avg.	TD	LG
Arnold, flk	9	20	357	17.9	4	91 UK
Scott, se	11	19	374	19.7	1	93 FL
N. Brown, te	11	12	253	21.1	2	58 VU
C. Jones, flk	10	9	158	17.6	2	36 UK
Walker, tb	11	7	70	10.0	0	31 GT
Womack, fb	11	5	75	15.0	0	31 SC
Stewart, fb	10	5	39	7.8	3	14 OM
Kay, te	11	4	52	13.0	0	19 AU
Junior, se	10	3	49	16.3	0	23 AM
Stargell, te	3	1	16	16.0	0	16 AM
Buckler, se	2	1	9	9.0	0	9 VU
GEORGIA	11	86	1452	16.9	12	93 FL
Opponents	11	150	1829	12.2	7	54 FL

OFFENSIVE LEADERS	Plays	Rush Yds.	Pass Yds.	Total Yds.	Play Avg.	Game Avg.
Walker, tb	281	1616	70	1686	6.0	153.3
Belue, qb	251	63	1314	1377	5.5	125.2

PUNT RETURNS	No.	Yds.	Avg.	TD	LR
Woerner, cb	31	488	15.7	1	67 CL
Bell, cb	1	16	16.0	0	16 AU
McShea, de	1	13	13.0	0	13 SC
Gilbert, de	0	27	27.0	1	27 AU
GEORGIA	33	544	16.5	2	67 CL
Opponents	16	8	0.5	0	4 UT

KICKOFF RETURNS	No.	Yds.	Avg.	TD	LR
Woerner, cb	9	232	25.8	0	71 GT
Walker, tb	6	119	19.8	0	29 CL
C. Jones., flk	2	43	21.5	0	23 CL
Womack, fb	2	15	7.5	0	13 TC
Scott, se	1	11	11.0	0	11 AU
Kay, te	1	10	10.0	0	10 UK
N. Brown, te	1	9	9.0	0	9 VU
GEORGIA	22	439	20.0	0	71 GT
Opponents	34	604	17.8	0	38 AU

PUNTING	No.	Yds.	Avg.	LP
Malkiewicz, p	26	979	37.7	57 FL
Broadway, p	31	1147	37.0	55 AM/TC
Team	1	16	16.0	16 SC
GEORGIA	58	2142	36.9	57 FL
Opponents	74	2928	39.6	68 UT

INTERCEPTIONS	No.	Yds.	TD	LR
Hipp, saf	8	104	0	32 SC
Woerner, cb	5	129	0	98 CL
Fisher, cb	3	36	0	25 FL
Williams, cb	2	41	0	23 OM
Miles, de	1	18	0	18 CL
Gilbert, de	1	13	0	13 TC
Bell, cb	1	12	0	12 AM
B. Kelly, saf-rov	1	11	0	11 OM
Payne, dt	1	4	0	4 VU
Thurson, lb	1	0	0	0 GT
GEORGIA	24	368	0	98 CL
Opponents	10	103	1	32 OM

SCORING	TD	FG	P.A.T.'s K	P	R	SAF	PTS
Walker, tb	15						90
Robinson, pk		16×22	36×36				84
Belue, qb	5						30
Arnold, flk	4						24
Stewart, fb	4						24
C. Jones, flk	2						12
N. Brown, te	2						12
Woerner, cb	1						6
Norris, tb	1						6
Young, tb-fb	1						6
Scott, se	1						6
Simon, tb	1						6
Gilbert, de	1						6
Junior, se				1			2
GEORGIA	38	16×22	36×36	1		1	316
Opponents	15	7×10	10×11	2		1	127

1980 GEORGIA DEFENSIVE STATISTICS

PLAYER, Position	Total Tackles	Solo	Assists	Sacks	Caused Fumble	Recov. Fumble	Caused Inter.	Tackles Behind Line of Scrim.
Taylor, lb	107	63	44		2	1		1
Ros, lb	100	59	41	1		1	1	
Weaver, dg	96	57	39	2	1	3		2
Hipp, saf	84	44	40			1		
Payne, dt	81	53	28	7	2	1		5
McShea, de	68	36	32	2		4	1	1
Welton, rov	61	34	27					
Thurson, lb	45	24	21					1
Woerner, cb	48	32	16		2			
Carver, de	46	27	19	1	1		1	2
Fisher, cb	40	23	17					
Creamons, dg	40	23	17	1		1		5
Forts, lb	38	21	17					1
Crowe, dg	41	26	15	1	1			1
Miles, de	34	19	15	1		2		2
Parks, dg	33	15	18	1		2	1	1
Bobo, de	34	18	16					2
Williams, cb	27	15	12			2		
Lindsey, dt	21	10	11	1				1
B. Kelley, saf-rov	21	8	13					
Gilbert, de	16	12	4	2				
Bell, cb	14	7	7					
Middleton, lb	10	6	4					
Jackson, dg,	8	4	4	1				
Jones, lb	7	5	2					
S. Kelly, cb	6	3	3					
Bouchillon, de	3	1	2					
Hoage, rov	1	0	1			1	1	

*Eleven games. Bowl games do not count in NCAA statistics.

TEAM STATISTICS*

	GA	OPP
1st Downs Rushing	119	90
1st Downs Passing	60	87
1st Downs Penalties	10	13
TOTAL 1ST DOWNS	**189**	**190**
No. Attempts Rushing	594	487
Yards Gained Rushing	3002	1858
Yards Lost Rushing	355	318
NET YARDS RUSHING	**2647**	**1540**
Average Rushing Per Game	240.6	140.0
TD's Rushing	24	7
Number Passes Attempted	172	300
Number Passes Completed	86	150
Number Passes Had Intercepted	10	24
NET YARDS PASSING	**1452**	**1829**
Average Passing Per Game	132.0	166.3
TD's Passing	12	7
Number Plays Pass & Rush	766	787
TOTAL OFFENSE	**4099**	**3369**
Average Yards Per Game	372.6	306.3
Number Opponent Passes Intercepted	24	10
Yards Interceptions Returned	368	103
Number Punts	58	74
Yards Punted	2142	2928
Number Punts Had Blocked	0	2
Punting Average	36.9	39.6
Number Punts Returned	33	16
Yards Punt Returned	544	8
Number Kickoffs Returned	22	34
Yards Kickoffs Returned	439	604
Number Penalties	53	45
Yards Penalized	469	460
Number Fumbles	31	32
Number Own Fumbles Lost	11	20

SCORE BY QUARTER

								Avg.
Georgia	68	99	76	73	=	316	=	28.7
Opponents	3	43	40	41	=	127	=	11.5

THIRD DOWN CONVERSIONS (BY QUARTER)

							Eff.
Georgia	21×47	21×46	13×44	18×42	=	73×179	= 41%
Opponents	11×42	19×52	15×38	20×44	=	65×176	= 37%

TIME OF POSSESSION (BY QUARTER)

Georgia	84:32	77:24	84:11	82:07	=	328:14
Opponents	80:28	87:36	80:49	82:53	=	331:46

*11 games. Bowl games do not count in NCAA statistics.

Honor Roll

HERSCHEL WALKER, Tailback

UPI NCAA Back of the Year
Football Writers All-America (*1st freshman ever*)
Kodak All-America (*1st freshman ever*)
Associated Press All-America
United Press International All-America
NEA All-America
Walter Camp All-America
Sporting News All-America
Football News All-America (*2nd team*)
Nashville Banner Player of the Year
SEC Sports Journal Player of the Year
UPI SEC Offensive Player of the Year
UPI All-SEC Team (*1st freshman ever*)
Associated Press All-SEC Team
SEC Sports Journal All-SEC Team
MVP 1981 Sugar Bowl

SCOTT WOERNER, Defensive Back

Kodak All-America
United Press International All-America
NEA All-America
Walter Camp All-America
Football News All-America
Associated Press All-America (*2nd team*)
UPI All-SEC Team
Associated Press All-SEC Team
SEC Sports Journal All-SEC Team
Hula Bowl
Senior Bowl

REX ROBINSON, Placekicker

Football Writers All-America
United Press International All-America
NEA All-America
Walter Camp All-America
Football News All-America
UPI All-SEC Team
Associated Press All-SEC Team
SEC Sports Journal All-SEC Team
Senior Bowl

JEFF HIPP, Safety

United Press International All-America (*2nd team*)
UPI All-SEC Team
Associated Press All-SEC Team
SEC Sports Journal All-SEC Team
Hula Bowl
Japan Bowl

TIM MORRISON, Offensive Guard

Football News All-America (*2nd team*)
UPI All-SEC Team
Associated Press All-SEC Team
SEC Sports Journal All-SEC Team
Japan Bowl

NAT HUDSON, Offensive Tackle

Jacobs Blocking Award (*SEC Best Blocker*)
UPI All-SEC Team
SEC Sports Journal All-SEC Team
Associated Press All-SEC (*2nd team*)
East-West Shrine Game
Senior Bowl

BUCK BELUE, Quarterback

Associated Press All-SEC Team

JIMMY PAYNE, Defensive Tackle

UPI All-SEC Team

EDDIE WEAVER, Defensive Guard

Associated Press All-SEC Team

COACH VINCE DOOLEY

Chevrolet NCAA Coach of the Year
UPI NCAA Coach of the Year
Walter Camp NCAA Coach of the Year
Kodak NCAA Coach of the Year
  (*American Football Coaches Assn*)
Football Writers Association NCAA
  Coach of the Year
Nashville Banner SEC Coach of the Year

TEAM

Associated Press National Champion
United Press International National Champion
Grantland Rice National Champion
McArthur Bowl National Champion
Stegeman Cup National Champion
Chicago Tribune National Champion

HERSCHEL WALKER
Game by Game

	Att.	Yds.	Avg.	TD	Lg	TD Runs
Tennessee	24	84	3.5	2	16	16, 9
Texas A&M	21	145	6.9	3	76	76, 1, 1
Clemson	23	121	5.3	0	20	—
TCU	9	69	7.7	0	41	—
Ole Miss	11	44	4.0	0	25	—
Vanderbilt	23	283	12.3	3	60	60, 48, 53
Kentucky	31	131	4.2	1	18	2
South Carolina	43	219	5.1	1	76	76
Florida	37	238	6.4	1	72	72
Auburn	27	77	2.9	1	18	18
GA Tech	25	205	8.2	3	65	1, 23, 65
	274	1,616	5.9	15	76	
Notre Dame	36	150	4.2	2	23	1.3
Total	310	1,766	5.7	17	76	

1980 Georgia Cheerleaders

STANDING L-R: Jerry Landers, Mableton, Ga.; Jim Brown, Dalton, Ga.; Barry Odom, Riverdale, Ga.; Chris Hunt, Warner Robins, Ga.; Lee Bonner, Decatur, Ga.; Doug Padgett, Athens, Ga.
KNEELING L-R: Ann Kelly, Savannah, Ga.; Gena Farr, Greenville, S.C.; Deidre Cummins, Decatur, Ga.; Denise Cummins, Decatur, Ga.; Donna Morrison, Bogart, Ga.; Scottie Johnston, Chamblee, Ga.

Miss Georgia Football and Court, 1980

L-R: Karen Hokanen, Spartanburg, S.C.; Gena Farr, Greenville, S.C.; Ann Kelly, Savannah, Ga.; Lee Ann Hileman, Lawrenceville, Ga.; Elizabeth Morgan (Miss Georgia Football 1980), Atlanta, Ga.; Lisa Popham, Piedmont, S.C.; Buffie Lee, Waycross, Ga.; Rhonda Pearlman, Charleston, S. C.

PHOTO CREDITS

Athletic Association, University of Georgia—i, 5, 6-7, 8-9, 17, 18-19, 20, 22-23, 24-25, 27, 28, 34, 37c, 38, 39, 40, 41, 42, 43, 46, 51, 91, 94a, 98, 100b, 101, 111, 150-151, 157a, b, 158, 159, 184, 194, 200, 214-215, 224.

Bennett, Fred—155b.

Cribb, Jimmy—3, 35, 53, 175, 176-177, 182, 183, 199.

Downs, Wingate—vi-vii, 33, 37a, b, 76-77, 94b, 95, 99, 100a, 106, 107, 109, 115, 155c, 164-165, 173, 179, 180, 185, 192-193, 196, 221.

Ellison, Travis—112.

Fortune, Frank—187.

Fowlkes, Richard—223a, b.

McIntyre, Perry—80-81, 85, 86-87, 90, 149, 160-161, 162, 168-169, 181.

Miller, Randy—96, 97, 154, 155a, 166.

Moore, R. D.—153.

Powers, Pat—60-61.

Rowland, Mary Ann—70, 72, 75.

Sanders, Clate—4-5, 45, 47b, 48-49, 59, 103, 197, 218-219, 225.

COLOR

Athletic Association, University of Georgia—119b, 125b, 126, 130.

Cribb, Jimmy—139a.

Downs, Wingate—118a, b, 122a, 125a, c, 127, 128-129, 131a, b, 134, 138, 139b, 140-141, 143, 146-147, 148.

Fitzgerald, Ellen—119a, 124, 131c, 132-133.

McIntyre, Perry—117, 120-121, 122b, 123, 135, 136-137, 142a, b, 144, 145.

ILLUSTRATIONS by Jack Davis.

ACKNOWLEDGMENTS

I would like to thank the following people, in no particular order, for their help in writing this book:

—Red Bullock, my first coach at Wrightsville High School, who made me realize everybody can rise to some accomplishment in athletics, no matter what their level of ability.

—Jerry Pryor, of the *Wrightsville Headlight*, for whom I wrote my first newspaper article.

—Bryan Lumpkin, the kind editor of the *Athens Banner-Herald*, who hired me as a sportswriter in 1960.

—Wallace Butts, for his colorful style which I will always appreciate.

—John E. Drewry, a dean who never lost touch with his Henry Grady School of Journalism matriculants.

—John Underwood, of *Sports Illustrated*, who has provided short course after short course in sportswriting at his home in South Miami.

—Joel Eaves, who gave me my first job in athletics.

—Dan Kitchens, who has been reviewing my work since I was editor of the *Red and Black*.

—Spec Towns, who yelled at me to run harder.

—Claude Felton, a solid pro.

—Diane Horton, whose job it is to keep me from having a nervous breakdown.

—Vince Dooley, a winner, who understood when I invaded his Mobile privacy.

—Bill Hartman, Jr., for whom I've worked for years and never considered a boss.

—Johnny Broadnax, who so vividly remembers athletic detail, back to the time when he was supposed to have gone to Georgia Tech to play for John Heisman.

—John Stegeman, a devoted and detailed researcher.

—Dan Magill, the funniest man who has ever lived. I've never told him that I love him, but I do.

—Bill Hale, my "listening" editor. And Jack Needle, who "listens" too.

—My parents, Mr. and Mrs. James L. Smith, who live by the rules.

—The 1980 Georgia football team, which made it all possible, and the legions of Georgia football fans I hope will relive 1980 in this book, not just for now, but forever. That is how long the memory will last.